The 60-Second Calm

The 60-Second Calm

Fast Tools for Stress, Anger, and Panic Moments

Selma Ravik

Mindful Pages

Published in 2026

ISBN: 9788169888356 (PB)
ISBN: 9788169888349 (eBook)

Published by

Mindful Pages
Imprint of Alpha Editions LLC
312 W. 2nd St #1834
Casper, WY 82601, USA

Content

Introduction vii

Chapter 1 The 60-second decision gap 1

Chapter 2 Your personal escalation map 27

Chapter 3 Breath resets that work 49

Chapter 4 Attention shifts in seconds 80

Chapter 5 Anger pauses without suppression 107

Chapter 6 Panic tools for real moments 128

Chapter 7 What to avoid during escalation 162

Chapter 8 Fast recovery after conflict 193

Chapter 9 Daily practice for pressure moments 215

Chapter 10 Calming with other people present 248

Chapter 11 Tools for work and public pressure 279

Chapter 12 Your personal 60-second plan 300

About the Author 326

Introduction

There is a particular kind of moment in which a whole life can seem to narrow to a single impulse.

A message appears on your phone and your chest tightens before you have finished reading it. Someone questions your judgement in a meeting and heat rises through your neck as though your body has been summoned to battle. A loved one says the one sentence that always finds the bruise, and suddenly your mind is not thinking so much as firing. Or panic arrives without permission: heart racing, breath catching, the world slightly unreal, your body behaving as if danger has stepped into the room even when nothing visible has changed.

These moments rarely announce themselves politely. They do not ask whether you have time. They do not wait until you are rested, eloquent, wise, well-fed, or emotionally prepared. They arrive in kitchens, cars, offices, queues, bedrooms, school corridors, train platforms, crowded shops, quiet cafés, inboxes, meetings, and ordinary Tuesday afternoons. They arrive when you are trying to be reasonable. They arrive when you have already promised yourself that next time you will handle things better.

The paradox of intense emotion is that it feels like an emergency and often is not. Yet your next move can create a real emergency in seconds.

One sharp email can damage months of trust. One raised voice can turn a difficult conversation into a wound. One rushed "fine" can close a door that needed to stay open. One accusation, one impulsive decision, one dramatic exit, one message sent while your nervous system is shouting can give a passing surge a long afterlife.

This book is about that narrow space.

Not the whole of emotional life. Not your entire personality. Not the complex history of why certain things affect you. Not a grand promise that you will become serene in all circumstances. This book is concerned with the practical, urgent, highly usable gap between the first surge and the next action.

That gap may be brief. It may be untidy. It may not feel dignified. It may last only a few seconds at first. But it is real, and it can be trained.

The 60-Second Calm is written for people who function well much of the time, perhaps even impressively well, but who sometimes get hijacked by stress, anger, or panic and later wonder, "Why did I do that?" It is for the person who can give sensible advice to everyone else, then still sends the defensive reply. It is for the person who appears capable, composed, and in control, yet privately knows the speed with which a difficult moment can take over the body. It is for the person who does not need a lecture on being calmer, but needs a usable sequence when calm is not immediately available.

The central idea is simple: in the first minute of escalation, your job is not to solve your life. Your job is to prevent the moment from getting worse.

That is a radical reduction, and it matters.

Most people ask too much of themselves during emotional surges. They try to understand everything, explain everything, defend everything, decide everything, and sound mature while doing it. They attempt moral excellence while their body is in alarm. They demand insight while their attention has narrowed. They try to reason with panic, debate with anger, negotiate with shame, and perform competence under physiological pressure.

No wonder willpower fails.

Willpower is a noble tool in the wrong time zone. It belongs to moments when the thinking mind has room to move. Under escalation, the body often accelerates before the mind catches up. Heart rate rises. Muscles prepare. Breathing changes. Attention narrows. Threat-detection sharpens. Speech becomes faster, harder, thinner, or disappears altogether. The mind begins to treat possibility as certainty. A criticism becomes humiliation. A delay becomes rejection. A sensation becomes danger. A disagreement becomes disrespect. A look, a pause, a notification, a tone of voice can suddenly feel enormous.

This is not a character defect. It is a state.

A state is not an excuse, but it is an explanation. And when you understand a state, you can work with it more intelligently.

One of the most damaging myths about calm is that it is mainly a matter of being a better person. This belief is not only inaccurate; it is unhelpful. It turns every surge into a moral examination. It makes people ashamed of the very signals they need to notice. It implies that if you were mature enough, healed enough, spiritual enough, disciplined enough, or kind enough, your body would not react.

But bodies react. Nervous systems mobilise. Old patterns appear quickly. Words rush towards the mouth. Hands reach for phones. The mind rehearses arguments. The chest tightens. The stomach drops. The room becomes too small. You may want to attack, disappear, explain, please, control, correct, leave, prove, confess, accuse, or fix everything immediately.

The question is not whether such impulses arise.

The question is whether they get to drive.

This book treats calm not as a mood, a personality trait, or a decorative lifestyle preference, but as a sequence of small actions that can be practised before you need them. Calm, in the sense used here, does not mean feeling peaceful. It does not mean liking what is happening. It does not mean agreeing, surrendering, smiling through resentment, or breathing prettily while someone behaves badly. Calm means having enough internal space to choose the next safe move.

Sometimes that move is silence.

Sometimes it is one sentence.

Sometimes it is stepping away.

Sometimes it is putting the phone down.

Sometimes it is slowing your exhale.

Sometimes it is feeling your feet and widening your gaze.

Sometimes it is saying, "I want to answer well. Give me a minute."

Sometimes it is doing absolutely nothing dramatic until the wave has passed.

This is not passivity. It is power with a steering wheel.

The first minute of escalation has three priorities: reduce intensity, widen attention, and choose the smallest safe next action. These priorities will appear throughout the book because they are the backbone of the method.

First, reduce intensity. You do not need to feel calm before you begin. In fact, waiting to feel calm is one reason people stay trapped. You begin with the body because the body is already involved. A longer exhale, a change in posture, contact with the ground, a slower turn of the head, unclenching the jaw, placing both feet on the floor — these are not sentimental gestures. They are signals. They tell the nervous system, in a language older than words, that there may be more options than attack, escape, collapse, or frantic repair.

Second, widen attention. Escalation narrows the world. It pulls you towards the threat target: the message, the person, the sensation, the imagined consequence, the sentence you cannot stop replaying. Narrow attention can be useful in genuine danger, but in ordinary conflict and panic spikes it often becomes a trap. Widening does not mean ignoring the problem. It means allowing your mind to receive more information. The room. The floor. The air on your skin. The neutral objects around you. The fact that this is one moment, not the whole story. The fact that urgency is not always accuracy.

Third, choose the smallest safe next action. Not the perfect action. Not the cleverest answer. Not the final decision. The smallest safe action is the move that reduces future regret. It may be delaying a reply, asking for a minute, leaving the draft unsent, taking one sip of water, lowering your voice, naming one fact, or postponing the conversation until both people can think. This book is deliberately suspicious of grand emotional performances during surges. When your state is high, smaller is usually wiser.

Do less, slower.

That phrase may sound modest, but in heated moments it can change the entire outcome.

Many people do not ruin things because they feel too much. They ruin things because they act too quickly while feeling too much. Emotion itself is not the enemy. Anger can protect dignity. Fear can alert you to vulnerability. Panic, though deeply uncomfortable, is often the body's alarm system misfiring rather than proof that catastrophe is unfolding. Stress can show that something matters, that a limit is being reached, or that a demand has exceeded current capacity. These signals deserve respect. But signals are not instructions.

Anger may say, "This matters."

The impulse may say, "Say it now, hard."

Those are not the same thing.

Panic may say, "Something feels wrong."

The interpretation may say, "I am in danger."

Those are not the same thing.

Stress may say, "There is too much happening."

The urge may say, "Rush, snap, agree, escape, decide immediately."

Those are not the same thing.

The work is to separate the signal from the action.

This distinction is especially important because modern life is built to collapse the gap between feeling and doing. A notification invites an instant reply. A social platform rewards outrage before reflection. Work culture often confuses speed with competence. Family systems may reward familiar roles: the explainer, the fixer, the appeaser, the fighter, the silent one. Digital communication removes the natural cooling spaces that once existed between reaction and response. You can now turn a ten-second surge into a permanent record.

The nervous system has not evolved as quickly as the send button.

That is why this book is practical by design. It does not ask you to become a different person before you can begin. It gives you tools for real moments, including the inconvenient ones: when other people are present, when you cannot leave the meeting, when panic makes breathing feel strange, when anger makes pausing feel like losing, when the message is already drafted, when your body is ahead of your values.

You will learn to map your personal escalation pattern. This matters because people do not all surge in the same direction. Some move outward: arguing, accusing, correcting, controlling, becoming louder or sharper. Some move inward: freezing, pleasing, numbing, shutting down, pretending, disappearing behind "I'm fine." Some become hyper-capable, performing competence so convincingly that nobody sees the cost. Some become urgent and over-explanatory, trying to secure certainty from another person who may not be able to give it. Some replay the moment for hours afterwards, constructing better arguments for a conversation that has already ended.

Your pattern is not your identity. It is your starting map.

Once you know your early signs — the jaw clench, the heat in the face, the tight chest, the shallow breath, the electric hands, the racing thoughts, the blankness, the urge to flee, the sudden need to win — you can intervene earlier. Early is everything. A tool used at a three is more effective than a tool used at a nine. The point is not to monitor yourself obsessively. The point is to recognise the first reliable signal and treat it as a cue.

A cue is kinder than a criticism.

Instead of "What is wrong with me?" you learn to ask, "What is my body preparing to do?"

Instead of "I must calm down immediately," you learn to ask, "What would reduce the intensity by five per cent?"

Instead of "How do I solve this?" you learn to ask, "What is the next safe move?"

These questions are small enough to be usable under pressure. That is their strength.

The tools in this book are intentionally brief. Breath resets. Attention shifts. Grounding methods. Anger pauses. Panic interruption techniques. Digital delay rules. Repair scripts. One-minute rehearsal drills. Boundary sentences. Meeting resets. Recovery sequences. Personal planning methods. Each tool is designed to earn its place in real life, not in an idealised wellness routine that collapses the moment life becomes loud.

Breathing, for example, is often presented as a cure-all, which is both exaggerated and irritating. Breath is not magic. It is a lever. Used well, it can help shift the body out of high alarm. Used badly, it can become another pressure: breathe deeper, breathe perfectly, breathe until you feel calm. For someone in panic, forcing huge breaths may increase discomfort. For someone in anger, being told to "take deep breaths" can feel patronising or silencing. This book takes a more precise approach. It uses breath as a discreet, structured intervention, especially through comfortable exhales and small steady patterns that reduce urgency without demanding instant tranquillity.

Grounding is treated with the same practicality. It is not an instruction to deny what you feel. It is a way of reconnecting with what is physically present so the mind is not trapped inside threat imagery. Feet on the floor. Hands against a surface. Eyes naming neutral objects. Peripheral vision. Texture. Temperature. The weight of the body in the chair. These are ordinary anchors, and their ordinariness is the point. In a surge, the ordinary can become a bridge back to choice.

Anger receives particular attention because anger is often misunderstood. Some people are frightened of it and suppress it until it leaks out sideways. Others trust it too completely and let it justify damage. Neither approach is good enough. Anger can be a fierce messenger. It can show that a boundary has been crossed, that something unfair has occurred, that a value is being threatened, or that exhaustion has stripped away your usual diplomacy. But anger's first suggested action is not always wise. The art is to keep the information and delay the injury.

A pause is not surrender.

A pause is how you keep your intelligence attached to your intensity.

Panic also deserves a clear, non-dramatic approach. Panic can feel catastrophic precisely because it is so physical. A racing heart, air-hunger, trembling, unreality, dizziness, heat, cold, pressure, or a sense that something terrible is about to happen can make the body feel untrustworthy. The fear of the sensations then fuels more sensations, and the spiral tightens. In those moments, long explanations are not enough. You need a way to stop adding frightening meanings to an already activated body. You need to return to what is happening now, in plain terms, without demanding that every sensation vanish at once.

This book does not ask you to diagnose yourself. It does not replace professional support, medical advice, therapy, crisis care, or treatment for ongoing anxiety, trauma, panic disorder, or health concerns. Some symptoms need medical attention. Some patterns need skilled support over time. Some environments are genuinely unsafe and require more than self-regulation. The tools here are not a substitute for getting help when help is needed.

But many daily surges are not solved by analysis alone. They are altered by timing, practice, and the ability to interrupt the next regrettable action.

That is the territory of this book.

A major theme you will meet is that avoiding the wrong move is often as important as choosing the right one. During escalation, people frequently reach for strategies that appear sensible but secretly intensify the state. They over-explain. They demand certainty. They scan their symptoms. They force deep breaths. They try to win the entire argument immediately. They send the message to relieve the tension of not sending it. They seek reassurance in a way that keeps fear alive. They replay the conflict under the illusion that rumination is preparation.

Some forms of "coping" are just the surge wearing a clever hat.

This book will help you spot those traps. It will show you how to delay high-impact decisions and messages, how to draft without sending, how to close rumination loops, and how to recover after conflict without starting a second conflict inside your own head. It will also help you repair when you do not handle something well, because you will not always handle things well. Nobody does. The aim is not an immaculate emotional record. The aim is shorter surges, fewer regrets, quicker repair, and a growing trust that you can return to yourself.

That last phrase matters: return to yourself.

When people describe emotional hijacking, they often speak as though they briefly became someone else. "I was not myself." "I do not know what came over me." "I could hear myself saying it and could not stop." "I knew I should not reply, but I did." "I felt like I had to get out." "I could not think." These descriptions are not signs of weakness. They are signs that state can temporarily overpower intention.

The solution is not to despise yourself for having a nervous system.

The solution is to build bridges back.

Those bridges must be practised before the storm. Skills rarely appear under pressure if they have only been admired in theory. Reading about calm is not the same as rehearsing it. Understanding a tool is not the same as being able to reach for it when your chest tightens and your pride is on the line. This is why the later chapters focus on daily practice: one-minute drills, automatic cues, mild stress rehearsal, and simple tracking. You will learn to practise while the kettle boils, while waiting for a lift, before opening messages, after getting into the car, before meetings, or during ordinary transitions. Calm becomes more available when it is woven into the day rather than reserved for emergencies.

The practice is deliberately humane. You are not trying to become a self-regulation machine. You are not trying to optimise every breath or turn your inner life into a productivity project. You are creating familiarity. The body trusts what it recognises. A breath pattern practised in neutral moments is easier to use in a tense one. A pause phrase spoken aloud before you need it is easier to say when your voice wants to sharpen. A grounding method rehearsed in a queue is easier to access when panic begins to pull the room away from you.

Repetition reduces the distance between knowledge and action.

Another important part of this work is learning to stay calm with other people present. Many emotional tools work beautifully in solitude and collapse in company. Conflict is relational. Pressure has witnesses. Meetings have hierarchies.

Families have history. Public situations have embarrassment. Digital exchanges have ambiguity. A method that only works when you are alone in a quiet room is useful, but incomplete.

You will learn how to listen without preparing your counterattack, how to set a boundary without delivering a lecture, how to de-escalate without conceding your position, and how to stay steady when another person is not. This is a mature form of calm: not fragile peace dependent on perfect conditions, but steadiness that can remain available in imperfect human weather.

The book also addresses work and public pressure because many surges happen where composure is expected but support is limited. In meetings, calls, presentations, customer-facing roles, interviews, reviews, and fast-moving digital exchanges, people often feel they must respond instantly. A pause can seem risky. Silence can feel exposed. Yet the most composed people are not those who never feel pressure; they are those who know how to buy a beat without making it look like a collapse.

A beat is sometimes all you need.

One breath before answering. One sip of water. One glance at your notes. One sentence: "Let me think about that for a moment." One slower exhale while someone else is speaking. One decision not to reply until you have read the message twice. These moves are small, but they protect judgement. They help you remain someone you respect after the moment has passed.

By the final chapter, you will build your own 60-second plan. Not a complicated menu with twenty-seven techniques. Under pressure, variety can become another burden. You need a small set of reliable tools: one breath reset, one grounding method, one anger pause, one panic response, one digital delay rule, one recovery step, and a few phrases that sound like you. The aim is not to copy someone else's calm. The aim is to design a plan that fits your patterns, your environments, your relationships, and your real triggers.

A good plan is boring in the best possible way.

It is simple enough to remember when your mind is crowded. It is practical enough to use in public. It is respectful enough to preserve your relationships. It is firm enough to protect your boundaries. It is flexible enough to survive bad days.

Because there will be bad days.

Progress does not mean you never surge. It means you notice sooner. It means you recover faster. It means fewer words need repairing. It means your body can be activated without your behaviour becoming reckless. It means you can feel anger without becoming cruel, fear without obeying every catastrophic story, stress without letting urgency make all your decisions. It means you begin to trust the gap.

The gap is where the work lives.

Between the message and the reply.

Between the insult and the counterattack.

Between the sensation and the story.

Between the urge and the action.

Between the raised voice and the next sentence.

Between "I can't stand this" and "I can take one breath."

In that gap, you do not need to become perfectly calm. You only need to become slightly more available to choice.

That is enough to begin.

The next time a surge rises, your body may still move first. Your heart may speed up. Your thoughts may sharpen or scatter. Your breathing may change. Your old pattern may lean forward, ready to take over. This book will not remove that first wave from human life, and it should not pretend to. The first wave is not always yours to choose.

The next move can be.

That is the promise of the 60-second calm: not instant peace, not emotional perfection, not a life without conflict or fear, but a trained, practical return to agency at the moment agency matters most.

Chapter 1
The 60-second decision gap

The criticism is small. Almost disappointingly small, once viewed from a distance. A colleague says your last response sounded abrupt. A partner asks why you forgot something you promised to do. A friend replies with a tone that may or may not mean anything. Nothing has exploded. Nobody has declared war. The room is still the room, the phone is still in your hand, the conversation is still recoverable.

Yet inside, something has already moved. Your jaw tightens. Heat climbs into your face. Your thoughts begin arriving too quickly, each one carrying evidence for why you are right, misunderstood, cornered, attacked, embarrassed, or unsafe. The sentence you were going to say calmly becomes sharper while it is still forming. The reply you should leave alone becomes almost magnetic. You can feel the send button waiting like a small trap.

Then comes the strange part: a moment that is not truly an emergency begins to behave like one. The body acts before the wiser part of the mind has assembled itself. You are not weighing options; you are being pulled by them. Attack seems clean. Shutdown seems protective. Over-explaining seems necessary. Agreeing too quickly seems easier than enduring the pressure. Later, when the heat has gone, the whole scene may look absurdly different. But in the moment, it has the force of truth.

This is the narrow territory where many regrets begin. Not because people lack values. Not because they do not care. Often, the opposite is true: they care so much that their system surges before their judgement can organise the care into a useful response. The gap between what you feel and what you do next may be brief, but it carries consequences far beyond its size. A passing state can choose words that the steadier self would never have approved.

The difficulty is that intensity changes the meaning of things. A neutral pause can become rejection. A question can become accusation. A delay can become disrespect. A bodily sensation can become proof that something is wrong. When pressure rises, the mind does not simply think harder; it often thinks narrower. It edits the scene around the threat. It reaches for old interpretations. It prepares a defence before checking whether defence is needed. The door may still be open, but inside the body, the locks have started turning.

This matters because the first movement after a surge is rarely private. It lands somewhere. It lands in an inbox, across a kitchen table, inside a meeting, on a child, on a partner, on a colleague, on yourself. A rushed sentence can become the centre of the conversation. A defensive reply can create the very distance it was trying to prevent. A silent withdrawal can be mistaken for contempt. A frantic apology can erase the boundary that needed to be named. Under pressure, people often do not merely express distress; they recruit the moment into making their distress larger.

The work, then, is not to become untouched by stress, anger, or panic. That would be an inhuman target and a useless one. The work is to understand the surge as a short-lived state with a beginning, a middle, and a point at which choice can be recovered. A state can be powerful without being permanent. It can be convincing without being accurate. It can deserve attention without deserving obedience. This distinction is severe, merciful, and practical.

Willpower alone is too fragile for this work. Telling yourself to calm down when your body is accelerating is like asking a door to stop slamming after the wind has already taken it. The command may be sensible, but it is badly timed. Moral resolve, clever self-talk, and good intentions all have their place, yet they often arrive late to a fast-moving physical event. The wiser move is to stop treating calm as a personality test and start treating it as an order of operations.

The path begins with what happens in surges: how the body accelerates, how perception narrows, and how speech and impulse can shift before reflection catches up. From there, the limits of willpower become clearer, not as failure, but as a sign that the sequence is wrong. Then the minute itself comes into focus as a field of priorities: lower the heat, widen the view, and protect the next action from becoming another problem.

So the real question is not whether you can avoid ever being triggered, startled, offended, frightened, or overwhelmed. You cannot build a life on that fantasy. The sharper question is this: when the surge begins and the old move reaches for the wheel, what happens in the space before you let it drive?

What happens in surges

A surge begins before it becomes a story.

That is why it can feel so unfair. One moment you are ordinary, available, reasonably yourself. The next, your body has moved ahead of you. Your chest tightens, your voice changes, your face heats, your hands become restless, your stomach drops, your thoughts gather speed. You may not yet know whether you are angry, frightened, ashamed, embarrassed, cornered, or overwhelmed, but your system has already started preparing for something.

This is the first truth to grasp: intense emotion is not only a feeling. It is a whole-body event.

When stress, anger, or panic rises quickly, the body does not wait for a full committee meeting of the mind. It acts on impressions. Tone of voice, facial expression, pace, memory, expectation, bodily sensation, and context all combine at high speed. Your system asks a primitive and urgent question: *Is there a threat here?* It may not be a threat to your physical safety. It may be a threat to belonging, dignity, control, certainty, competence, reputation, or emotional security. The body does not always distinguish neatly between these categories in the first rush. It responds to significance.

This is why a minor criticism can feel enormous. The actual words may be mild: "That came across a bit harshly," or "You said you would do it yesterday," or "Can we talk about what happened?" On paper, nothing dramatic has occurred. But the body is not reading a transcript. It is reading the moment through everything attached to it: previous arguments, old humiliations, tiredness, fear of being judged, fear of being trapped, fear of disappointing someone, fear of being controlled, fear of losing face. A small spark lands on dry material.

Then perception begins to narrow.

In a calmer state, you can hold several possibilities at once. Perhaps the person is tired. Perhaps they chose their words badly. Perhaps there is something useful in the criticism. Perhaps there has been a misunderstanding. Perhaps you need to listen before answering. But in a surge, the mind often stops behaving like a spacious room and starts behaving like a spotlight. It shines on the most threatening interpretation and leaves the rest in darkness.

This narrowing is one reason emotional surges feel so convincing. You are not merely having a thought; you are having a thought inside a body that is preparing to defend itself. The body gives the thought volume. A possibility becomes a certainty. A concern becomes evidence. A delay becomes rejection. A question becomes an attack. A look becomes contempt. A sensation becomes danger. The mind does not say, "I am currently in a heightened state and may be interpreting this through a threat filter." It says, "This is what is happening."

That is the dangerous elegance of a surge. It simplifies.

It removes nuance exactly when nuance is most needed. It reduces the other person to their worst-sounding sentence. It reduces your options to the most urgent ones. It reduces the future to what might happen if you do not act now. This is why people often become more absolute when escalated. Words like "always," "never," "everyone," "nothing," and "fine" appear with suspicious confidence. The mind reaches for clean conclusions because ambiguity feels unbearable under pressure.

Speech changes too.

Some people become faster. Their sentences crowd one another, each one trying to outrun discomfort. They interrupt, correct, defend, accuse, explain, justify, or demand an answer immediately. They may hear their own voice getting sharper and still feel unable to soften it. The pressure seems to need an exit, and the mouth becomes the nearest door.

Others go quiet. Not thoughtfully quiet, but locked quiet. Words vanish. The face becomes still. The body may feel heavy, numb, distant, or absent. The person may appear calm from the outside while internally they are flooded. This can be confusing in relationships because silence is easily misread. One person experiences it as self-protection; the other experiences it as punishment, indifference, or rejection.

A third pattern is compliance. The surge does not always push people into attack or withdrawal. Sometimes it pushes them into immediate agreement. "Yes, fine." "It does not matter." "Do whatever you want." "I am sorry, I am sorry, I am sorry." The aim is not truth; the aim is escape from intensity. The person may surrender a boundary, accept blame they have not considered, or promise something unsustainable because the pressure of the moment feels more urgent than the cost of the promise.

These patterns may look different, but they share a common feature: the body is trying to reduce threat quickly.

Attack tries to push the threat away.

Shutdown tries to disappear from it.

Appeasement tries to soothe it.

Control tries to organise it.

Over-explaining tries to make it understand.

Escape tries to get distance from it.

None of these moves is automatically wrong in every situation. There are moments when firm speech matters, when leaving is wise, when explanation is needed, when calming another person is kind, when decisive action is appropriate. The problem is not that the body offers protective strategies. The problem is that, during a surge, it may offer them too early, too strongly, and without enough information.

This is where impulse control changes.

In a settled state, you may know perfectly well that sending the message is unwise. You may know that raising your voice will not help. You may know that agreeing too quickly will create resentment later. You may know that leaving without a word will deepen the conflict. But knowing is not the same as accessing that knowledge under pressure. During escalation, the distance between impulse and action shrinks. The hand moves towards the phone. The sentence leaves the mouth. The door closes. The decision is made because making any decision feels better than staying inside the discomfort.

Surges are impatient.

They do not like waiting for context. They do not like slow truths. They do not like the sentence, "Let me think." They prefer immediate relief, even if that relief creates later damage. This is why the first minute matters so much. Not because everything can be healed in sixty seconds, but because much can be protected there. The first minute is often when the preventable harm either happens or does not happen.

To work skilfully with surges, you need to stop treating them as mysterious moral collapses. They are not random explosions from nowhere. Most have a recognisable shape.

There is usually a trigger, though it may be obvious or subtle. A message, a tone, a memory, a sensation, a demand, a mistake, a criticism, a crowded room, a raised eyebrow, a silence. Then there is bodily acceleration: breath shifts, muscles prepare, heat rises, energy gathers or drains. Then comes interpretation: the mind decides what the moment means. Then comes impulse: defend, flee, freeze, fix, please, prove, control, confess, accuse. Then comes action, unless something interrupts the sequence.

The key word is *sequence.*

A surge can feel instant, but it is still made of parts. Those parts may move quickly, but they are not the same thing. The trigger is not the interpretation. The sensation is not the story. The impulse is not the action. The emotion is not the behaviour. Once these are separated, even slightly, choice begins to return.

This distinction is essential because normalising a surge must never become excusing its consequences. It is true that the body can accelerate before the mind catches up. It is also true that harmful words and actions still matter. You can understand why you snapped and still take responsibility for snapping. You can understand why you shut down and still recognise the effect of disappearing mid-conversation. You can understand why panic made you seek reassurance and still notice when repeated checking keeps the fear alive. Explanation is not absolution. It is leverage.

Shame is poor leverage.

When people look back on a surge, they often attack themselves with the same intensity they brought to the original moment. "I am ridiculous." "I always ruin things." "I cannot trust myself." "What is wrong with me?" This may feel like accountability, but it is usually another form of escalation. It keeps the body in threat. It turns the self into the enemy. It makes the next surge more loaded because now the person is not only reacting to the moment; they are reacting to the fear of becoming that version of themselves again.

A better approach is more exacting and more humane: "What happened in my sequence?"

Where did the body first signal acceleration?

What meaning did the mind attach?

What impulse appeared?

What did I do next?

What would have interrupted the chain earlier?

These questions do not flatter you, but they do not crush you either. They turn the surge into something observable. And what can be observed can be trained.

Imagine a person receiving a brief comment after a presentation: "The opening felt a little unclear." The comment is not cruel. It may even be useful. But the person has been running on poor sleep, has been anxious about seeming competent, and has a long history of feeling exposed when judged. Their body reacts before their professional self can assemble a measured response. Heat rises. Their shoulders tighten. Their mind translates the comment into, "They think I failed." Then the impulse arrives: defend. They begin listing reasons the opening had to be that way, correcting the other person's impression, speaking faster, adding details nobody asked for.

From the outside, they may look arrogant.

Inside, they feel under threat.

Now imagine a different person receiving the same comment. Their body reacts with a drop rather than a push. Their mind translates the words into, "I have disappointed them." The impulse is not to argue, but to disappear. They smile tightly, say, "Yes, you are right," and stop contributing for the rest of the meeting. Later, they replay the comment for hours and decide they should avoid presenting next time.

From the outside, they may look agreeable.

Inside, they feel unsafe.

The trigger is the same. The surge moves differently. That is why generic advice often fails. "Speak up" may be useful for one person and disastrous for another in that moment. "Take a pause" may sound simple, but one person needs a pause to prevent attack, while another needs a pause to prevent self-erasure. One person needs to soften the push. Another needs to stay present instead of vanishing. The tool must match the pattern.

This is why your body cues matter. The earliest signal is often more reliable than the story that follows. Stories can be elaborate, persuasive, and wrong. The body cue is simpler. Jaw tight. Face hot. Throat closing. Fingers tapping. Vision narrowing. Breath held. Chest tight. Stomach dropping. Sudden blankness. Sudden urgency. Sudden certainty. These are not commands. They are dashboard lights.

A dashboard light does not tell you the whole repair. It tells you to stop driving as though nothing is happening.

At first, noticing these cues may feel awkward. Many people only recognise a surge after they have already acted. They know they were escalated because of the email they sent, the tone they used, the promise they made, the silence they imposed, the apology that was really panic, or the argument they kept alive long after it should have rested. But with practice, recognition moves earlier. You catch the heat before the sentence. You catch the breath-hold before the reply. You catch the tunnel vision before the decision. That is progress.

Not dramatic progress. Useful progress.

There is a quiet dignity in catching yourself one inch earlier than last time. It may not look impressive to anyone else. No one applauds the message you did not send. No one sees the insult you swallowed, the unnecessary confession you delayed, the defensive paragraph you left in drafts, the extra breath you took before answering. But these private interruptions are the architecture of a calmer life. They are how trust is rebuilt with yourself.

The point is not to eliminate surges. That would make you less human, not more mature. The point is to stop being surprised by your own acceleration. When a surge rises, you can learn to recognise the pattern: the body moves, the mind narrows, the story hardens, the impulse leans forward. This recognition does not make the feeling pleasant. It gives you a place to stand.

And that place matters.

Because once you can say, "This is a surge," you are no longer completely inside it. Some part of you has stepped back far enough to name the weather. Not control it perfectly. Not end it on command. Not become instantly serene. Just name it.

This is the first opening in the 60-second decision gap. The surge says, "Act now." Recognition says, "Not yet."

Why willpower fails fast

"Just calm down" is one of the most common instructions given in the very moment it becomes least useful.

It sounds sensible from a distance. It appeals to the responsible adult within us, the part that believes we ought to be able to master ourselves by deciding to do so. It assumes that calm is mainly a matter of character: choose better, think harder, be kinder, be stronger, be more reasonable. Yet in the heat of escalation, this command often lands like asking someone to solve a puzzle while the table is shaking. The instruction is not wrong in principle; it is wrong in timing.

A surge changes the conditions under which self-control must operate. When you are settled, you can reflect, compare options, weigh consequences, remember your values, consider another person's perspective, and choose your words with care. Under pressure, those capacities may still exist, but they are no longer operating in calm weather. They are being asked to work while the body is accelerating, attention is narrowing, and urgency is rising. The mind is not sitting in a quiet room making a clean moral choice. It is trying to steer while the engine is revving.

This is why many people are confused by their own reactions. They know better. They genuinely do. They may have read the books, taken the advice, apologised before, promised themselves change, and rehearsed the mature version of the conversation in their head. Then the moment arrives, the old heat rises, and the better plan seems to vanish behind the immediate need to defend, escape, fix, prove, explain, or shut everything down.

The failure is not always knowledge. Often, the failure is access.

Willpower depends on access to the very capacities that surges temporarily make harder to use. It asks for perspective when the mind has narrowed. It asks for patience when the body is demanding speed. It asks for careful speech when the mouth has become the pressure valve. It asks for restraint when the hand is already reaching for the phone. It asks for generosity when the other person has been reduced, at least briefly, to the threat they appear to represent.

This does not mean people are helpless. It means the strategy must match the state.

The mistake is treating escalation as though it were merely a thinking problem. If you could only remind yourself of the right idea, you would behave differently. If you could only say the right sentence in your mind, the feeling would obey. If you could only be disciplined enough, the surge would stand down. But intense emotion is not simply a mistaken thought wandering through the brain. It is an organised bodily state. Muscles, breath, posture, facial expression, memory, attention, and interpretation are all involved. A purely verbal command often fails because it is trying to reason with a system that is already preparing to act.

Consider anger. You may tell yourself, "Do not raise your voice." A useful instruction, certainly. But if your chest is tight, your jaw is clenched, your breath is high, and your attention has locked onto the most insulting part of what was said, the instruction has arrived late. It is trying to stop the final behaviour without addressing the build-up beneath it. The voice does not sharpen in isolation. It sharpens as part of a chain.

The same is true of panic. "There is nothing to worry about" may be accurate, yet it can feel useless when the heart is racing and the breath feels unreliable. The body is producing sensations that seem to demand interpretation. The mind, desperate to make sense of them, may reach for frightening explanations. In that state, calm self-talk can become one more argument to lose: "I know I should not be worried, but I still feel worried, so perhaps something really is wrong." The attempt to think panic away can sometimes tighten the loop.

Stress has its own version. You tell yourself to be patient, but the unread messages, unfinished tasks, waiting people, noise, tiredness, and inner pressure gather into a single demand: hurry. Hurry your answer. Hurry your decision. Hurry your apology. Hurry your escape. The body begins to confuse speed with safety. Willpower says, "Slow down." The state says, "There is no time."

This is why calm must be understood as a sequence, not a virtue.

A virtue is something you either appear to possess or not possess. A sequence is something you can follow when conditions are difficult. This distinction removes a great deal of unnecessary shame. If you believe calm is proof of goodness, then every surge becomes an accusation. If you understand calm as a sequence, then a surge becomes a cue to begin again at the right point.

The right point is usually not the most sophisticated thought. It is the simplest physical shift that reduces intensity enough for thought to become useful again.

That may sound too modest, especially to people who are used to solving problems with intelligence. But in the first minute of escalation, modesty is a strength. You are not trying to become wise all at once. You are trying to lower the internal temperature by a small amount. You are trying to create a fraction more space between impulse and action. You are trying to make the next sentence less damaging than it might have been. That is not glamorous work. It is effective work.

The body often needs evidence before the mind can believe it has options. A slower exhale gives evidence. Feet pressing into the floor give evidence. Unclenching the hands gives evidence. Turning the gaze away from the single threat target gives evidence. Taking one sip of water gives evidence. Dropping the shoulders gives evidence. These are not magic tricks. They are small messages sent through the body: not so fast, not so narrow, not yet.

Only then does reasoning become more available.

This is the order many people reverse. They try to think their way into calm, then become frustrated when the body does not obey. A better order is to shift physiology enough that thinking can return. The aim is not to bypass the mind, but to help it come back online in a usable way. Once intensity has dropped even slightly, self-talk becomes less like shouting into a storm and more like giving direction in a room where someone can hear you.

This also explains why moral resolve can fail under pressure even in people who care deeply about doing the right thing. Values are essential, but values need access routes. A person may value patience and still snap when exhausted and cornered. A person may value honesty and still appease when conflict feels unbearable. A person may value courage and still withdraw when shame floods the system. Values do not disappear in those moments, but they may be temporarily outrun by protective patterns.

The task is to make values reachable under pressure.

That requires cues simpler than principles. A principle might be, "I want to communicate respectfully even when I am upset." Good. Necessary. But in the middle of a surge, that sentence may be too large to use. A cue is smaller: "Exhale before answering." "Feet." "Draft, do not send." "One sentence only." "Pause, then speak." "Look around the room." "Lower the pace." These cues are not childish. They are precision tools for a narrowed state.

The more escalated a person becomes, the more simple the cue must be.

This is difficult for people who pride themselves on complexity. They want insight at the very moment they need structure. They want to understand the whole relationship while they are struggling not to send one message. They want to analyse the roots of panic while their body is pleading for steadiness. They want to resolve the entire argument while their tone is becoming dangerous. There will be time for insight later. During the surge, the work is smaller and more urgent: reduce the chance of making things worse.

This is not anti-intellectual. It is intellectually honest.

A clear mind recognises its own state limits. It knows that some moments are poor conditions for major decisions, sweeping statements, final judgements, or emotional verdicts. It knows that the feeling of certainty under pressure is not always trustworthy. It knows that urgency can be a bodily sensation rather than a reliable instruction. It knows that the first answer is not always the truest one.

Willpower fails fast because it is often asked to stand alone. It is treated like a single heroic guard at the gate, expected to hold back years of habit, bodily acceleration, fear, pride, shame, and impulse by force of command. No wonder it tires. It was never meant to do the whole job without support.

Support looks like design.

It means deciding before the surge what you will do when the surge comes. It means building a short path from cue to action. It means making the safer move easier than the reactive one. It means placing friction between impulse and consequence: phone down, draft unsent, room left kindly, one breath taken, one phrase rehearsed, one hand on the table, one minute claimed before answering. The point is not to become rigid. The point is to reduce reliance on last-second heroics.

The most reliable calm is often pre-decided.

This is why people who manage pressure well do not necessarily have stronger feelings of peace. Many have simply built better procedures. They know how to pause without looking lost. They know how to delay a reply without making a drama of it. They know how to let the first wave pass before trusting the first interpretation. They know that a fast body should not be allowed to write permanent policy.

The same principle applies in ordinary domestic life. Imagine someone being criticised for forgetting a task. Their immediate impulse is to defend: "I have had a lot on, you know." The sentence may be true, but the tone carries a second message: back off. If they rely on willpower alone, they may try to suppress the defensiveness while their whole body continues to prepare an argument. The pressure leaks through anyway. But if they have a cue, the sequence changes. Feet on the floor. Exhale. One beat. Then perhaps: "You are right, I missed it. I need a minute before we talk about it properly."

That is not perfect serenity. It is a better next move.

Notice what happened there. Calm did not arrive as a feeling first. It arrived as a structure. The structure protected the relationship long enough for the person to regain choice. That is the practical genius of sequencing: behaviour can become wiser before emotion becomes comfortable.

This is essential because many people wait to act differently until they feel different. They assume they must feel calm in order to speak calmly, feel brave in order to hold a boundary, feel safe in order to stop seeking reassurance, feel certain in order to delay a decision. But emotional readiness is often unreliable in the first minute. A better standard is behavioural readiness: Can I do one small thing that does not feed the surge?

One small thing is enough to interrupt the old machinery.

Not always completely. Not elegantly. Not with cinematic transformation. But enough to create a gap. A longer exhale may not erase anger, but it can soften the first sentence. Looking around the room may not end panic, but it can reduce the sense of being trapped inside the sensation. Putting the phone face down may not resolve the conflict, but it can prevent a message from becoming a wound. Saying, "I need a moment," may not solve the issue, but it can keep the issue from being buried under the way it is discussed.

This is the discipline beneath the 60-second calm. It is not the discipline of forcing yourself to feel differently on command. It is the discipline of respecting the order in which humans change state. Body first, attention next, action smallest.

When people misunderstand this, they often become harsh with themselves. They treat every escalation as proof that they are weak. They compare their heated interior with someone else's composed exterior. They assume that if the feeling is still present, the tool has failed. But a tool has not failed because discomfort remains. A tool succeeds when it reduces the authority of the discomfort over behaviour.

That is a different standard, and a far more useful one.

You may still feel angry and choose not to wound. You may still feel panicked and choose not to obey every catastrophic interpretation. You may still feel stressed and choose not to rush a decision that needs steadiness. You may still feel ashamed and choose not to disappear behind silence or excessive apology. The feeling may remain, but its power to dictate the next move has weakened. That weakening is calm in its early form.

Willpower wants to win the whole battle immediately. A sequence aims to change the next thirty seconds.

The sequence is humbler, and that is why it works better. It does not depend on becoming a different person at the peak of pressure. It depends on having a rehearsed way to interrupt acceleration before it becomes behaviour. It treats the surge as real, but not sovereign. It respects the body without surrendering judgement to it.

So when willpower fails, the answer is not to despise yourself and demand more force. Force is often part of the problem. The answer is to ask a more precise question: What cue would help my body shift before I ask my mind to choose?

That question changes everything. It moves calm out of the realm of personality and into the realm of practice. It turns self-control from a heroic last stand into a sequence of small, repeatable moves. It gives the next minute a structure.

And in a surge, structure is mercy.

The one-minute priorities

The first minute of escalation is not the time to solve everything. It is not the time to decide who is right, repair the whole relationship, prove your point, analyse your childhood, answer every accusation, explain your full intention, or make a final judgement about what this moment means. The first minute has a narrower duty: stop the surge from becoming damage.

This sounds simple until the body is under pressure. In a surge, everything feels urgent. The email wants answering. The criticism wants correcting. The panic wants checking. The accusation wants defeating. The silence wants filling. The discomfort wants relief, and it wants relief now. That urgency is persuasive because it arrives dressed as necessity. It says, "You must act." It rarely says, "I am an activated state looking for somewhere to discharge."

The discipline of the 60-second calm begins by refusing to give urgency automatic authority. Not ignoring it. Not mocking it. Not pretending it is not there. Simply refusing to let it become the manager of the next move. A surge may be loud, but loud is not the same as wise. The body may be preparing for action, but action still needs direction. Your task is to create enough internal room for direction to return.

There are three priorities in the first minute: reduce intensity, widen attention, and choose the smallest safe next action. They are deliberately ordered. The order matters because escalation is not just a thought problem. If the body is racing and attention has narrowed to a single threat, asking yourself to make a balanced decision is asking too much too early. You do not need a brilliant insight in the first few seconds. You need a usable sequence.

The first priority is to reduce intensity.

This does not mean forcing yourself into perfect calm. That expectation is one of the reasons people abandon tools too quickly. They try one breath, still feel angry, and decide breathing does not work. They press their feet into the floor, still feel panicked, and decide grounding has failed. They pause before speaking, still feel the urge to defend, and conclude that nothing has changed. But the aim is not to remove the feeling instantly. The aim is to lower the volume enough that the feeling no longer has total control of behaviour.

A small reduction is valuable. A five per cent shift can be the difference between sending and saving, shouting and speaking firmly, fleeing and stepping away clearly, collapsing into apology and naming the truth with steadiness. The early movement is often subtle. Your breath becomes slightly less trapped. Your shoulders drop by a fraction. Your jaw releases enough for your voice to sound less sharp. Your feet remind you that you are standing in a room, not inside a catastrophe. These tiny changes may not impress the dramatic part of the mind, but they can change the outcome of the next sentence.

Reducing intensity works best when it is physical and simple. Under pressure, complex instructions become another burden. "Regulate your nervous system" is not a usable command when you are already flooded. "Exhale slowly" is better. "Unclench your hands" is better. "Both feet on the floor" is better. "Sip water before replying" is better. "Lower your voice by one notch" is better. The body needs a signal it can understand quickly.

The mistake is to wait until you feel ready to begin. In real surges, readiness often comes after action, not before. You take the breath while still irritated. You look around the room while still anxious. You put the phone down while still convinced you should answer. You soften your grip while still wanting to win. These physical moves do not deny the emotion; they prevent the emotion from monopolising the whole system.

The second priority is to widen attention.

Escalation narrows the field. It pulls you towards the person's face, the message on the screen, the sensation in your chest, the sentence that stung, the imagined consequence, the argument you are building, the apology you are about to over-give. The mind becomes less interested in reality as a whole and more interested in the single piece of reality that appears to carry the threat. This narrowing can make the moment feel more certain than it is.

Widening attention interrupts that certainty. It does not solve the issue. It does not require you to become detached or indifferent. It simply brings more of the present moment back into view. The table. The floor. The window. The colour of the wall. The contact of your hands. The other person's full sentence, not just the sharpest word. The fact that you have time for one breath. The fact that you do not have to answer at the speed of your alarm.

When attention widens, options begin to reappear. You may notice that the person is not shouting, merely disappointed. You may notice that the message does not require an immediate reply. You may notice that panic is made of sensations, not proof. You may notice that anger is asking for a boundary, not necessarily a punishment. You may notice that silence is possible without being hostile. You may notice that you are about to respond to an old fear rather than the current facts.

A practical way to widen attention is to deliberately include the environment. Let your eyes move from the trigger to the wider space. Notice three neutral objects. Feel the weight of the body. Listen for a sound that is not part of the conflict. Use peripheral vision rather than staring at the source of pressure. These ordinary actions matter because they tell the mind there is more here than the threat. The surge says, "This is everything." Widening says, "This is one part of a larger moment."

This is especially useful before speaking. Speech under narrowed attention often becomes excessive. You may say too much, too fast, too hard, or too finally. You may make claims you do not mean once the heat has passed. You may diagnose the other person's motives, announce sweeping conclusions, or offer promises designed only to end the discomfort. Widening creates a small delay between inner pressure and outer language. That delay is not weakness. It is quality control.

The third priority is to choose the smallest safe next action.

This is where many people make the first minute too ambitious. They want to choose the correct action, the mature action, the healing action, the impressive action, the action that proves they have grown. But during escalation, the best action is often much smaller than the ego prefers. The smallest safe next action is the move least likely to create fresh harm while you are still activated.

It may be not sending the message. It may be saying, "I need a minute." It may be turning your phone face down. It may be asking someone to repeat the question more slowly. It may be standing up and getting water. It may be saying, "I want to answer, but not sharply." It may be leaving the room with a clear return point: "I am going to step away for ten minutes, then come back." It may be writing the reply in notes rather than in the message thread. It may be doing nothing visible at all while you let the first wave pass.

The smallest safe action protects the future from the present state. It recognises that not every emotion deserves an immediate performance. Some truths are better spoken after the body has slowed. Some decisions are better made after sleep, food, movement, or distance. Some replies are more accurate twenty minutes later. Some apologies are cleaner when they are not panic in formal clothing. Some boundaries are stronger when they are not delivered as an attack.

"Do less, slower" is the plainest expression of this priority.

Doing less does not mean caring less. It means refusing to let a heightened state multiply consequences. Slower does not mean passive. It means giving judgement a chance to catch up. In many pressure moments, the most powerful act is subtraction: fewer words, fewer claims, fewer decisions, fewer explanations, fewer taps on the screen, fewer dramatic gestures. You are not shrinking from the moment. You are removing fuel.

This principle is particularly important with digital communication. A message can feel like a private discharge of emotion, but it travels. It lands. It can be reread, forwarded, screenshotted, stored, interpreted without tone, and used as evidence of a state you no longer occupy. The body wants relief; the send button offers relief with consequences attached. The one-minute priority is not to craft the perfect reply. It is to prevent the reactive reply from becoming the event.

The safest digital move is often to separate writing from sending. Draft the message somewhere else. Remove the recipient while composing. Set the phone down after reading. Read the message twice before answering. Ask whether a reply is required now or merely desired by the surge. The distinction matters. Many messages are not urgent until an activated body declares them urgent.

The same principle applies to speech. A conversation can survive a pause far better than it can survive a damaging sentence. People often fear that pausing will look weak, evasive, or cold. But a clear pause can be deeply respectful. "I need a moment so I do not answer badly" is not avoidance. "I want to think before I respond" is not defeat. "I hear you, and I need a minute" is not abandonment. These phrases protect the relationship from the unedited version of the surge.

The first minute also requires you to lower your standard of success. This is not a lowering of integrity; it is a lowering of fantasy. Success may not look like feeling peaceful. It may not look like resolving the argument. It may not look like making the other person understand. Success may be leaving the room without slamming the door. Success may be sending nothing. Success may be keeping your voice steady enough. Success may be noticing panic without feeding it a catastrophic story. Success may be delaying a decision you badly want to make from the peak of emotion.

That is not small in the life of a relationship. It is not small in the life of a workplace. It is not small in the life of a person trying to trust themselves. Many painful patterns continue because people underestimate the dignity of prevention. They want transformation to look dramatic, when often it looks like the absence of a familiar regret.

The one-minute priorities also help prevent a common trap: trying to use the wrong tool at the wrong stage. Insight is valuable, but not when the body is in full acceleration. Conversation is valuable, but not when speech is turning into a weapon. Problem-solving is valuable, but not when urgency is narrowing the options. Apology is valuable, but not when it is being used to escape discomfort rather than take responsibility. Boundary-setting is valuable, but not when it is being delivered as punishment.

Timing changes the quality of an action.

A sentence spoken after one breath may land differently from the same sentence fired from heat. A boundary named after a pause may sound clear rather than cruel. An apology offered after the body steadies may sound accountable rather than frantic. A decision made after the first wave passes may reflect values rather than pressure. The content matters, but state matters too. The same words can carry different force depending on the body they come from.

This is why the 60-second gap is not merely a calming technique. It is an ethical space. It is where you protect other people from being made responsible for your unfiltered state, and where you protect yourself from decisions that do not represent your steadier judgement. It is where dignity is preserved in small increments. It is where freedom begins to reappear, not as a grand ideal, but as the ability to refrain from the next harmful move.

The three priorities can be remembered as a simple internal movement: lower, widen, choose.

Lower the intensity.

Widen the field.

Choose the smallest safe next action.

Even when the mind is crowded, this sequence is short enough to use. It does not require perfect emotional literacy. It does not require you to understand every origin of the reaction. It does not require the other person to behave well first. It gives you something to do with your own state before your state starts doing things through you.

There will be times when you remember too late. That is part of learning. You may catch yourself after the message is sent, after the tone has sharpened, after the silence has stretched too long, after the panic checking has already begun. Even then, the sequence is still useful. Reduce intensity now. Widen attention now. Choose the smallest safe repair now. The gap can reopen at many points. Missing the first opening does not mean the whole moment is lost.

Over time, the aim is to catch the surge earlier and intervene more cleanly. The body starts to recognise the pattern. The first heat in the face becomes a cue. The first breath-hold becomes a cue. The first urge to type becomes a cue. The first rush of certainty becomes a cue. Instead of discovering the surge only through its consequences, you begin to notice it while there is still room to steer.

The one-minute priorities are not glamorous. They are not complicated. They will not make every conflict graceful or every panic spike easy. They will not remove the need for later conversations, deeper repair, practical boundaries, medical care when appropriate, or longer emotional work. Their strength is more immediate than that. They help you cross the most combustible part of the moment without handing it a match.

A surge says, "Do something now."

The 60-second calm answers, "Not just anything."

That answer is the beginning of choice.

Chapter 2
Your personal escalation map

Most people recognise their escalation pattern too late. They see it after the message has been sent, after the tone has sharpened, after the apology has become excessive, after the room has gone quiet, after the body has finally slowed enough to reveal what just happened. The evidence arrives in the aftermath: the look on someone's face, the heavy silence, the regret in the stomach, the familiar thought, *I did it again.*

Yet the surge was not invisible. It had early signals. It almost always does.

The trouble is that early signals are easy to dismiss because they seem too small to matter. A tight jaw. Heat in the cheeks. A pressure behind the eyes. A breath held without noticing. Fingers gripping the phone. A sudden need to prove the point. A wish to leave the room. A blankness that drops like a curtain. These are not dramatic events, so they are often ignored. But in emotional pressure, the small signs are the useful ones. By the time the signs become obvious to everyone else, the easiest moment for intervention has usually passed.

Your personal escalation map begins with a more honest kind of attention. Not self-surveillance. Not anxious monitoring. Not turning every feeling into a project. It is the practical skill of noticing what your system tends to do before it takes over. The body often speaks before the mind can explain. It gives clues in muscle, breath, temperature, posture, pace, and impulse. Those clues are not the problem. They are the earliest invitation to regain choice.

This matters because no two people escalate in exactly the same way. One person becomes louder, quicker, more certain, more prosecutorial. Another becomes quiet, agreeable, distant, almost absent. Someone else becomes charming and competent, performing control while panic rises behind the eyes. Another begins to explain, then explain the explanation, then defend the explanation against imagined judgement. These patterns can look like personality, but very often they are protection. They are the moves the body has learnt to make when pressure feels unsafe.

A map is not a verdict. That distinction is essential. The purpose is not to label yourself as angry, avoidant, needy, dramatic, cold, weak, difficult, oversensitive, or defensive. Those labels may feel powerful, but they are usually too crude to be useful. A map is more precise. It asks: where does the surge begin, how does it travel, what does it make me want to do, and where does it usually cause trouble? Precision gives you leverage. Shame merely gives the old pattern more fuel.

The first layer of the map is physical. Before there is a full story, there is often a bodily cue. Anger may arrive as heat, forward motion, pressure in the chest, a hardening of the face, or a forceful readiness to speak. Panic may arrive as breathlessness, unreality, shaking, dizziness, a racing heart, or a frightening sense that something must be fixed immediately. Stress may arrive as tight shoulders, shallow breathing, restless scanning, impatience, or a clenched concentration that squeezes the world into tasks and threats. These cues do not diagnose the whole moment, but they tell you that your state is shifting.

The second layer is behavioural. Under pressure, people tend to repeat a small set of moves. They debate, please, blame, withdraw, perform competence, seek certainty, become sarcastic, over-apologise, over-function, go silent, rush decisions, or try to control the emotional weather of everyone in the room. These moves are not random. They usually promise relief. Debate promises safety through winning. Pleasing promises safety through approval. Withdrawal promises safety through distance. Blame promises safety through certainty. Competence promises safety through appearing unaffected. The promise is seductive because it is immediate. The cost often arrives later.

This is where the map becomes personal. General advice can only go so far because the same instruction can help one person and harm another. "Speak up" may be exactly right for the person who disappears, but dangerous for the person who already attacks. "Take space" may protect one relationship, while giving another person permission to vanish without repair. "Say what you feel" may create honesty for one person and become an unfiltered discharge for another. The tool has to meet the pattern. To choose well in sixty seconds, you need to know what your system usually reaches for when you are no longer choosing carefully.

The question beneath this work is beautifully severe: what do you do when you are not choosing?

That question removes the fantasy version of self-improvement. It does not ask what you believe on a calm morning. It does not ask what you admire in emotionally skilled people. It asks what happens when the pressure rises, when your pride is touched, when someone sounds disappointed, when your body mistakes discomfort for danger, when panic offers a catastrophic story, when anger offers a weapon disguised as clarity. The answer may be uncomfortable, but it is also liberating. Once the pattern is visible, it is no longer fate.

There is also compassion in the map, though not the soft kind that excuses everything. Real compassion tells the truth without turning the self into an enemy. It can say, "I learnt to go quiet because conflict once felt unsafe," and also, "My silence can still hurt people now." It can say, "I defend quickly because criticism feels exposing," and also, "My defensiveness blocks repair." It can say, "I please because I fear disconnection," and also, "My false agreement creates resentment later." This is the mature ground: understanding without evasion, responsibility without self-attack.

As you begin mapping your escalation pattern, the aim is not to catch every signal perfectly. The aim is to move recognition earlier. At first, you may notice the pattern only after the fact. Then perhaps halfway through. Then at the first sharp sentence forming in your mind. Then at the heat in your face before the sentence. Then at the breath you were holding before the heat. Each earlier point gives you more room. You are not trying to become emotionless. You are learning the route your emotion usually takes so you can stop treating every surge as a surprise.

The doorway into this chapter is simple: your body has been giving you information, and your behaviour has been leaving clues. The task now is to read both with discipline. Not to judge the map. Not to decorate it. To see it clearly enough that the next surge does not have to travel the same road unchecked.

Spotting early body cues

The body usually tells the truth before the story becomes convincing.

A surge rarely begins with a complete sentence in the mind. It begins lower down, earlier than language, in the small physical changes people are trained to ignore. The jaw tightens. The shoulders lift. The breath becomes shallow. The face grows hot. The hands become restless. The stomach drops. The throat narrows. The body leans forward or pulls away. Something in the system has already shifted, even if the mind is still pretending that everything is normal.

These early cues matter because they arrive before behaviour hardens. Once you are already shouting, shutting down, over-explaining, apologising too quickly, typing furiously, or trying to escape, the surge has momentum. It can still be interrupted, but the work is harder. Early body cues are useful precisely because they are unimpressive. They do not look like drama. They look like a held breath, a clenched hand, a sudden stillness, a rush of heat, a need to move, a small internal flinch. That is why they are easy to miss, and why learning to notice them changes everything.

Most people look for emotional awareness in the wrong place. They wait until they can name the feeling clearly: anger, fear, panic, shame, resentment, dread, embarrassment. But by the time the label is obvious, the body may already be several steps into escalation. A better question is not, "What emotion am I having?" but, "What is my body beginning to do?" That question is faster, cleaner, and less likely to become tangled in analysis.

The body does not speak in essays. It speaks in signals.

A tight jaw may be the beginning of anger, determination, fear, or restraint. A tight chest may be panic, grief, pressure, or dread. A blank mind may be shock, overwhelm, shame, or a protective shutdown. The aim is not to interpret the cue perfectly on first contact. The aim is to notice that a cue has appeared. You do not need to know the whole meaning of the dashboard light before you stop driving as though nothing is happening.

This is where many people lose valuable time. They notice a physical signal and immediately begin arguing with it. "I should not feel this." "This is stupid." "I am overreacting." "I need to be fine." "Nothing is happening." These responses may sound like attempts at control, but they often increase pressure. The body is already activated; now it is being criticised for being activated. The result is a second surge on top of the first: the original reaction, followed by shame or frustration about the reaction.

A wiser response is simpler: "Something is rising."

That sentence does not dramatise the moment. It does not excuse any behaviour. It does not require you to understand the entire emotional history beneath the cue. It merely marks the beginning of a shift. In the 60-second calm, that is enough. The earlier you can say, "Something is rising," the more choices remain available.

Early cues vary from person to person, but they often cluster around several areas: breath, muscle tension, temperature, movement, attention, voice, and impulse. Breath is one of the most common. Some people hold it without noticing. Others breathe high in the chest. Some begin to sigh, gulp air, or feel as though they cannot get a satisfying breath. In anger, the breath may become forceful and ready for speech. In panic, the breath may feel urgent, unreliable, or strangely insufficient. In stress, it may become shallow and efficient, as if the body has decided there is no time for a full inhale or exhale.

Muscle cues are equally revealing. The jaw clamps. The tongue presses against the teeth. The shoulders rise towards the ears. The hands close into fists or grip a phone too tightly. The stomach braces. The legs become ready to move. The back stiffens. Some people feel a forward surge, as though their body wants to close distance and confront. Others feel a backward pull, as though their body wants to vanish from the room. These are not random sensations. They are preparation.

Temperature cues can be particularly noticeable in anger and embarrassment. Heat in the face, ears, neck, or chest can signal that the system is moving quickly. Some people experience the opposite: cold hands, a chilled feeling, or a drained sensation, especially when fear or shutdown is rising. Neither cue is more legitimate than the other. The important thing is to learn your own pattern rather than borrowing someone else's.

Movement cues often reveal the direction of the surge. Anger may bring pacing, pointing, leaning in, rapid gestures, or a sudden need to stand. Panic may bring fidgeting, scanning exits, touching the chest, checking the body, or repeatedly adjusting position. Stress may bring restless efficiency: opening apps, checking messages, tidying unnecessarily, rushing between tasks, or moving too quickly for the actual situation. Shutdown may look like reduced movement, stillness, heaviness, numbness, or a collapse in facial expression.

Attention cues are more subtle but extremely important. When a surge begins, attention often narrows. You may lock onto one sentence, one look, one bodily sensation, one possible outcome, one perceived insult, one unfinished task. The rest of the world fades. This narrowing can make the moment feel more dangerous, more urgent, and more certain than it really is. One early cue, then, is not physical in the obvious sense but perceptual: the room gets smaller. The issue becomes everything.

Voice cues are another early warning. You may speak faster, louder, flatter, sharper, quieter, or with forced politeness. Your words may become clipped. Your tone may carry contempt before your conscious mind has admitted anger. You may laugh in a way that is not amusement. You may say "fine" with a meaning that is nowhere near fine. You may begin sentences before you have decided whether they are wise. The voice is often the body's pressure made audible.

Impulse cues may be the most useful of all. An impulse is not yet an action. That makes it precious. The urge to reply immediately, leave abruptly, correct every detail, apologise excessively, demand reassurance, make a sweeping decision, prove your innocence, send a long explanation, or shut the conversation down is a cue. It is not an instruction. When you learn to recognise impulses as body signals rather than commands, the decision gap opens.

Anger and panic often have different flavours, though they can overlap. Anger tends to bring a forward push. It says, "Move towards. Say it. Stop this. Correct them. Make them understand. Do not let this stand." The body may feel hot, pressurised, energised, and certain. Panic often brings a trapped urgency. It says, "Get out. Check. Fix this. Find certainty. Something is wrong. Do something now." The body may feel shaky, breathless, unreal, dizzy, or flooded with alarming sensations. Both states can narrow attention. Both can make immediate action feel necessary. But their early cues may ask for different responses.

This is why naming the body cue is more useful than judging the emotion. "My chest is tight." "My face is hot." "My jaw is locked." "My breath is high." "My hands are restless." "My attention has narrowed." "I want to send something now." These observations are plain enough to use under pressure. They do not require a deep psychological explanation. They simply locate you in the sequence.

The skill is to notice without making a case.

Many people turn body awareness into a courtroom. They gather evidence for why they are justified, unsafe, wronged, weak, ridiculous, or doomed. This is not spotting cues; it is building a story around cues. The first task is much more restrained. Notice the signal. Name it in ordinary language. Let it be information. Nothing more is required in that first beat.

For example, imagine someone standing in a kitchen while a partner says, "You forgot again." The words are familiar. Before the person has consciously decided to defend themselves, their body has already begun. Jaw tight. Heat in the face. Breath held. Attention fixed on the word "again." The old interpretation arrives: "They think I am useless." The impulse follows: attack back, list everything they have done wrong, prove that the criticism is unfair. If the person only notices the surge at the point of speech, the first sentence may already be loaded. But if they catch the jaw, heat, and breath-hold, there is a small opening. Not a perfect calm. An opening.

Or imagine someone in a shop queue feeling panic rise. Nothing visible has changed. Still, the body begins to send signals: chest tight, air unsatisfying, hands tingling, vision slightly narrowed, urge to leave. The mind may rush to interpret: "I am going to faint," "I cannot handle this," "I need to escape now." Spotting early body cues changes the relationship to the moment. The person can say, "This is the start of a panic surge. My breath feels tight. My feet are on the floor." That does not make the sensations vanish instantly, but it interrupts the leap from sensation to catastrophe.

The cue is the hinge.

Before the cue is noticed, the surge feels like reality. After the cue is noticed, the surge becomes an event happening in the body. Still uncomfortable, still powerful, but more observable. That small shift matters because observation creates distance. Distance creates choice. Choice creates the possibility of a different next move.

A common fear is that noticing body cues will make them worse. Some people worry that paying attention to a tight chest or racing thoughts will intensify anxiety. That can happen when attention becomes obsessive checking. There is a difference between noticing and monitoring. Noticing is brief, practical, and linked to action. Monitoring is repetitive, fearful, and asks the body for constant reassurance. The aim is not to stare at the sensation. The aim is to receive the signal and use it.

Think of it as glancing at the weather before choosing how to travel. You do not stand at the window for an hour arguing with the rain. You notice what is present and adjust.

The same applies to early cues. "My throat is tight" is useful if it leads to a slower exhale, a sip of water, or a pause before speaking. "My throat is tight, why is it tight, what if it gets worse, what if I cannot cope, what does this mean?" is no longer cue recognition. It is escalation wearing the clothes of self-awareness.

To make cue-spotting practical, keep the language concrete. Avoid grand interpretations at the beginning. Instead of "I am being disrespected," try "My face is hot and I want to interrupt." Instead of "I am losing control," try "My breath is fast and my thoughts are speeding up." Instead of "They are judging me," try "My stomach dropped when they said that." Concrete language slows the jump from signal to story. It keeps you close to what can actually be worked with.

The body cue also helps you avoid the trap of blaming the trigger for the entire reaction. Triggers matter, of course. Some words, environments, behaviours, and dynamics genuinely are difficult. Some conversations need boundaries. Some relationships need repair. Some situations are not healthy. But if all attention goes to the trigger, you may miss the only part you can influence in the next sixty seconds: your own sequence. The cue brings responsibility back into reach without pretending the outside world is irrelevant.

This balance is important. Spotting body cues is not a technique for tolerating mistreatment. It is not a way of making yourself smaller, quieter, or endlessly accommodating. It is the opposite. When you recognise your early signals, you are less likely to hand your boundary to anger and let anger deliver it badly. You are less likely to let panic turn uncertainty into emergency. You are less likely to let shame make you disappear when you need to stay present. The cue helps you act with more precision.

At first, you may only identify your cues after the moment has passed. That still counts. After a tense exchange, ask plainly: Where did I feel it first? What changed in my breathing? What happened in my hands, jaw, chest, stomach, or voice? Did I move towards, pull away, freeze, please, explain, or rush? What was the first physical sign that I was no longer settled? This kind of review should be brief. The purpose is learning, not self-punishment.

Over time, the review moves closer to the moment itself. You begin to notice during the conversation, not only afterwards. Then you begin to notice before the first reactive sentence. Eventually, a cue that once passed unnoticed becomes unmistakable. The jaw tightens and a small inner voice says, "Here it is." The breath catches and you know to slow down. The urge to type a paragraph becomes the warning, not the instruction. That is the map coming alive.

There is no need to collect dozens of cues. In fact, too many can become clutter. You need the earliest reliable ones. For some people, that is the jaw and the hands. For others, breath and chest. For others, heat and urgency. For others, blankness and withdrawal. Choose the cues that consistently appear before your least helpful behaviours. Those are your practical entry points.

A useful body cue is not the most dramatic sensation. It is the one that gives you time.

This is why subtle cues deserve respect. The held breath before the sharp reply matters more than the shouting that comes later. The first urge to apologise may matter more than the resentment that follows false agreement. The moment your attention locks onto the send button may matter more than the regret after sending. The early cue is where the pattern is still soft enough to shape.

The work is not glamorous. It is intimate, repetitive, and exact. It asks you to become less impressed by your own stories and more attentive to the body that generates them under pressure. It asks you to stop treating physical signals as inconveniences and start treating them as messages. It asks you to notice the beginning before the behaviour becomes the headline.

The next time a surge rises, your body may still move first. That is not failure. The question is whether you can catch its movement one moment earlier than before. A breath held. A hand clenched. A face heating. A tunnel forming. An urge appearing.

There, at the first honest signal, the map begins.

Naming your default moves

Everyone has a move they tend to make when pressure rises and choice narrows.

It may not look dramatic. It may not even look emotional from the outside. One person argues with clean logic and calls it clarity. Another agrees too quickly and calls it keeping the peace. Someone withdraws and calls it needing space. Someone becomes painfully efficient and calls it coping. Someone blames, jokes, performs confidence, apologises repeatedly, goes cold, over-explains, changes the subject, or reaches for their phone with the private certainty that this message must be answered now.

These moves are not random. They are the body's preferred escape routes. Under stress, anger, or panic, the system reaches for whatever has most often promised relief. Relief from uncertainty. Relief from shame. Relief from being misunderstood. Relief from conflict. Relief from feeling trapped. Relief from the unbearable few seconds in which the body is activated and no one has fixed it yet. The move may not solve the situation, but it offers something seductively immediate: a way not to feel this particular pressure quite so directly.

A default move is what you do when you are no longer fully choosing.

That sentence deserves respect, not panic. A default move is not proof that you are weak, cruel, immature, broken, or doomed to repeat yourself. It is a learned pattern. It may once have helped you get through difficult rooms, unpredictable moods, demanding adults, humiliating criticism, unsafe conflict, social embarrassment, or periods when being agreeable, invisible, clever, forceful, funny, or self-sufficient was the safest available option. Patterns often begin as protection. They become problems when they keep protecting you from the wrong thing.

The aim is not to shame the move. The aim is to name it.

Naming matters because unnamed patterns move quickly. They hide inside justification. They borrow the voice of common sense. They sound like personality. "I am just honest." "I do not like drama." "I am only trying to explain." "I cannot leave things unresolved." "I work better under pressure." "I hate confrontation." "I need people to understand me." "I am fine." These statements may contain truth, but they may also conceal a surge strategy. The question is not whether the story is reasonable. The question is whether the move gives you more choice or less.

One common default move is debating. This person tries to think and talk their way out of the surge. They correct details, challenge wording, present evidence, defend motives, and treat the conversation as though winning the case will calm the body. Sometimes the facts matter. Sometimes correction is needed. But in escalation, debate can become a way of avoiding vulnerability. The person is not only seeking truth; they are trying to reduce the feeling of being accused, exposed, or out of control.

Debating often feels powerful in the moment because it creates structure. It turns emotion into argument. It gives the mind a task and gives the body somewhere to send its pressure. The cost is that other people may feel cross-examined rather than heard. A partner's hurt becomes a point to refute. A colleague's feedback becomes a courtroom. A friend's concern becomes an error to correct. The debater may later insist, sincerely, "I was only explaining," while the other person remembers the experience as being pushed away by words.

Another default move is pleasing. Pleasing seeks safety through agreement, softness, helpfulness, apology, or self-erasure. It says yes before it knows whether yes is true. It accepts blame before checking the facts. It rushes to soothe the other person's disappointment, anger, silence, or discomfort. Pleasing can look kind, but in a surge it is often fear wearing good manners.

The danger of pleasing is delayed resentment. A person may escape the heat of the immediate moment by becoming agreeable, only to feel trapped later by the promise, apology, or concession they made while activated. They may say, "It is fine," when it is not fine. They may say, "Do not worry about it," while the body stores the injury. They may say, "I understand," when they have not had time to understand anything except the need to make the pressure stop. Pleasing protects the present minute by borrowing trouble from the future.

Blaming is another familiar route. It moves discomfort outward. Rather than staying with the complexity of the moment, blame locates the problem entirely in someone else: their tone, their timing, their selfishness, their incompetence, their lack of care. Sometimes another person really has behaved badly. Clear responsibility matters. But blame becomes a default move when it arrives too fast, too completely, and with too much certainty. It refuses the discomfort of asking, "What part of this belongs to me?"

Blame is attractive because it reduces ambiguity. It creates a hard edge where the mind can rest. If they are entirely wrong, you do not have to feel exposed. If they are the problem, you do not have to examine your own impulse. If their behaviour explains everything, your next move can feel justified before it has been considered. The cost is that blame often inflames the very conflict it claims to clarify. It may produce a temporary sense of strength, but it rarely produces repair.

Withdrawal takes a different path. It seeks safety by reducing contact. The person goes quiet, leaves the room, becomes unavailable, stops replying, turns emotionally flat, or retreats behind a wall of "nothing is wrong." Withdrawal can be necessary when a situation is truly unsafe or when a pause is clearly communicated and followed by return. But as a default surge move, it often creates confusion and distance. What feels like self-protection from the inside may feel like punishment from the outside.

Withdrawal is especially tricky because it can look calm. A person who withdraws may not raise their voice, send sharp messages, or make dramatic accusations. They may appear controlled. Yet internally, the system may be flooded, frozen, ashamed, panicked, or furious. Silence then becomes a container for everything unsaid. The other person is left guessing. The issue remains unresolved, but now it has acquired another layer: the hurt of disappearance.

Performing competence is one of the more socially rewarded default moves. Under pressure, this person becomes capable, composed, useful, impressive, organised, perhaps even charming. They solve, manage, reassure, take charge, produce, tidy, answer, and keep functioning. From the outside, they may look admirable. Inside, they may be using competence to outrun feeling.

This move can be hard to name because it often produces good results. Tasks get done. People are reassured. Problems appear handled. But the body still pays. The person may never pause long enough to register fear, anger, grief, or exhaustion. They may become resentful that others rely on their steadiness, while also feeling unable to stop performing it. Competence is valuable. Performed competence under escalation is different. It is less a strength than a hiding place decorated as a strength.

Over-explaining is closely related to both debating and pleasing. It tries to secure safety through being fully understood. The person adds context, then more context, then a clarification, then a clarification of the clarification. They try to close every possible gap where judgement could enter. They may believe that if they can just make the other person see the whole picture, the discomfort will end.

Sometimes explanation is necessary. But over-explaining during a surge usually has a desperate quality. It does not trust one clear sentence. It keeps adding words because the body still feels unsafe. The listener may become tired, defensive, or overwhelmed. The over-explainer then feels even less understood, which fuels the urge to continue. A move meant to create connection can become a wall made of language.

Another default move is rushing to certainty. This appears often in panic, but also in conflict and stress. The person wants the answer now: Are we okay? Am I ill? Are you angry? Is this ruined? What should I do? What does this mean? Certainty feels like oxygen. The trouble is that reassurance gathered under pressure often does not last. The body asks again. The mind checks again. The question returns in a slightly different form. The move promises relief but trains the system to distrust uncertainty even more.

Control is another route. It tries to reduce internal chaos by organising the outside world. The person gives instructions, sets rules, manages timing, edits other people's emotions, insists on a particular process, or tries to force the conversation into a form that feels safer. Some structure is useful, especially in conflict. But control becomes a default move when flexibility disappears and other people become obstacles to emotional relief.

Sarcasm and humour can also be default moves. A sharp joke can release pressure without admitting pain. A sarcastic remark can express anger while preserving deniability. A laugh can cover embarrassment. A witty deflection can prevent closeness. These moves may be socially skilled, even entertaining, but under escalation they often keep the real issue out of reach. The person avoids exposure, but also avoids being accurately known.

None of these moves should be treated as a villain. Each is an attempted solution. Debate tries to protect truth. Pleasing tries to protect connection. Blame tries to protect dignity. Withdrawal tries to protect safety. Competence tries to protect functioning. Over-explaining tries to protect against misunderstanding. Certainty-seeking tries to protect against fear. Control tries to protect against chaos. Humour tries to protect against vulnerability. Every default move carries an intelligence. The problem is that the intelligence is incomplete.

The move protects one value while endangering another.

Debate may protect accuracy while endangering warmth. Pleasing may protect harmony while endangering honesty. Blame may protect self-respect while endangering accountability. Withdrawal may protect space while endangering trust. Competence may protect performance while endangering emotional truth. Over-explaining may protect intention while endangering clarity. Certainty-seeking may protect immediate comfort while endangering resilience. Control may protect order while endangering respect. Humour may protect dignity while endangering intimacy.

This is why naming your default move must be done without self-shaming. Shame narrows attention and pushes you straight back into the old strategy. The blamer blames themselves. The pleaser apologises for having needs. The withdrawer disappears from the work. The debater builds a case against their own debating. The competent performer turns self-awareness into another performance. Shame does not free the pattern. It rehearses it.

A better question is: "What is this move trying to do for me?"

That question slows judgement and reveals function. If your default is debating, it may be trying to protect you from feeling falsely accused. If your default is pleasing, it may be trying to protect you from disconnection. If your default is withdrawal, it may be trying to protect you from overwhelm. If your default is blame, it may be trying to protect you from shame. If your default is competence, it may be trying to protect you from collapse. Once you see the function, you can choose a cleaner way to meet the same need.

The second question is sharper: "What does this move cost?"

Every default move has a bill. The bill may come as conflict, distance, resentment, exhaustion, confusion, mistrust, regret, or loneliness. It may come as a private loss of self-respect. It may come as a relationship in which people tiptoe around your defensiveness, cannot reach you through your withdrawal, rely too much on your competence, or stop believing your "fine." The cost is not mentioned to punish you. It is mentioned because mature change requires honest accounting.

The third question is the most useful under pressure: "What do I do when I am not choosing?"

This question belongs at the centre of your escalation map. It catches the pattern before the personality story takes over. You may think of yourself as honest, kind, calm, independent, responsible, relaxed, thoughtful, or resilient. Those identities may be real. But under pressure, a different script may run. Naming that script gives you the chance to interrupt it.

You might discover, "When I am not choosing, I prosecute."

Or, "When I am not choosing, I disappear."

Or, "When I am not choosing, I agree."

Or, "When I am not choosing, I perform."

Or, "When I am not choosing, I send a paragraph."

Or, "When I am not choosing, I demand reassurance."

Or, "When I am not choosing, I become certain too quickly."

The wording should be plain. Not poetic. Not diagnostic. Not cruel. You are not trying to produce a perfect psychological profile. You are trying to create a label short enough to remember during a surge. "I prosecute" is more usable than a long theory about your relationship with criticism. "I disappear" is more usable than a detailed analysis of avoidance. "I perform" is more usable than an elegant essay on pressure and identity. Under escalation, the best labels are practical.

Once named, the move can become a cue. If you hear yourself building a case, you can recognise the debating move. If you feel the automatic "yes" rising, you can recognise pleasing. If your body starts to go numb and your eyes search for an exit, you can recognise withdrawal. If your voice becomes brisk and polished while your chest tightens, you can recognise performed competence. The move itself becomes the alarm bell.

This is a major shift. Previously, the default move felt like the solution. Now it becomes information.

The moment you can say, "This is my move," you are not completely possessed by it. Some observing part has returned. You may still feel the pull. You may still choose badly sometimes. But the move has lost a little invisibility, and invisible patterns are the hardest ones to change. Naming brings the pattern into the room where choice can reach it.

It is important to recognise that people often have more than one default move. You may debate at work, please in family conflict, withdraw with a partner, and perform competence in public. You may attack when you feel disrespected but appease when you fear abandonment. You may become controlling under stress and reassurance-seeking under panic. The aim is not to force your entire emotional life into one category. The aim is to identify the moves that show up most reliably in specific contexts.

Context matters. Your body may not react the same way to a manager's criticism as it does to a partner's disappointment. A text message may activate a different pattern from a face-to-face conversation. Panic in a crowded shop may produce escape, while panic at home may produce checking. Anger with a stranger may be easier to contain than anger with someone whose opinion matters deeply. The map should be specific enough to be useful.

A strong escalation map often sounds like this: "When I feel criticised by someone I care about, my chest tightens, I become very certain they are being unfair, and I start defending every detail." Or: "When someone seems disappointed in me, my stomach drops, I agree too fast, and later I feel resentful." Or: "When I feel trapped in a conversation, my mind goes blank, I get quiet, and I leave without explaining when I will return." These sentences join body cue, interpretation, and default move. That is the beginning of practical self-knowledge.

The purpose of this work is not to remove your protective instincts. It is to update them. You may still need to speak firmly, take space, explain yourself, apologise, organise, ask for reassurance, or use humour. None of these actions is inherently wrong. The difference is whether the action is chosen or automatic, proportionate or excessive, clear or loaded, connected to the present or dragged in by old pressure.

A chosen pause is different from withdrawal.

A clear boundary is different from blame.

A concise explanation is different from over-explaining.

A sincere apology is different from appeasement.

A steady answer is different from performed competence.

A request for support is different from panic-driven reassurance-seeking.

The same outer behaviour can carry a different quality depending on whether it comes from choice or compulsion. That quality is what people often feel, even when they cannot name it. They can sense when an apology is really a plea for the discomfort to stop. They can sense when silence is not reflection but punishment or fear. They can sense when explanation has become defence. They can sense when competence is being used to avoid honesty. Naming your move helps you bring the behaviour back into alignment with intention.

There is humility in this, and also freedom. Humility because you have to admit that your first impulse is not always your wisest guide. Freedom because you no longer have to obey that impulse simply because it arrives with force. You can respect the protective move without letting it run the entire moment.

The next time pressure rises, listen for the familiar script. It may arrive as a tone in your voice, a posture in your body, a sentence in your mind, a hand reaching for the phone, an urge to fix the other person's feeling, a need to win, a need to vanish, a need to be seen as fine. Do not attack it. Name it.

"This is my default move."

That naming is not the end of the surge. It is the first clean interruption.

Chapter 3
Breath resets that work

The meeting has already tightened before anyone raises a voice. A question lands badly, not because it is cruel, but because it touches the place where pressure has been gathering all morning. Your face warms. Your mind starts drafting a defence. Someone else is still speaking, but you are no longer fully listening; you are preparing. The answer forming in your mouth is accurate enough to justify itself and sharp enough to cause trouble.

Your breath has changed too. Perhaps you are holding it. Perhaps it has climbed high in the chest. Perhaps the exhale has become short, as if your body has decided there is no spare time for release. Nobody else can see the full event. To them, you may look composed, attentive, mildly tense at most. Inside, the body has begun to vote for speed.

This is the moment where breath is often misunderstood. People talk about breathing as though it were a spell: take a deep breath and become calm. But a pressured body does not always respond well to grand instructions. A forced inhale can feel intrusive. A huge breath can create more discomfort than relief. A person already panicking may become more frightened by trying to breathe "properly" and failing. A person in anger may experience the instruction to breathe as a demand to swallow the truth. Breath helps most when it is treated not as magic, but as a lever.

The central tension is precision. Breath can steady the system, but only when it matches the state you are actually in. Stress, anger, and panic do not all ask for the same kind of breathing. A body full of heat and forward pressure needs a different entry point from a body gripped by air-hunger and alarm. The aim is not to perform calm for other people, nor to smother the emotion before it has been understood. The aim is to create one usable beat between activation and action.

That beat matters because breath sits close to the border between the voluntary and the automatic. Much of the body's alarm response happens before deliberate thought has caught up, yet breathing gives you a small handle on the physical state. You may not be able to decide your way out of panic in a single command. You may not be able to reason anger into elegance while your jaw is locked and your chest is pressurised. But you can often alter the rhythm slightly. Slightly is enough to begin.

There is a particular danger in making breath too heroic. People imagine that a useful breath must be deep, dramatic, cleansing, visible, and immediately transformative. That belief creates failure where none is needed. In real pressure, the most useful breath is often discreet. It does not announce itself. It does not require closing your eyes, escaping the room, or turning the moment into a performance. It may be no more than a softer inhale, a longer exhale, a small pause before speech, or a deliberate refusal to chase the next breath in panic.

This is why comfort matters. A breath reset that makes you dizzy, strained, embarrassed, or more focused on symptoms is not serving the moment. Calm is not proven by how intensely you can breathe. It is supported by the smallest adjustment that tells the body, *there is no immediate need to accelerate further*. The breath should give the nervous system evidence of safety, not another task to fail. A good reset feels like easing a grip, not winning a contest.

The path begins by recognising when breath is the right lever and when it is being asked to do too much. From there, the emphasis shifts towards exhale-led changes that are quiet enough for ordinary life and gentle enough not to create fresh alarm. Anger then requires its own kind of pause: a breath that slows the rush without silencing the message. Panic requires even more care, because the urgent demand for "more air" can pull a person into fighting the very sensations they need to steady.

So the question is not, "Can I breathe my way into perfect calm?" That question is too large and too crude. The sharper question is this: when pressure rises and the next word, message, or movement is about to carry the surge forward, can your breath create one clean beat before the moment chooses for you?

When breathing helps

Breath is one of the few tools that can meet a surge where it begins: in the body.

That is why it is so often recommended, and also why it is so often badly taught. People are told to breathe as though breathing were a universal command, equally useful in every emotional state and every body. They are told to take a deep breath when they are angry, panicking, embarrassed, overstimulated, or trying not to cry. The advice is familiar enough to sound wise. Yet many people have discovered, quietly and with some irritation, that it does not always work. Sometimes it helps. Sometimes it does nothing. Sometimes it makes the moment worse.

The problem is not breath itself. The problem is the fantasy attached to it.

Breath is not magic. It does not erase conflict, cure fear, settle every argument, or turn a frightened body into a peaceful one on command. It cannot make an unfair situation fair. It cannot make a harsh email kind. It cannot make a person listening badly suddenly understand you. It cannot remove the need for boundaries, repair, rest, medical care when appropriate, or difficult decisions. Breath should never be asked to do the work of a whole life.

But breath can do something more modest and, in the first minute of escalation, more useful. It can reduce intensity enough for choice to return.

That is the proper promise. Not transformation. Not instant serenity. A shift.

When a surge rises, the body often changes its breathing before the mind has named the emotion. Anger may make the breath forceful, shallow, or held behind clenched speech. Panic may make the breath feel urgent, cramped, unreliable, or impossible to satisfy. Stress may make breathing tight and efficient, as though the body has decided there is no time to exhale fully. These patterns are not moral failures. They are part of the body's preparation for action.

The breath then becomes both signal and lever. It signals that the state has changed, and it offers a small handle by which that state may be influenced.

This is why breath can help faster than reasoning in the early phase of escalation. Reasoning asks the mind to slow down while the body is still accelerating. Breath speaks in a more physical language. A softened exhale, a slower rhythm, a brief pause before replying, or a return to steadier breathing tells the body that the moment may not require immediate attack, escape, collapse, or frantic repair. The message is not, "Everything is fine." That would be too large, and often untrue. The message is smaller: "There is no need to make this worse in the next few seconds."

Small messages matter.

A breath reset works best when it is matched to the moment. This is the point many people miss. They treat breathing as one technique, when it is really a family of techniques. The breath that helps before answering a tense question in a meeting may not be the same breath that helps during a panic spike. The breath that softens anger should not make you feel silenced. The breath that steadies panic should not involve forcing in more air when the body is already alarmed by breathing sensations. Precision is kinder than intensity.

The first question, then, is not "How do I breathe correctly?" It is "What is my state asking for?"

If the body is heated and pushing forward, the breath may need to create a pause before speech. If the body is panicked and chasing air, the breath may need to become smaller and steadier rather than bigger. If the body is stressed and rushing, the breath may need to lengthen the exhale just enough to interrupt speed. If the body is numb or shut down, breath may need to be paired with grounding, movement, or contact with the environment rather than used alone.

Breath helps when it reduces pressure. It does not help when it becomes pressure.

This distinction is crucial. Many people turn breathing into a performance. They try to do it perfectly. They monitor each inhale. They worry whether the breath is deep enough, slow enough, smooth enough, calm enough. They begin checking whether the tool is working while they are doing it. That kind of effort can become another layer of escalation. The person is no longer breathing to steady the body; they are trying to prove they can control the body. Panic especially can feed on this kind of struggle.

A useful breath reset should feel workable, not impressive.

In ordinary life, the best breathing tools are often discreet. You should be able to use them while sitting in a meeting, standing in a queue, listening to a partner, reading a difficult message, waiting for a call, or walking down a corridor. They should not require a ritual setting or perfect privacy. A tool that only works when the room is quiet, nobody is watching, and you already feel safe is too fragile for pressure moments.

Imagine a tense meeting. Someone questions your decision in a way that sounds dismissive. You feel the familiar heat rising. Your mind begins collecting evidence. The first answer forming in your mouth is not wrong, exactly, but it carries more force than the situation deserves. In that moment, the breath reset is not there to make you delighted with the criticism. It is there to prevent your body from handing your voice a weapon.

You do not need to close your eyes. You do not need to announce that you are calming yourself. You do not need to perform visible serenity. You simply notice the breath has become tight, then let one exhale run slightly longer than the inhale. The shoulders soften by a fraction. The jaw loosens enough to change the tone. The reply that comes next is still firm, but it is less loaded. That is breath doing its proper job.

It has not solved the meeting. It has protected the next sentence.

That is enough.

Breath is especially helpful when the main danger is acceleration. The more rapidly a moment is gathering speed, the more valuable a breath-led interruption becomes. Anger accelerates speech. Stress accelerates decisions. Panic accelerates interpretation. A breath reset introduces a small counter-rhythm. It says, "Not at the speed of alarm." It does not deny the feeling; it changes the pace at which the feeling becomes action.

This is why longer exhales are so useful for many people. Not exaggerated, theatrical exhales. Not forced emptying. Just a comfortable extension of the out-breath. The exhale naturally carries a quality of release. It gives the body a chance to downshift without demanding a huge inhale. For a person already tense, a giant inhale can feel like adding pressure to a crowded room. A gentle exhale is often more acceptable, more discreet, and more effective in the first minute.

The word "gentle" matters. Breath work becomes counterproductive when it becomes aggressive. Forcing the breath, counting with rigid perfection, holding beyond comfort, or trying to overpower panic through technique can make the body feel even less safe. The body does not respond well to being bullied into calm. It responds better to cues of steadiness, space, and control.

Breath also helps when you are on the edge of saying more than you mean. Many regrettable words are not born from deep conviction but from unregulated speed. They are spoken while the body is trying to discharge pressure. A single breath before speech can interrupt that discharge. It can turn a sharp sentence into a clear one. It can turn a defensive paragraph into one honest line. It can turn a contemptuous tone into a boundary that still leaves room for repair.

This is not politeness for its own sake. It is accuracy. Speech from a surge is often inaccurate in proportion, even when it contains a truth. You may have a valid concern, but the surge exaggerates the delivery. You may need to say no, but the surge adds punishment. You may need to apologise, but the surge adds panic and self-erasure. Breath creates a beat in which the message and the emotional force behind it can be separated.

The aim is not to become soft when firmness is needed. A good breath reset does not take away your backbone. It gives your backbone cleaner alignment.

This is particularly important for anger. Some people resist breathing during anger because they believe it means backing down. They hear "breathe" as "swallow it," "be nice," or "make the other person comfortable." That is a poor use of breath.

The purpose is not to erase anger's information. Anger may be showing you that something matters, that a limit has been crossed, or that a truth needs to be spoken. Breath simply slows the impulse to deliver that truth in a way that creates extra damage.

The breath does not silence the boundary. It protects it from becoming an attack.

Panic needs a different caution. When panic is present, the breath can become frightening because the person may already be highly aware of it. They may feel they cannot get enough air. They may chase bigger breaths, sigh repeatedly, or become preoccupied with whether breathing is normal. In that state, the instruction to "take a deep breath" can backfire. It may intensify attention on the sensation and increase the feeling of struggle.

During panic, breath helps when it is steady and small. The goal is not to gulp relief. The goal is to stop fighting the breath. A gentler rhythm can reduce the sense that every sensation requires urgent correction. Instead of trying to force the body into calm, the person practises staying with a manageable breath long enough for the alarm to lose some of its authority.

Breath is less helpful when it becomes the only tool. Some moments require attention shifts, grounding, movement, words, boundaries, or leaving the situation safely. If you are in a conversation where someone is becoming cruel, breathing may help you stay steady, but it is not a substitute for setting a limit. If you are exhausted, overstimulated, and underfed, breathing may help in the moment, but it is not a substitute for restoration. If panic symptoms are new, severe, or medically concerning, breathing techniques should not be used to dismiss the need for appropriate help. A tool is strongest when it knows its place.

This is the mature view of breath: useful, limited, practical, and powerful within its proper range.

Breath helps when the body needs a signal of "not immediate danger." It helps when the next action matters and the state is moving too quickly. It helps when words are about to outrun wisdom. It helps when panic is turning sensation into catastrophe. It helps when anger has a valid message but an unsafe delivery system. It helps when stress has convinced you that speed is the only answer.

It helps most when used early.

A breath reset after an argument may support recovery. A breath reset before the first sharp sentence may change the whole conversation. A breath reset after sending the message may calm the aftermath. A breath reset before sending may prevent the aftermath. Timing gives the tool its power.

This is why breath belongs inside the 60-second decision gap. It is not a decorative wellness habit added to the edges of life. It is a practical intervention at the exact point where body state threatens to become behaviour. The breath becomes a hinge between surge and choice.

The skill is not complicated. The discipline is remembering to use it before the moment has fully taken over. That remembering becomes easier when breath is tied to cues: the hot face, the clenched jaw, the tight chest, the hand reaching for the phone, the urge to interrupt, the sudden need to escape, the first rush of certainty. Each cue can become an invitation to breathe in a way that fits the state.

Not because breathing fixes everything.

Because it may stop you from adding one more problem.

That is the standard. It is plain, humane, and demanding enough. A breath reset is successful when it gives you one cleaner beat, one softer edge, one less reactive sentence, one moment in which the body receives evidence that it does not have to accelerate further. The feeling may still be there. The issue may still need dealing with. The person may still be difficult. The message may still need an answer.

But now, perhaps, not from the peak of the surge.

Quick exhale techniques

The quickest way to make breathing unhelpful is to turn it into a performance.

People often imagine a calming breath as something large, impressive, and unmistakable: a great inhale, a dramatic pause, a long theatrical release. That may look convincing from the outside, but in a real surge it can feel forced, awkward, or even alarming. If you are already tense, a huge inhale can make the chest feel tighter. If you are panicking, chasing a bigger breath can make breathing feel more urgent. If you are angry, an obvious breathing exercise may feel like a humiliating attempt to contain yourself while the issue remains alive and unresolved.

Quick exhale techniques take a different route. They do not ask you to breathe more. They ask you to release more completely, more comfortably, and more deliberately. The emphasis is not on filling the body with air, but on helping the body let go of the pressure it is already holding. In the first minute of escalation, that distinction matters. A person in a surge rarely needs another demanding instruction. They need a small physical cue that says, *slow the pace; there is no need to act at full alarm.*

The exhale is useful because it naturally belongs to release. You do not have to believe anything special for this to be true in practice. You can feel it in ordinary life. A sigh after completing a task. A long breath out before answering a difficult question. The softening that follows laughter. The small release after setting down a heavy bag. The out-breath is already associated with lowering effort. A quick exhale technique simply makes that existing doorway more deliberate.

The first principle is comfort. Not depth. Not perfection. Comfort.

If a breathing pattern makes you strain, gulp, tense your shoulders, push air out aggressively, or become preoccupied with whether you are doing it correctly, it is too much for the moment. A good exhale technique should feel like loosening a tight knot, not pulling harder on it. The breath should remain manageable. It should not create dizziness, air hunger, or a sense of failure. In pressure moments, the best technique is often the one you can do quietly without anyone noticing.

This is especially important because many people over-inhale when trying to calm down. They hear "breathe" and instinctively pull in a large breath. But the body may already be braced. The chest may already be lifted. The throat may already be tight. Adding a big inhale can increase the sensation of pressure. An exhale-led approach begins where the body can often cooperate more easily: by letting a little air leave, then allowing the next inhale to arrive without chasing it.

The simplest technique is the longer-out breath.

Breathe in gently through the nose or mouth, whichever feels natural. Then let the out-breath last a little longer than the in-breath. Not twice as long. Not according to a rigid count if counting makes you tense. Just slightly longer. Think of the exhale as a slow closing of a door rather than a forceful push. The point is not to empty yourself completely. The point is to lengthen the release enough for the body to notice a change in pace.

This can be done anywhere. Before answering a message. While someone is still speaking. In a meeting. In a queue. At a doorway before entering a room. Sitting in a parked car before going inside. You do not need to close your eyes or change posture dramatically. Let the inhale be ordinary. Give the exhale a little more time. That is all. Its power lies in its lack of drama.

A second technique is the silent sigh.

This is not the heavy sigh that communicates irritation to everyone nearby. It is private. Take a small, easy inhale and release it as though you were quietly fogging a mirror, but with the mouth barely open or the breath softened through the nose if that feels more discreet. The jaw loosens. The tongue rests. The throat releases. The shoulders may drop slightly. This works well when the body has become tight around speech, especially when you are about to answer too quickly.

The silent sigh is useful because anger and stress often gather in the jaw, mouth, throat, and chest. A pressured person may hold the breath while preparing to speak, then release words with too much force. The silent sigh interrupts that chain. It gives the mouth something to do before it becomes a weapon. It lets the voice return with less heat in it. The issue may still matter. The boundary may still need to be spoken. But the first sentence no longer has to carry the full pressure of the body.

A third technique is the downshift breath.

This is a small breath in, followed by an exhale that softens in stages. You inhale comfortably, then breathe out as though easing down through two or three gears. The exhale starts normally, then slows, then softens again near the end. There is no need for a visible pause. You are simply refusing to rush the release. This can be particularly helpful when stress has made everything feel hurried. The body has begun to treat speed as safety. The downshift breath offers a different rhythm.

Use it before a decision. Use it before pressing send. Use it before walking into a conversation that already feels charged. Use it when you notice your hands moving faster than the situation requires. The technique is not there to make you passive. It is there to stop urgency from pretending to be wisdom.

A fourth technique is the phrase-length exhale.

This is useful when counting feels mechanical or annoying. Choose a short phrase that naturally fits on an out-breath, such as "not yet," "slow the next move," or "one beat." You do not need to say it aloud. Let the phrase ride silently on the exhale. The phrase should be short enough that you do not strain to finish it. Its purpose is to pair breath with intention. The breath lowers speed; the phrase reminds you not to act from the peak of the surge.

This technique is particularly helpful for digital triggers. You read a message and feel the immediate rise: heat, offence, panic, urgency, the need to answer. Instead of trying to compose the perfect response in that state, let one phrase-length exhale happen before your thumbs begin. "Not yet." The words are not a solution. They are a barrier. They place a small strip of space between impulse and consequence.

A fifth technique is the nose-softening exhale.

This works well for people who dislike mouth breathing or feel self-conscious breathing visibly in public. Inhale gently through the nose. Exhale through the nose as if warming the upper lip, slow and quiet. Let the face soften while the air leaves. The important detail is not the nose itself; it is the quality of the exhale. Small, steady, unforced. This breath is discreet enough for meetings, public transport, classrooms, shops, and family conversations where you do not want your regulation strategy to become the centre of attention.

For anger, the exhale needs dignity. Many people resist calming techniques because they fear losing their edge. They believe that if they breathe, they are surrendering. This is a misunderstanding. The right exhale does not remove your position. It protects the delivery. It stops anger from recruiting your voice before your judgement has approved the sentence. A longer out-breath before speaking can turn "That is ridiculous" into "I do not agree with that." It can turn "You never listen" into "I need you to hear this properly." The truth is not weakened. It is made cleaner.

For panic, the exhale needs gentleness. Panic often creates a frightening relationship with breath. The person may feel unable to get enough air, then try to compensate by pulling in more. That chase can make the breath feel even less satisfying. During a panic spike, the aim is not to force a big calming breath. The aim is to stop struggling with the breath. A small inhale followed by a soft, slightly longer exhale can be more useful than a dramatic breathing exercise. The body needs steadiness, not a contest.

This is why exhale techniques should never become aggressive. Do not push the air out until you feel emptied. Do not hold the breath beyond comfort. Do not count so rigidly that the count becomes another pressure. Do not keep repeating a technique that is making you feel worse. A breathing tool is not a moral exam. If a pattern creates dizziness, strain, or alarm, make it smaller. Return to ordinary breathing. Add grounding. Feel your feet. Look around the room. The purpose is regulation, not obedience to a method.

The best exhale is often barely noticeable.

That may disappoint the part of the mind that wants proof. Under pressure, people often want a technique to feel powerful immediately. They want the surge to drop away in a single breath. Sometimes a breath reset does create a quick, visible shift. Often, it creates something subtler: a slight reduction in speed, a little less pressure in the voice, a small delay before action, a softer jaw, a clearer next sentence. These changes are easy to underestimate because they do not feel dramatic. But they may be exactly what protects the moment.

Think of the exhale as a brake, not a cure.

A brake does not decide where the vehicle should go. It does not repair the road. It does not explain why the journey became difficult. It simply prevents speed from becoming danger. That is what a quick exhale technique does in a surge. It slows the internal momentum so that your next move is less likely to be driven by acceleration alone.

The timing matters. Use the exhale at the first cue, not after the entire pattern has taken over. Hot face: exhale. Tight jaw: exhale. Hand reaching for the phone: exhale. Sudden certainty: exhale. Voice about to sharpen: exhale. Chest tightening in panic: soften the breath rather than chase it. The cue does not need a long analysis. It needs a small interruption.

A good practice is to attach exhale resets to ordinary transitions. Before opening a message, breathe out slowly. Before answering a difficult question, breathe out. Before entering the house after a stressful day, breathe out. Before starting the car, breathe out. Before replying to a partner's comment that touches a nerve, breathe out. These are not grand rituals. They are rehearsals. They teach the body that an exhale belongs between stimulus and response.

Over time, this makes the technique easier to reach under pressure. A breath pattern practised only during crisis may feel foreign when crisis comes. A breath pattern practised in ordinary moments becomes familiar enough to use when the body is loud. Familiarity is one of the hidden strengths of calming skills. The body trusts what it recognises.

There is no single perfect exhale technique. The right one is the one that fits your body, your setting, and your surge pattern. If you become sharp and fast, choose a technique that slows speech. If you become panicked and air-hungry, choose one that is small and gentle. If you become frozen, pair the exhale with contact: feet on the floor, hand on the table, eyes open to the room. If you become digitally reactive, pair the exhale with a physical delay: phone down, message unsent, one breath before any reply.

The technique should serve the next action. That is the standard.

Breathing for its own sake may become abstract. Breathing to protect the next sentence is concrete. Breathing to delay a message is concrete. Breathing to soften the jaw before setting a boundary is concrete. Breathing to stop panic from turning sensation into catastrophe is concrete. In the 60-second calm, breath is not decoration. It is a practical lever placed exactly where escalation begins to become behaviour.

A quick exhale technique succeeds when it gives you a little more room.

Not complete peace. Not spiritual radiance. Not instant emotional mastery. A little more room. Enough to hear the other person's full sentence. Enough to notice that the message can wait. Enough to feel panic without obeying every frightening interpretation. Enough to speak firmly without striking. Enough to choose the smallest safe next action.

The next time pressure rises, resist the temptation to inhale your way out of it with force. Start smaller. Let the breath leave. Let it leave slowly enough to change the pace. Let the body receive the message that no immediate explosion is required.

One ordinary exhale can become the first refusal to escalate.

Breath for anger heat

Anger is rarely still. It has motion in it.

It rises, presses, leans forward, gathers in the jaw, tightens the chest, sharpens the eyes, and pushes language towards the edge of the mouth. Even before a person speaks, anger has often organised the body into readiness. The shoulders may square. The breath may become short and forceful. The face may heat. The hands may want to gesture, point, grip, type, or strike the table for emphasis. The mind begins to move quickly, collecting evidence and preparing a case. The body is not merely feeling anger; it is preparing to act from anger.

This is why anger can be so convincing. It arrives with energy. It creates focus. It seems to clarify what matters. In a moment of insult, unfairness, dismissal, betrayal, or repeated frustration, anger can feel like the first honest thing in the room. It cuts through hesitation. It says, "No. This is not acceptable." That message may be important. Anger often appears where a value, boundary, need, or dignity has been touched.

The danger is that anger does not only deliver information. It also delivers momentum.

Momentum is where the trouble begins. The truth inside anger may be useful, but the speed of anger can corrupt the delivery. A valid complaint becomes an accusation. A needed boundary becomes a threat. A clear refusal becomes contempt. A sentence that could have opened a difficult conversation becomes the sentence that shuts it down. Anger may point towards something real, yet still push you to handle it in a way that creates avoidable damage.

Breath for anger heat is not about becoming meek.

This must be said plainly, because many people resist calming tools for anger for exactly this reason. They imagine that breathing means backing down, being nice, letting the other person get away with it, becoming passive, or swallowing the point. They have been told to "calm down" in tones that were dismissive, patronising, or controlling. No wonder breath can sound like surrender.

But the right breath does not erase anger. It gives anger a cleaner channel.

The aim is not to remove the fire from the message. The aim is to stop the fire from burning the whole conversation down. A breath reset for anger should preserve strength while reducing speed. It should help you stay firm without becoming cruel, direct without becoming reckless, honest without becoming excessive. Anger does not need to vanish before you speak. It needs to stop driving faster than your judgement can steer.

Anger heat often changes breathing in recognisable ways. Some people hold the breath while listening, then release speech in a burst. Some breathe high in the chest, as though the body is bracing for impact. Some shorten the exhale, which keeps the system feeling charged and unfinished. Some inhale sharply before interrupting. Some speak while half-breathing, pushing words out on pressure rather than choosing them with care. The breath becomes tied to the urge to act.

That tie can be interrupted.

The most useful anger breath is usually not deep, dramatic, or obvious. It is a pause-breath: one deliberately placed breath between the rise of heat and the next sentence. It does not require privacy. It does not require a special posture. It does not require closing the eyes, which may feel unnatural or unsafe during conflict. It simply places a small physical event where the old pattern would normally rush straight into speech.

The pause-breath begins with noticing the moment before you speak. That is the whole skill. The jaw locks. The chest presses. The sentence forms. The body leans towards the reply. Instead of letting the sentence leave immediately, you take a small, ordinary inhale and a slower, controlled exhale. The exhale should be comfortable, not forced. Think of lowering the heat by one notch rather than putting the fire out. Then speak, if speaking is still the smallest safe next action.

The breath is not a delay for the other person's comfort. It is a delay for your accuracy.

Anger loves overstatement. It reaches for "always," "never," "you do not care," "this is typical," "I knew you would," and other sentences that feel powerful while the body is hot and look clumsy later. The pause-breath gives you a chance to remove the unnecessary injury from the necessary truth. You may still say, "I am not willing to be spoken to like that." You may still say, "I disagree." You may still say, "This matters to me." You may still say, "I need this to change." But you are less likely to add the extra sentence that turns firmness into damage.

There is a difference between a boundary and a blast.

A boundary defines what is acceptable, what will happen next, or what you are willing to continue. A blast releases pressure. In anger, the blast can disguise itself as honesty. It may contain real feeling, but its primary purpose is discharge. The body wants relief, and the other person becomes the place where that relief is thrown. Breath gives you the chance to ask, without many words, "Am I about to set a boundary, or am I about to unload?"

That question can change the next minute.

One simple practice is the "before-the-first-word" breath. Use it when you feel the first sentence coming with too much force. Keep your mouth closed for one beat. Let the inhale be small. Let the exhale be longer than the inhale. On the exhale, soften the jaw just enough to change the tone. Then begin with fewer words than anger wants. Not a speech. Not a verdict. One clear sentence.

For example: "I need a moment before I answer that."

Or: "I do not agree, but I want to respond carefully."

Or: "That landed badly with me. Give me a second."

Or: "I am too heated to discuss this well right now."

These sentences are not weak. They are disciplined. They protect the point from being buried under the delivery.

Another useful pattern is the "hands-and-exhale" reset. Anger often collects in the hands. You may grip your phone, clench your fists, press your fingers into your palm, or gesture more sharply than you realise. Place both hands flat on a surface, or let them rest open by your sides if you are standing. Then exhale slowly enough to feel the hands soften. The body receives a message: no immediate strike, no immediate typing, no immediate escalation. The hands stop leading the argument.

This technique is especially useful with digital anger. A message arrives, and the body wants action through the thumbs. The reply forms quickly because the phone makes speed feel normal. The anger says, "Answer now, before they think they have won." The pause-breath says, "Not at the speed of heat." Put the phone down. Exhale. Let your hands leave the device. You may still reply later, firmly and clearly, but you have broken the chain between anger and instant publication.

A third pattern is the "lower-the-voice" breath. Many people focus on the words they should say and forget that tone carries the state. You can use the same sentence with a different force and create a different outcome. Before speaking, take a small inhale and let the exhale lower the pace of your voice. Not artificially slow. Not cold. Simply less driven. The goal is not to sound calm when you are not calm; the goal is to sound responsible for the force you are bringing into the room.

This matters in close relationships. With a partner, parent, sibling, friend, or child, anger often has a history attached. The body may not only be responding to this moment but to a pattern of moments. A remark may touch old frustration. A repeated habit may feel like proof that nothing changes. A small provocation may carry the weight of every time you felt unheard. In those moments, anger tries to make the current sentence carry the entire archive.

Breath helps you reduce the load.

Imagine a partner says, "You are overreacting." The phrase lands badly. Heat rises. Your mind immediately gathers the evidence: all the times you have not overreacted, all the times they dismissed you, all the reasons this is unfair. The first impulse is to strike back: "You always do this. You never listen." That sentence may feel justified, but it is unlikely to move the conversation towards anything useful.

A pause-breath creates a different path. Small inhale. Longer exhale. Jaw softens. Hands open. Then: "Do not call it overreacting. I want you to listen to what I am actually saying." The anger remains. The boundary remains. But the delivery has less shrapnel.

This is the heart of breath for anger heat: it protects the message from the surge.

It also protects your future self. The heated self often borrows against the steadier self's account. It spends words the steadier self must later repay. It says the exaggerated thing, sends the dramatic message, makes the sweeping threat, and then leaves the calmer self to manage the consequences. A breath before speech is a small act of loyalty to the person you will be after the heat has passed.

The breath should be brief because anger does not tolerate elaborate rituals well. If the technique is too complicated, anger will reject it. If it feels humiliating, anger will mock it. If it takes too long, anger will insist that the other person is getting away with something. Use the smallest intervention that changes the pace. One breath. One loosened jaw. One exhale through the nose. One hand unclenched. One beat before answering.

The aim is to make the breath acceptable to the angry body.

Do not ask anger to become peaceful. Ask it to wait one second before choosing a weapon. That is a more realistic request. In that second, the body can shift just enough for the next move to become more deliberate. Not perfect. Deliberate.

Some people worry that pausing will make them lose the argument. But a pause often increases authority. Reactive anger may feel strong, yet it can weaken your position because it gives the other person a reason to focus on your tone rather than your point. A steady boundary is harder to dismiss. A clear sentence is harder to deflect. When anger is disciplined by breath, it becomes more difficult for the issue to be buried under the style of delivery.

This is not about managing appearances for their own sake. It is about preserving influence. The way you carry anger affects whether the truth inside it can be heard, whether repair remains possible, and whether you respect yourself afterwards. Heat may announce that something matters. Breath helps you decide how that mattering should enter the world.

There are moments when the safest next action is not to keep talking. Breath can help you recognise that too. If the body remains highly charged after a pause-breath, if the voice still wants to sharpen, if the mind is rehearsing insults, if the hands are restless and the chest is tight, the smallest safe action may be to step away with clarity. The breath then supports a pause phrase: "I am too angry to do this well. I am going to take a break and come back." That is not abandonment if you return. It is containment.

Containment is one of the most underrated strengths in emotional life.

To contain anger is not to deny it. It is to hold it without letting it spill everywhere. A contained anger can speak. It can refuse. It can insist. It can protect. It can demand repair. An uncontained anger often becomes so loud that the original need disappears beneath the impact. Breath is one of the simplest ways to begin containment in the body before it is demanded in words.

Practise when the stakes are low. Use the pause-breath when mildly annoyed by a delay, a noise, a small interruption, or a message that irritates you. Do not wait for the largest conflict to learn the tool. Anger has habits. It is easier to shape those habits in small heat than in full blaze. Each low-stakes rehearsal teaches the body that a breath does not mean defeat. It means command.

The phrase to remember is: *slow before strong*.

Strength without slowness often becomes force. Slowness without strength may become avoidance. Together, they create steadiness. The pause-breath gives anger enough slowness to become useful strength rather than uncontrolled force. It lets you stay in contact with what matters while refusing to let the first surge decide the method.

The next time anger rises, do not argue with the fact that it has arrived. Notice the heat. Notice the push. Notice the sentence forming. Then place one breath between the surge and the sound of your voice.

That breath is not surrender.

It is the moment anger stops being the driver and becomes information you can use.

Breath for panic spikes

Panic does not ask politely for your attention. It storms the body, rearranges the meaning of ordinary sensations, and makes the next few seconds feel as though they must be handled urgently. The heart races, the chest tightens, the breath feels unreliable, the hands may tremble, the room may seem strange, and the mind begins looking for an explanation dramatic enough to match the intensity of the body.

This is why panic is so convincing. It does not feel like a thought. It feels like evidence.

Breathing becomes especially charged during panic because the breath is often part of the alarm. A person may feel unable to get enough air, even while air is still moving. They may take repeated big breaths, sigh frequently, yawn, gulp, or keep testing whether the next breath feels satisfying. When it does not, the fear rises. The body asks for more air. The mind interprets the discomfort as danger. The next breath becomes a test, and the test itself keeps the panic alive.

This is the first rule of breath during panic: do not turn breathing into a struggle.

Many people instinctively try to defeat panic by taking huge breaths. They pull air in forcefully, lift the chest, tense the shoulders, and search for a dramatic sense of relief. This is understandable. When the body feels air-hungry, "more air" seems like the obvious answer. But panic often does not respond well to force. The harder you chase the perfect breath, the more important breathing becomes in your attention, and the more frightening each imperfect breath may feel.

A panic breath reset must therefore be gentler than an anger breath reset. Anger often needs slowing before speech. Panic needs reassurance without wrestling. The aim is not to prove that you can control every sensation. The aim is to stop treating every sensation as an emergency requiring immediate correction.

The phrase to remember is: steady and small.

Steady and small means you do not need to fill the lungs dramatically. You do not need to inhale as deeply as possible. You do not need to hold the breath for long periods or count with rigid precision. You do not need to make the breath impressive. You are simply teaching the body that breath can continue without being chased, forced, examined, or feared.

During a panic spike, the most useful breath may look almost ordinary from the outside. A small inhale. A soft exhale. A brief pause while the next inhale arrives by itself. Then again. Not perfect. Not theatrical. Just less frantic than the alarm wants it to be.

This matters because panic often creates a cruel loop. A sensation appears: tight chest, fast heart, dizziness, unreality, tingling, heat, trembling, or breath discomfort. The mind adds a frightening meaning. That meaning increases fear. Fear increases bodily activation. The activation produces more sensations. The sensations seem to confirm the frightening meaning. Around it goes.

Breath can interrupt this loop, but only if it is used as a signal of steadiness rather than a frantic attempt to remove every sensation.

A helpful starting point is to stop asking, "Can I get a perfect breath?" and begin asking, "Can I let the next breath be smaller than my panic wants?" Panic tends to demand more: more checking, more air, more certainty, more escape, more reassurance. A small breath is a quiet refusal to obey that demand. It says, "I do not have to match the intensity of the alarm."

This does not mean ignoring the body. It means changing the relationship to the body.

One practical approach is the soft-exhale reset. Let the inhale arrive gently, through the nose or mouth, without pulling hard. Then let the exhale be slightly longer and softer, as though you are releasing warmth from the chest rather than pushing air out. Keep the shoulders low if you can. Let the jaw loosen. Do not empty the lungs completely. Do not force. The exhale should feel like lowering the volume, not squeezing the body.

If counting helps, keep it simple and flexible. A gentle in-breath and a slightly longer out-breath is enough. If counting makes you tense, abandon the count. The body does not need arithmetic; it needs steadiness. A person in panic can easily turn counting into another performance, then panic because the count was not perfect. That is not regulation. That is pressure.

Another useful method is the "allow the next breath" practice. Instead of trying to take the next breath aggressively, let the body begin it. You soften the belly or ribs as much as possible, release the jaw, and wait a brief moment for the inhale to come in its own time. This can feel strange at first, especially if panic has made you believe you must supervise every breath. But allowing the breath to arrive helps reduce the sense that breathing is a task you must manually control.

The purpose is to rebuild trust with an automatic function.

Breathing has been happening all day without your management. Panic narrows attention until this ordinary process feels fragile and urgent. A gentle breath reset reminds the body that breathing does not require constant checking. The breath may still feel uncomfortable for a while. That is allowed. The goal is not instant comfort. The goal is less struggle.

There is a strong difference between noticing breathing and monitoring breathing. Noticing is brief and practical: "My breath feels tight; I will soften the exhale." Monitoring is fearful and repetitive: "Is it better now? What about now? Was that breath normal? Why did that one feel strange?" Monitoring keeps the threat loop alive. It makes the breath the centre of the universe. During panic, the breath should be used as an anchor, not an obsession.

If the breath feels too charged to focus on directly, use indirect breathing. This means pairing breath with grounding so the mind is not staring at the sensation. Place both feet on the floor. Let the exhale soften while you feel pressure through the soles of the feet. Rest a hand on a table, chair, or your own thigh and exhale while noticing contact. Look at a neutral object and let the breath leave while your eyes stay open. This prevents the breath from becoming a private tunnel of anxiety.

Panic narrows the world inward. Grounded breathing brings the world back in.

This is especially important during air-hunger sensations. Air-hunger can feel frightening, but the instinct to keep taking larger and larger breaths often makes the experience more urgent. A steadier approach is to breathe less dramatically, not more dramatically. Let the inhale be modest. Let the exhale be unforced. Keep attention partly outside the body: feet, hands, surface, room, sound, object. The message is, "I can feel this and remain here."

That sentence is more useful than "I must make this stop immediately."

Trying to make panic stop immediately often gives panic more authority. It tells the body that the sensations are unacceptable and must be removed before life can continue. A calmer goal is to reduce cooperation with the panic spiral. You may still feel the sensations. Your heart may still be fast. The breath may still feel imperfect. The room may still feel slightly odd. But if you stop adding fear, checking, and forced breathing to the sensations, the spike has less fuel.

Breath for panic is therefore not a rescue mission. It is a de-escalation.

A rescue mission says, "I must get out of this state now." De-escalation says, "I can lower the struggle around this state." Rescue grabs. De-escalation steadies. Rescue demands proof. De-escalation offers repetition. Rescue treats the sensations as enemies. De-escalation treats them as uncomfortable signals moving through the body.

This distinction can change the entire tone of the moment.

Imagine you are sitting in a cafe when panic begins to rise. At first, it is subtle: a flutter in the chest, a slight unreality, a feeling that your breath is not satisfying. Then the mind leaps: "What if something is wrong?" You inhale sharply. The breath still does not feel right. Now the room feels too bright, the exit becomes important, and your body wants immediate escape.

A forceful breathing strategy might intensify the focus: big inhale, check, no relief, fear; bigger inhale, check, still no relief, more fear. A steadier strategy is smaller. Feet on the floor. Eyes open. One hand around the cup, noticing warmth or texture. A gentle inhale. A soft, slightly longer exhale. No demand that the next breath feel perfect. A simple phrase: "This is panic rising. I do not need to chase it." The sensations may continue, but the spiral has been interrupted.

The breath is not the only tool in that moment. It works with attention, contact, and interpretation. Panic tools are strongest when combined lightly. Breath steadies the rhythm. Grounding reconnects you with the environment. Plain language reduces catastrophic meaning. Together, they reduce the sense of being trapped inside the alarm.

The language you use around breath matters. Avoid dramatic inner commands such as "I cannot breathe," unless there is a genuine medical emergency requiring immediate help. Panic often borrows extreme language, and extreme language feeds fear. More useful phrases are concrete and current: "My breathing feels tight." "This is uncomfortable." "Air is moving." "I am exhaling now." "I can let the next breath be small." These sentences do not argue with the body. They keep the mind from turning discomfort into catastrophe.

Breath for panic should also avoid harsh self-talk. Telling yourself, "Stop it," "This is ridiculous," or "Calm down now" adds conflict to an already activated body. The body is not reassured by contempt. A steadier tone works better: "This is a panic spike." "I can slow the struggle." "I do not need a perfect breath." "Small and steady." This is not sentimental. It is efficient. Panic needs less threat, not more.

There are times when breathing techniques are not enough, and that must be respected. If symptoms are new, severe, unusual, connected to a medical condition, or genuinely worrying, appropriate medical advice or urgent support may be necessary. A breathing tool should not be used to dismiss real health concerns. Nor should it be treated as a substitute for professional help when panic is frequent, disabling, or linked to trauma. Practical self-regulation and proper care are not rivals.

Within its proper place, however, breath can be a powerful early intervention.

It helps most when used before panic has recruited the whole mind. The first cue may be a tight chest, a strange breath, a sudden wave of unreality, a racing heart, a rush of heat, or the urge to escape. That cue is not a command. It is the moment to become smaller, steadier, more grounded. The earlier you soften the breath, the less likely you are to spend the next minute feeding the fear.

A useful panic breath has several qualities. It is gentle. It is repeatable. It keeps the eyes open if closing them makes the sensations larger. It does not require perfect counting. It does not involve gulping. It does not chase relief. It gives the body a rhythm and gives the mind something plain to do. Most importantly, it does not become the whole event. You breathe, ground, look, name, and continue.

Continue does not always mean stay exactly where you are. Sometimes the smallest safe action is to step to a quieter place, sit down, loosen tight clothing, drink water, or move slowly. The difference is whether the movement is chosen or panicked. A breath reset can create enough steadiness to leave with care rather than bolt, ask for support rather than plead for rescue, or stay present for one more moment rather than obeying the first catastrophic interpretation.

This is what makes steady, small breathing so dignified. It does not promise that panic will feel pleasant. It does not pretend that sensations are easy. It simply refuses to let the alarm set the terms of the entire moment.

The body says, "More, faster, now."

The breath answers, "Small, steady, here."

That answer may not end the spike instantly. It may not make you feel brave. It may not erase every sensation. But it can stop the breath from becoming another battlefield. It can reduce the fear layered on top of the feeling. It can give you one clean moment in which you are not chasing, checking, forcing, or fleeing.

In panic, that is no small thing.

The next time your breathing feels urgent and unsatisfying, resist the instinct to fight for the biggest breath you can find. Let the breath become less dramatic. Let the exhale soften. Let the next inhale arrive without being dragged in. Keep part of your attention in the room, on your feet, on your hands, on something steady outside the alarm.

Panic may still rise.

You do not have to rise with it.

Chapter 4
Attention shifts in seconds

Why does one sentence sometimes become the whole world?

A message appears, a tone changes, a sensation rises, and suddenly the rest of the room disappears. The chair beneath you, the air around you, the ordinary sounds nearby, the possibility that there may be more than one explanation for what is happening: all of it retreats. What remains is the threat target. The criticism. The silence. The look. The tightness in the chest. The imagined consequence. The thing that must be fixed, answered, escaped, explained, or defeated immediately.

The strange part is that this narrowing can feel like clarity. It does not usually announce itself as a state change. It arrives as certainty. "I must deal with this now." "They meant that." "This is going to go badly." "I cannot stand this feeling." "I need an answer." The mind feels focused, but it may be focused in the way a torch is focused in a dark room: bright in one place, blind everywhere else.

This is the central tension of attention under pressure. The same capacity that helps you detect what matters can, under stress, shrink the moment until only danger appears real. Narrow attention is not useless. In genuine threat, it can be protective. But in emotional surges, it often over-serves the alarm and under-serves judgement. It makes urgency feel like truth. It makes one interpretation feel final. It makes the next action feel compulsory when it may only be familiar.

The cost is rarely confined to the private mind. Narrow attention changes speech, posture, timing, and choice. A person who has locked onto one phrase may stop hearing the rest of the sentence. A person who has locked onto a bodily sensation may begin treating discomfort as proof of danger. A person who has locked onto an imagined outcome may rush to prevent a future that has not happened. The world becomes smaller, and behaviour follows the size of that world.

This matters because widened attention is often the missing step between body regulation and wise action. Breath can lower intensity, but if the mind remains fixed on the threat, the surge can quickly rebuild itself. You may breathe once, then stare again at the message that offended you. You may exhale, then return to rehearsing the argument. You may feel your feet for a moment, then climb straight back into the story that made the body accelerate. Without an attention shift, the system keeps feeding from the same source.

Grounding is often misunderstood at this point. It is not an escape from reality. It is a return to more of reality. When you notice the pressure of your feet, the texture under your fingers, the edge of a table, the colour of a wall, or the ordinary sound beyond the conflict, you are not pretending the problem does not exist. You are refusing to let the problem occupy the entire field. That refusal is not denial. It is proportion.

Attention can move quickly when given a simple enough task. The route begins with recognising narrowing: the tunnel, the urgency, the sense that one thing has become everything. Then grounding offers contact with the physical present, not as a ritual, but as a practical anchor. From there, the field can widen: eyes, ears, body, room, neutral details, other possibilities, enough space for the thinking mind to return before speech or decision takes over.

The question to carry forward is severe and useful: when you feel certain that something must be fixed this instant, are you seeing the moment clearly, or are you seeing it through a tunnel?

Narrowing and tunnel vision

Stress has a way of shrinking the world.

Not literally, of course. The room remains the same size. The phone is still only a phone. The other person is still a whole person, not merely the sentence they have just spoken. The future has not collapsed into one fixed outcome. Yet inside a surge, it can feel as though the mind has been pulled through a narrow opening. Everything that is not threat becomes less available. Everything that might be threat becomes brighter, louder, and more convincing.

This is tunnel vision in emotional form. It is not always dramatic. Sometimes it is no more than rereading the same message until one phrase becomes unbearable. Sometimes it is staring at a person's expression and deciding, with sudden certainty, what they must be thinking. Sometimes it is feeling a tightness in the chest and becoming unable to attend to anything except what the sensation might mean. Sometimes it is the sense that a conversation must be fixed immediately, before the silence, uncertainty, or discomfort becomes impossible to tolerate.

Tunnel vision is not simply concentration. Concentration can be chosen, flexible, and useful. Tunnel vision is narrower than that. It has a trapped quality. The mind does not feel as though it is focusing because focus is helpful; it feels as though it cannot afford to look away. The threat target becomes the centre of everything. The rest of reality is still present, but it has lost influence.

This matters because narrowed attention often masquerades as truth.

When stress pulls attention into threat-scanning, the mind begins to search for danger, rejection, disrespect, failure, illness, embarrassment, loss, or conflict. It does not search neutrally. It searches with an agenda. It looks for what confirms the alarm. A delayed reply becomes evidence of distance. A brief criticism becomes evidence of incompetence. A bodily sensation becomes evidence that something is wrong.

A partner's tired tone becomes evidence of contempt. A colleague's question becomes evidence of attack.

The frightening part is not only that the mind finds these interpretations. The frightening part is that, under pressure, they feel complete.

A calmer mind might say, "There are several possible explanations." A narrowed mind says, "This is what it means." A calmer mind might say, "I can wait before responding." A narrowed mind says, "I must fix this now." A calmer mind might say, "This sensation is uncomfortable." A narrowed mind says, "This sensation is dangerous." A calmer mind might say, "That comment stung." A narrowed mind says, "They are against me."

The state speaks in absolutes.

The body often participates before the mind has caught up. Eyes may fix on one point. The face may harden. The jaw may lock. The breath may become shallow or held. The shoulders may lift, the chest may tighten, and the body may lean towards or away from the source of pressure. Hands may grip a phone, a steering wheel, a mug, a chair, a sleeve. Movement may become restless, hurried, or unusually still. The body is no longer simply occupying the moment; it is preparing for the moment to become a problem.

Speech narrows too. This is one of the clearest signs that tunnel vision has taken hold. Words become faster, sharper, more repetitive, or more final. People begin to argue from a single interpretation. They stop asking questions and start presenting conclusions. They interrupt because waiting feels unsafe. They over-explain because being misunderstood feels intolerable. They accuse because ambiguity feels too exposed. They say "always" and "never" because the mind has lost access to the softer, truer middle.

Other people may hear the narrowing before you do. They may notice that your tone has changed, that you are not responding to what they actually said, that you have seized on one phrase and ignored the rest. This can be infuriating because, from inside the tunnel, you may feel unusually clear. You may believe you are finally seeing the issue properly. In reality, you may be seeing one part of it with too much intensity and the rest with too little attention.

Time perception can narrow as well. A surge often creates false immediacy. The mind insists that the next few seconds are decisive. You must reply now. You must know now. You must leave now. You must make them understand now. You must settle the question now. The pressure of "now" becomes so strong that delay feels like danger, even when delay would be the wiser move.

This is one reason people make decisions in states they later barely recognise. They send the message because not sending feels unbearable. They agree because conflict feels too hot. They accuse because uncertainty feels weak. They leave because staying with the conversation for another minute feels impossible. The action is not chosen from the full field of options; it is chosen from inside the tunnel, where only the most immediate relief looks available.

The phrase "I must fix this now" is especially revealing. Sometimes immediate action is genuinely needed. There are moments when safety, care, or basic responsibility require speed. But in many emotional surges, "I must fix this now" is not a fact. It is a state cue. It tells you that urgency has entered the body and attention has narrowed around the discomfort. The problem may be real. The timing demanded by the surge may not be.

This distinction is vital. If you treat "I must fix this now" as truth, you may obey the surge. If you treat it as a cue, you gain a small opening. You can say, "Urgency is here." That sentence changes the relationship to the moment. It does not deny the issue. It simply stops urgency from disguising itself as wisdom.

Worst-case certainty is another sign of narrowing. Under stress, the mind often jumps past possibility and lands in prediction. "This will ruin everything." "They will never trust me again." "I cannot cope." "I am going to lose control." "This conversation is already broken." "Something is seriously wrong." The words may vary, but the pattern is similar: the mind chooses the most threatening interpretation and then behaves as though the choice has already been verified.

Worst-case thinking can feel protective. It seems to prepare you. It says, "If I imagine the worst, I will not be caught off guard." But in a surge, worst-case certainty usually narrows behaviour. It makes you defensive, avoidant, frantic, controlling, or overly compliant. Instead of preparing you for reality, it may prepare you for a fear and make you act as though the fear is already happening.

This is how tunnel vision creates self-fulfilling trouble. A person fears rejection, then responds with accusation, which creates distance. A person fears being judged, then over-explains until others become impatient. A person fears panic sensations, then monitors the body so intensely that the sensations feel larger. A person fears conflict, then withdraws without explanation, creating the very rupture they hoped to avoid.

The tunnel does not merely distort perception. It can shape the next event.

That is why noticing narrowing is not a minor skill. It is the doorway to de-escalation. Before you can widen attention, you have to recognise that attention has narrowed. This recognition is not always comfortable. It requires humility. It asks you to consider that the certainty you feel may be partly state-driven. It asks you to stop treating intensity as proof. It asks you to admit that your mind, under pressure, may be editing the scene.

A useful sign is disproportionate focus. Are you unable to stop thinking about one sentence? Are you rereading a message even though you already understand the words? Are you staring at the person's face for signs of threat? Are you scanning your body for symptoms? Are you rehearsing a future argument with increasing conviction? Are you treating a pause, tone, delay, or sensation as though it contains the whole answer? These are not failures. They are signs that the field has narrowed.

Another sign is shrinking language. The more narrowed the state, the less flexible the language often becomes. "I cannot." "They always." "This never." "I have to." "There is no way." "It is ruined." "I need to know." "I cannot stand it." Such phrases may not be lies, but they are rarely the whole truth. They show that the mind is reaching for hard edges because soft complexity feels unsafe.

The body gives signs too. A tunnel often has a posture. The head moves forward. The eyes fix. The breath tightens. The hands grip. The stomach braces. The voice narrows into speed, sharpness, flatness, or forced calm. A person may stop noticing temperature, sound, colour, space, and contact with the floor. The present moment becomes reduced to the problem alone.

This is why sensory awareness is so central to widening later. Tunnel vision is not just a thinking style; it is an embodied narrowing. You cannot always think your way out of it by arguing with the interpretation. Sometimes the fastest way to loosen the tunnel is to bring in more physical reality: the floor, the chair, the light, the wall, the sound of a kettle, the pressure of the hands, the space behind and beside you. The body needs evidence that the world is larger than the threat target.

But before widening comes the recognition: "My attention has narrowed."

This phrase is plain enough to use under pressure. It does not require analysis. It does not demand that you decide whether your interpretation is right or wrong. It simply names the process. Once named, the narrowing loses a little authority. The thought may still be loud. The feeling may still be uncomfortable. The problem may still matter. But you are no longer completely fused with the tunnel.

There is dignity in this kind of noticing. It is not self-doubt in the weak sense. It is disciplined self-respect. You are refusing to hand your whole judgement to a state that has reduced the available evidence. You are saying, "Something in me is treating one part of the moment as the whole moment." That is a sophisticated observation, and it can be made in very ordinary language.

Imagine standing in a queue when the line stops moving. You are already late. Someone ahead seems to be taking too long. Heat rises. Your eyes fix on the delay. Your mind begins to build a story: nobody cares, this always happens, the whole day is ruined. Time seems to tighten. The body wants to sigh loudly, complain, abandon the queue, or send an irritated message to someone waiting. The delay is real. The tunnel is also real.

If you notice only the delay, you may obey the pressure. If you notice the narrowing, the moment changes. "My attention has locked onto this queue." That single recognition does not move the line. It does something more immediate: it stops the line from becoming your entire nervous system. It creates the possibility of feeling your feet, loosening your hands, hearing the room, and choosing the next action from a slightly wider field.

The same applies in conflict. Someone says, "You did not listen." The phrase lands hard. Your attention locks onto the accusation. You stop hearing the rest. Your body prepares a defence. A narrowed mind hears, "You are a failure." A wider mind might eventually hear, "They are upset about not feeling heard." The difference matters. One interpretation invites battle. The other may still be uncomfortable, but it leaves room for response.

Tunnel vision also appears in panic. The threat target may not be another person but an internal sensation. A tight chest becomes the whole world. A strange feeling in the head becomes the centre of attention. The person checks, interprets, checks again, and the checking magnifies the sensation. The room, the chair, the floor, the conversation, the weather outside, the ordinary continuity of life: all of it fades behind the question, "What is happening to me?" The sensation is real. The tunnel around it is what intensifies fear.

Noticing narrowing is not the same as dismissing concern. This distinction must be kept clear. If there is genuine danger, illness, abuse, or urgent responsibility, action may be needed. Emotional regulation should never become a way to minimise reality. But many surges occur in ambiguous, uncomfortable, or charged situations rather than immediate emergencies. In those moments, widening attention protects judgement. It helps you tell the difference between a real problem and a state-driven command.

Narrow attention says, "Only this matters."

Wider attention says, "This matters, and there is more here."

That "and" is powerful. It allows the problem to remain visible without becoming total. I am angry, and I can feel my feet. I am panicked, and I am sitting in this chair. I am criticised, and I can listen to the full sentence. I am under pressure, and I do not have to answer at the speed of fear. I feel urgency, and urgency is not the same as instruction.

The goal is not to become detached. Detachment is not always wise or possible. The goal is to become less captured. A captured mind has fewer options. A widened mind has more. It can delay, ask, clarify, breathe, pause, repair, leave safely, speak firmly, or do nothing for a few seconds. These choices may sound small, but they are impossible to access when attention has collapsed around one threat.

The first practice, then, is to learn your signs of narrowing. For some, it begins in the eyes: staring, scanning, reading and rereading. For others, it begins in language: certainty, absolutes, urgency. For others, it begins in time: the sense that a decision must be made immediately. For others, it begins in the body: leaning forward, holding breath, gripping, bracing. Your pattern is the one that matters.

When you catch it, do not scold yourself. Scolding narrows the field further. Simply name it: "Tunnel." "Narrowing." "My attention has locked on." "I am treating this as urgent." These are not magic words. They are markers. They show you the point at which the old sequence can begin to change.

The next movement will be grounding, because a narrowed mind needs contact with the physical present before it can reliably widen. But the essential first act is recognition. You cannot step out of a tunnel you refuse to admit you are in.

So when the next surge tells you that one sentence, one sensation, one silence, one message, or one possible outcome is the whole truth, pause long enough to ask: what has disappeared from view?

Fast grounding methods

Grounding is often misunderstood as a way to escape emotion. It is not.

Grounding is a way to return to the present moment with more of yourself available. When stress, anger, or panic narrows attention, the mind can become trapped inside the threat: the message, the argument, the sensation, the imagined consequence, the urgent story. Grounding does not deny any of that. It simply reintroduces the rest of reality. The floor is here. The hands are here. The room is here. The body is not only a storm of feeling; it is also standing, sitting, touching, seeing, hearing, breathing.

This matters because escalation often pulls people away from physical contact with the world. Not dramatically, perhaps. You may still be in the room, still answering questions, still holding your phone, still standing in a queue. But inwardly, attention has left the wider environment and narrowed around the perceived threat. The problem becomes the whole scene. The body becomes a collection of alarming signals. The future becomes one frightening prediction. Grounding helps restore proportion.

The word itself can sound too gentle for the intensity of real surges. When panic is rising, anger is hot, or stress is pressing hard, "ground yourself" may sound like advice from someone who has never felt the force of the moment. But effective grounding is not vague. It is specific, physical, and brief. It gives attention a simple job that the body can perform even when the mind is crowded.

A good grounding method answers one question: *Where can I place attention right now that is real, neutral, and physically present?*

That question is more useful than asking, "How do I stop feeling this?" Feelings do not always stop when commanded. Sensations do not vanish because you disapprove of them. Thoughts do not quiet down simply because they are unhelpful. But attention can often be moved a little. Not completely. Not perfectly. A little is enough. In the 60-second calm, a little movement of attention can interrupt the tunnel.

The simplest grounding method is contact.

Contact means deliberately noticing where your body meets something solid. Feet against the floor. Back against a chair. Hands on a table. Fingers around a mug. Thighs on a seat. Shoulder against a wall. These contact points are ordinary, which is exactly why they work. They require no belief, no performance, no special environment. They are physical facts available before the mind has settled.

Start with the feet. This is one of the most discreet and reliable anchors. Press both feet gently into the floor. Notice the difference between heel, toe, and the outer edges of the feet. Do not make a drama of it. Do not stamp. Do not turn it into an exercise everyone can see. Simply let the floor hold some of your attention. If you are standing, notice weight travelling down through the legs. If you are sitting, notice the soles inside your shoes or against the ground. The point is not to feel calm instantly. The point is to stop being entirely absorbed by the surge.

Feet are especially useful when urgency is rising. Panic says, "Get out." Anger says, "Move towards." Stress says, "Hurry." The feet say, "Here." They remind the body that not every impulse has to become movement. They create a small physical pause before the next action.

Hands are another strong anchor. They are often involved in escalation because they are so ready to act. Hands type the message, grip the steering wheel, clench into fists, point in argument, rub the face, check the pulse, open the app, push the door, reach for reassurance. Grounding through the hands interrupts this readiness. Place one hand on a surface and notice texture, temperature, pressure, and shape. Let the fingers spread slightly. Feel the table, the fabric, the cup, the chair arm, the sleeve, the phone case without using the phone.

This matters because the hands can either carry the surge forward or help contain it. A hand gripping a phone may be halfway to sending the message. A hand resting open on a table is doing something different. It is still active, but not reactive. It gives the body a physical instruction: stay with contact before action.

Eyes can also ground quickly, especially when attention has collapsed around one target. Look at something neutral and ordinary. Not the person's face if that is the trigger. Not the message that has set you off. Not your own symptoms in the mirror. Choose an object with no emotional charge: a door handle, a book spine, a corner of the room, a cup, a patch of light, the edge of a desk. Let your eyes rest there for a few seconds. Name it silently in plain language: "blue mug," "wooden table," "white wall," "black chair."

This is not childish. It is precise. The mind in a surge often runs on interpretation: threat, meaning, prediction, judgement. Naming a neutral object brings attention back to description. Description is calmer than interpretation because it asks less of the mind. "White wall" is not a story. "They hate me" is a story. "My chest feels tight" is closer to description. "Something terrible is happening" is interpretation. Grounding trains the mind to return to what is directly present before leaping into what it fears.

Sound can be useful too, though it must be chosen carefully. In a noisy or tense environment, sound may be part of the stress. But there is often at least one neutral sound available: distant traffic, a fridge hum, footsteps outside the room, a kettle, rain, typing, the rustle of clothing, your own breath leaving quietly. Listen for one sound that is not demanding anything from you. Let it exist for a few seconds without needing to interpret it.

Sound grounding can be particularly helpful when the eyes are too locked onto a trigger.

Temperature is another strong anchor. A cool glass, warm mug, cold tap, fresh air on the face, or the temperature of a surface under your palm can give the body a clear present-moment signal. This is especially useful during panic or derealisation, when the world may feel distant or unreal. Temperature has a blunt honesty. It does not require complex thought. The cup is warm. The water is cool. The air touches the skin. The body is here.

The best grounding methods are small enough to use without drawing attention. This is important. Many people avoid calming tools because they fear looking strange, weak, dramatic, or exposed. A tool that requires a visible ritual may be too awkward for a meeting, a public queue, a tense dinner table, or a difficult conversation. Fast grounding should fit into real life. Feet on the floor. Hand on the table. Eyes on a neutral object. One sound. One texture. One contact point.

Choose one sense and one location.

That rule prevents grounding from becoming cluttered. In a surge, people sometimes try to do too much. They scan the room, count objects, regulate breath, analyse feelings, relax every muscle, and monitor whether the tool is working. The effort becomes another stressor. Simpler is better. One sense. One location. Feet and pressure. Hands and texture. Eyes and colour. Ears and sound. Skin and temperature. Stay there briefly, then return to the next safe action.

The purpose is not to become fascinated by the object or sensation. The purpose is to give attention a stable place to land.

Imagine standing in a queue when impatience and panic begin to rise together. The line is barely moving. Your chest tightens.

Your thoughts start pushing: "I cannot be stuck here. I need to get out. This is taking too long." The body begins scanning for escape, and the mind begins treating the queue as a trap. A grounding response does not argue with the queue. It does not demand that you enjoy waiting. It brings attention to contact: feet inside shoes, weight on the floor, fingers touching the edge of a bag, the coolness of a bottle in your hand. One sense, one location. Stay for a few seconds.

The queue has not changed. Your relationship to the queue has.

That is the point. Grounding rarely changes the external situation immediately. It changes the amount of attention available to meet it. The mind that was fused with "I cannot stand this" now has at least one foot in physical reality. The body that was preparing to bolt now has evidence of contact. The urgency may still be there, but it is no longer the only signal in the system.

Grounding also helps in conflict. Suppose someone says something that lands sharply. Your attention locks onto the phrase. The body heats. The reply begins forming. Instead of staring harder at the person, you let one hand feel the table. You notice the pressure of your fingers. You keep your eyes open. You let the physical contact become a quiet anchor while you listen to the rest of the sentence. This does not mean you accept what was said. It means you do not let one phrase steal your whole nervous system.

This can prevent a common escalation error: responding to the most painful fragment rather than the full moment. When attention is grounded, it becomes easier to hear context, tone, uncertainty, or the possibility of asking a question before attacking. Grounding does not make you passive. It makes you less easily captured.

During panic, grounding must be handled with particular care. The anxious mind may try to turn any technique into checking. "Is this working? Do I feel better? Is my chest still tight? Am I calmer now?" That is not grounding. That is monitoring. Grounding should move attention towards the physical present, not towards constant evaluation of symptoms. If you use your feet as an anchor, stay with the pressure of the feet, not with repeated questions about whether panic has gone.

A useful phrase is: "Contact, not checking."

Contact says, "My hand is on the chair." Checking says, "Has this stopped the panic yet?" Contact says, "My feet are on the floor." Checking says, "Do I feel normal now?" Contact widens attention. Checking narrows it back around threat. The distinction may seem small, but in panic it can make the difference between interrupting the loop and feeding it.

Fast grounding should also be brief. Some people assume they must remain grounded for a long stretch or achieve a special state of calm. That expectation can make the tool feel burdensome. In a 60-second surge, a few seconds of grounded attention can be enough to create a gap. Feel the feet. Notice the hand. Name the object. Hear the sound. Then choose the next small action. Grounding is not a place to hide. It is a place to return from.

There are moments when grounding alone is not enough. If the body is highly activated, pair grounding with a soft exhale. If anger is pushing hard, pair grounding with a pause phrase. If panic is rising, pair grounding with plain language: "This is panic; I am here." If stress is demanding speed, pair grounding with a delay: "Not yet." Grounding is not in competition with other tools. It gives them a base.

The most common mistake is making grounding too abstract. "Be present" is a beautiful idea and a poor emergency instruction. "Feel your left foot on the floor" is better. "Notice the texture under your thumb" is better. "Name the object in front of you" is better. The body under pressure needs instructions that are concrete enough to follow. Abstraction belongs later, when the system has slowed.

Another mistake is using grounding to avoid necessary action. A person may keep grounding themselves in a conversation where a boundary is needed, or stay physically present in a situation they should leave. Grounding is not endurance training for unhealthy dynamics. It is not a way to tolerate what should be addressed. Its purpose is to help you act from steadiness rather than from panic, appeasement, anger, or collapse. Sometimes the grounded next action is to speak. Sometimes it is to leave. Sometimes it is to say no. Sometimes it is to pause before deciding.

A grounded person is not always a quiet person. A grounded person is more accurately located in the moment.

That location matters. When you are located, you can tell the difference between what is happening and what your surge is adding. You can feel anger without becoming only anger. You can feel panic without becoming only panic. You can hear criticism without becoming only the criticised self. You can stand in a queue without the queue becoming a personal catastrophe. You can read a message without letting the screen become the whole room.

This is not a soft skill. It is a hard interruption of emotional narrowing.

Practise grounding when nothing serious is happening. This is how the body learns the route. While waiting for a kettle, feel both feet. While sitting at a desk, notice the pressure of your hands. While walking through a doorway, look for one neutral object and name it. While standing in a queue, feel the weight shift through your legs. These tiny rehearsals make grounding less foreign when stress rises. A tool used only in crisis often feels clumsy. A tool woven into ordinary moments becomes available.

You do not need many grounding methods. You need a few that reliably fit your life. One for public places. One for conversations. One for digital triggers. One for panic sensations. For public places, feet are discreet. For conversations, hands are useful. For digital triggers, touch the phone but do not open it, then place it down and feel the surface beneath your palm. For panic, combine feet, eyes, and a soft exhale without staring inward at the breath.

Grounding is successful when it changes your relationship to the next moment. Not when it makes you perfectly calm. Not when it removes all discomfort. Not when it proves that you are in control of every sensation. It succeeds when it gives you one more point of contact, one less second of tunnel vision, one clearer pause before the next sentence, one small piece of reality beyond the threat.

That is enough to matter.

The next time your attention collapses around a message, a sensation, a criticism, a delay, or a fear, do not begin by arguing with the whole story. Start with contact. Feet. Hands. Eyes. Sound. Temperature. One sense, one location, a few seconds of honest noticing.

The world is larger than the threat target.

Grounding is how you let the body remember.

Widening your field

A surge makes the world feel smaller than it is.

The message becomes the whole room. The face across from you becomes the whole relationship. The tightness in your chest becomes the whole body. The one sentence that hurt becomes the whole conversation. Attention collapses around the threat target, and because the mind is looking so intensely at one thing, that one thing begins to feel like the only thing that matters.

Widening your field is the practice of bringing the rest of the moment back into view.

This does not mean pretending the trigger is harmless. It does not mean forcing yourself to be positive, detached, forgiving, agreeable, or serene. It does not mean floating above the problem as though you have no stake in it. Widening is much more practical than that. It is the deliberate act of expanding awareness beyond the single point your stress, anger, or panic has selected as urgent.

The threat target may still matter. It simply may not deserve the whole room.

When attention narrows, the mind often loses proportion. A difficult message feels like a disaster. A pause feels like rejection. A criticism feels like exposure. A sensation feels like danger. A delayed reply feels like proof. The more the mind stares, the more convincing the interpretation becomes. Widening interrupts that stare. It gives the thinking mind more material to work with: space, context, neutral details, body position, time, other possible meanings, and the simple fact that this moment is larger than the alarm.

One of the fastest ways to widen is through the eyes. Stress often fixes the gaze. You may stare at the screen, the person, the door, the floor, the symptom, the sentence. The eyes narrow, and the mind follows. To widen, let your gaze soften without closing your eyes. Notice not only what is directly in front of you, but what exists to the sides. Let peripheral vision come back. You do not have to look around dramatically. Simply allow the edges of the room to exist again.

Peripheral vision is useful because it changes the quality of attention. A fixed gaze can intensify threat. A softened gaze often reduces the sense of being locked onto one target. This is especially helpful before speaking. If you keep staring at the person or message that triggered you, the body may continue to treat it as the whole event. If your field widens, even slightly, your next sentence has a better chance of coming from more than the surge.

You can practise this in ordinary places. Look at an object directly, then allow the background to become noticeable without moving your head. Notice the wall behind it, the light around it, the space beside it, the colours at the edge of vision. Nothing mystical is happening. You are teaching attention that it can include more than the centre. Under pressure, that lesson becomes valuable.

Another method is the slow room scan.

This is not anxious scanning for exits, danger, or people's reactions. It is a deliberate, neutral sweep of the environment. Let your eyes move slowly across the room and name simple objects without interpretation: chair, window, cup, lamp, door, book, table, bag. Use plain language. The point is not to make the objects interesting. The point is to shift the mind from threat-story into direct noticing.

Direct noticing is powerful because it does not argue with the surge. Arguing often keeps attention attached to the threat. "I should not be upset." "This is not a big deal." "I must stop thinking about it." These inner sentences may be well-intentioned, but they still orbit the problem. A room scan does something cleaner. It gives the mind another task. It says, "Look. Include. Return to the larger scene."

Naming neutral objects also helps reduce emotional over-interpretation. In a surge, the mind becomes rich with meaning, often too rich. The eyebrow means contempt. The silence means abandonment. The body sensation means danger. The delayed email means disaster. Neutral naming brings attention back to description. "White door." "Wooden table." "Blue folder." "Glass of water." Description is steadier than prediction.

The scan should be slow enough to soften urgency but brief enough to remain practical. You are not trying to catalogue the room. You are trying to remind the body that the trigger is one part of the environment, not the whole environment. In a meeting, this may take only a few seconds. In a conflict at home, it may be the glance that keeps you from answering too sharply. In panic, it may be the first bridge back from internal alarm to external reality.

A third method is widening through sound.

When attention is locked onto a threat, sound often narrows too. You may hear only the other person's tone, only the blood rushing in your ears, only the imagined echo of the message you just read. To widen, listen for a sound that is not part of the surge. A distant car. A fridge hum. Footsteps. Rain. A chair shifting. A low background murmur. The sound does not need to be pleasant. It only needs to be present and not emotionally central.

Sound widening is especially useful when looking around would be too obvious or when your eyes are trapped by the situation. You can sit in a meeting and listen for the faintest neutral sound while someone else speaks. You can stand in a queue and notice the ordinary noise around you instead of being consumed by impatience. You can sit with panic and hear one external sound while allowing the body to remain uncomfortable. The point is not distraction. It is inclusion.

There is a crucial difference between widening and avoiding.

Avoiding says, "I will not deal with this." Widening says, "I will deal with this from a larger state." Avoiding uses attention shifts to escape responsibility. Widening uses attention shifts to recover judgement. Avoiding leaves the issue untouched because it is uncomfortable. Widening creates enough internal space to approach the issue more cleanly.

This distinction matters because some people mistrust calming tools. They fear that if they look away from the trigger, they are minimising it. If they notice the room, they are letting someone off the hook. If they soften their gaze, they are weakening their position. But narrowed attention is not the same as moral seriousness. You can care deeply and still widen. You can hold a boundary and still notice the floor. You can challenge unfairness and still hear the whole sentence. You can feel panic and still see the room.

Widening is not a betrayal of the truth. It is protection against a partial truth becoming total.

The most useful widening practices are small enough to use at the exact moment before action. Before replying, widen. Before accusing, widen. Before agreeing too quickly, widen. Before leaving abruptly, widen. Before searching symptoms, widen. Before sending the message, widen. The tool belongs at the hinge between urge and behaviour.

Suppose you receive a message that feels cold. Your attention locks onto one phrase. The mind begins building the case: they are annoyed, they are withdrawing, they are being unfair, they do not respect you. The body tightens and the reply begins forming. Widening interrupts the sequence. Look away from the screen. Notice the room around the phone. Feel the space to the left and right of you. Name three neutral things nearby. Let the message become an object within a larger environment, not a command centre for your whole nervous system.

The message may still need a reply. It may even deserve a firm reply. But the reply no longer has to come from the smallest version of the moment.

In conflict, widening helps you hear more accurately. When someone says something painful, attention often grabs the sharpest word and treats it as the full meaning. You stop listening. You begin preparing. You may answer a sentence the other person has not finished saying. A widened field gives you a better chance of staying with the whole communication: words, tone, context, your body, their state, the room, the pace. It does not guarantee agreement. It increases accuracy.

Accuracy is underrated in emotional moments. Many people aim for calm as though calm were the highest goal. But accuracy may matter even more. Can you accurately hear what was said? Can you accurately sense what your body is adding? Can you accurately tell whether the moment is urgent or merely uncomfortable? Can you accurately choose whether to speak, pause, leave, ask, delay, or repair? Widening helps because a narrowed mind cannot be fully accurate. It has excluded too much.

In panic, widening is often the difference between being trapped inside sensation and remaining connected to the world. Panic pulls attention inward: breath, heart, dizziness, unreality, heat, trembling, tightness. The person begins checking the body, then checking again, then interpreting every change. The field shrinks to symptoms. Widening reintroduces the outside: the floor, the wall, the person at the next table, the shape of a window, the temperature of a cup, the sound of traffic. These details do not argue that panic is pleasant. They remind the brain that sensation is not the whole scene.

A helpful phrase is: "There is more here."

Use it gently. Not as a slogan, but as an orientation. The chest is tight, and there is a chair beneath me. I feel angry, and there is light on the wall. I want to reply, and my phone is resting in my hand. I feel criticised, and I can hear the rest of the sentence. I feel urgency, and there is still space around me. The word "and" widens. It allows the surge to exist without becoming the entire truth.

Widening your field also changes time. A narrowed mind often feels trapped in immediacy. Now is all there is. The next action must happen now. The answer must arrive now. Relief must come now. Widening creates the sense that the moment has edges. There was a before. There will be an after. You do not have to spend the whole future in the emotional weather of this minute.

This is one reason widening is so effective before decisions. Decisions made inside a tunnel often serve the tunnel. They reduce pressure, prove a point, escape discomfort, or create the illusion of certainty. Decisions made from a wider field are more likely to serve your values. They may still be firm. They may still be difficult. But they are less likely to be merely reactive.

A practical way to widen before deciding is to change visual distance. If you are staring at a screen, look across the room. If you are staring at the person, briefly look at a neutral point and then return. If you are staring inward at a sensation, open your eyes and identify the farthest object you can see. Distance changes the feel of the moment. The mind that has been pressed against the trigger gains a little room.

Another way is to widen through posture. A surge often pulls the body into a shape: leaning forward, curling inward, bracing, collapsing, gripping. Without making a performance of it, let the body take up a little more balanced space. Both feet on the floor. Shoulders released by a fraction. Hands open. Head turning slightly rather than fixed. Posture and attention are linked. A body locked onto threat makes a widened mind harder to access.

This does not mean forcing yourself into an artificial pose of confidence. It means giving attention a body that is not completely organised around alarm. A small postural shift can say, "I am here, not trapped inside that one point." Again, the movement is modest. The modesty is part of why it works.

Widening can also include other possible meanings. This should come only after some physical widening, because trying to think flexibly too early can feel impossible. Once the body has a little more room, ask: "What else might be true?" Not as a way to excuse harm. Not as a way to deny your perception. Simply to loosen certainty. Perhaps the delay is not rejection. Perhaps the tone is tiredness. Perhaps the criticism has one useful piece. Perhaps the sensation is panic, not danger. Perhaps the urgency is a state cue, not a deadline.

The aim is not to find the most comforting interpretation. That can become another form of avoidance. The aim is to stop the most threatening interpretation from becoming the only one available. Emotional maturity is not always believing the best. It is refusing to let the worst case seize the whole field without evidence.

There will be moments when widening reveals that action is needed. You may widen and realise a boundary must be set. You may widen and choose to leave. You may widen and decide the message does deserve a response, just not the one your first surge wanted to send. You may widen and recognise that panic symptoms need care, rest, or medical advice if they are unusual or concerning. Widening does not predetermine softness. It improves contact with reality.

This is why it belongs in the 60-second calm. The goal is not to become passive. The goal is to recover enough field to choose the smallest safe next action. A narrow field produces narrow choices: fight, flee, freeze, fix, please, prove. A wider field produces more nuanced choices: pause, clarify, delay, breathe, ask, state a limit, ground, repair, or wait.

Practise widening when you are not escalated. Let your eyes soften while walking down a street. Notice peripheral vision while sitting at your desk. Name neutral objects while waiting for the kettle. Listen for background sound while travelling. Look at the farthest visible point when you feel mildly stressed. These small practices teach the body that attention can move. Under pressure, it will be easier to remember that the tunnel is not the only view.

A useful practice is to pair widening with common triggers. Before opening a difficult email, widen your gaze beyond the screen. Before entering a meeting, notice the room rather than only the people. Before answering a tense message, look away and name three neutral objects. Before discussing a charged issue, feel the space beside you and behind you. You are not trying to become calm in advance of life. You are creating a wider starting position.

The measure of success is not whether the feeling disappears. Widening succeeds when the threat target loses its monopoly. You still see the problem, but you also see the room. You still feel the sensation, but you also feel the feet. You still hear the criticism, but you also hear the full sentence. You still want relief, but you also recognise that not every immediate action is wise.

That shift may be brief. It may last only long enough to stop one sentence, delay one message, or ask one clarifying question. Brief is enough. The 60-second calm is built from brief openings used well.

The next time your attention fastens onto one point and the surge insists that nothing else matters, do not demand instant calm. Widen the field. Let the eyes soften. Include the edges of the room. Name what is neutral. Hear one ordinary sound. Feel the space around the threat.

The trigger may still be there.

But now it is no longer everything.

Chapter 5
Anger pauses without suppression

Anger has a reputation problem. It is either treated as dangerous and shameful, something to be buried quickly before it makes everyone uncomfortable, or it is treated as truth in its purest form, something that deserves immediate expression simply because it feels powerful. Both views are too crude. Anger is neither a monster to be locked away nor a wise ruler to be obeyed without question. It is a signal. Sometimes a fierce one. Sometimes a necessary one. Sometimes a distorted one. Always one that deserves handling with care.

The difficulty is that anger rarely arrives alone. It brings heat, speed, certainty, pressure, and a strong urge to act. It can make the body lean forward before the mind has decided what should happen. It can sharpen the tongue, harden the face, tighten the chest, and make one sentence feel as if it must be spoken now or something essential will be lost. In that state, pausing can feel almost insulting. The angry body says, "If I pause, I am giving in. If I soften, they win. If I wait, the point disappears."

But a pause is not surrender.

A pause is the space in which anger stops being a weapon and becomes information. It allows you to ask a more disciplined question: what is this anger trying to protect? It may be protecting dignity. It may be pointing towards a crossed boundary, a repeated disappointment, a hidden resentment, a genuine injustice, an unmet need, or exhaustion that has finally run out of patience. Those messages matter. They should not be dismissed simply because they arrive hot. Yet the action anger recommends in its first rush is not always the action that will best serve the message.

This is the central challenge of anger work: preserving the signal while delaying the impulse. Suppression fails because it teaches people to distrust their own limits. It pushes anger underground, where it often becomes resentment, coldness, sarcasm, contempt, sudden explosions, or a private fantasy of saying everything at last. Unfiltered expression fails because it often makes the delivery so forceful that the original point becomes harder to hear. One path erases the self. The other can injure the relationship. Neither is mature enough for real pressure.

A good anger pause sits between those two failures. It does not ask you to pretend you are fine. It does not ask you to become agreeable, charming, endlessly patient, or conveniently quiet. It asks for enough restraint to stop the first surge from choosing your words. There is a profound difference between silencing anger and containing it. Silencing says, "This must not exist." Containment says, "This matters, and I will not let it come out in a way that creates unnecessary harm."

This matters because anger often contains a valid complaint wrapped in an unsafe delivery system. The complaint may be clear: "Do not speak to me like that." "I need more support." "That was unfair." "I am not willing to keep having this conversation at this volume." "I said no." The unsafe delivery system adds the excess: the insult, the accusation, the sweeping judgement, the old grievance dragged into the present, the sentence designed to punish rather than clarify. A pause helps separate the message from the shrapnel.

The work begins by separating anger from action, because the feeling and the behaviour are not the same thing. From there, words become tools rather than sparks. A safe pause needs language that is short, natural, and strong enough to hold the moment without escalating it: not a lecture, not a performance of calm, not an apology for having a limit, but a clean sentence that buys time while preserving respect. The aim is not to remove anger from the conversation. The aim is to stop anger from damaging the very thing it is trying to defend.

The question, then, is not whether you should be angry. Sometimes you will be, and sometimes you should be. The sharper question is this: when anger rises with a truth in one hand and a match in the other, can you keep the truth and put down the match?

Separating anger and action

Anger can be honest without being wise about timing.

That is the first distinction. Many people confuse the arrival of anger with permission to act from anger. They assume that because the feeling is strong, the next impulse must be truthful. Because the body is hot, the sentence must be necessary. Because the point matters, the delivery must be justified. This is how anger becomes dangerous: not because it exists, but because it persuades people that intensity is the same as authority.

Anger often carries information worth taking seriously. It may signal that a boundary has been crossed, that a promise has been broken, that someone has been careless with your trust, that your effort has gone unseen, or that you have been accommodating for too long. It may appear when a value has been violated. It may rise when you feel dismissed, cornered, patronised, blamed, interrupted, or treated as though your needs are inconvenient. These signals matter. A life without anger would not be a healthier life; it would be a life with one of its warning systems disconnected.

But a warning system is not a steering wheel.

The signal says, "Something matters here." The impulse says, "Say it now, hard." Those are not the same thing. The signal may deserve respect. The impulse may need delay. This is the heart of separating anger and action: you do not have to deny the feeling in order to refuse its first instruction.

This distinction can feel unnatural at first because anger arrives with such physical confidence. It does not usually enter like a quiet suggestion. It rises in the chest, heats the face, tightens the jaw, sharpens the eyes, speeds up thought, and prepares the body to move towards the source of frustration. It can make stillness feel intolerable. It can make waiting feel like weakness. It can make a pause feel as though you are letting the other person win.

That is anger's trick. It makes speed feel like strength.

Yet the strongest anger is not always the fastest anger. Fast anger often spends itself in blunt force: accusation, sarcasm, contempt, overstatement, interruption, threat, dramatic exit, punishing silence, or the message written with shaking hands and sent before judgement can return. It may feel clean for a moment. It may even feel like relief. But relief is not the same as resolution. Sometimes the moment after the outburst is quieter only because damage has entered the room.

Anger wants an outlet. Wisdom wants an outcome.

Those two aims are not automatically aligned. An outlet is about discharge. It asks, "How do I get this pressure out of me?" An outcome asks, "What needs to happen next, and what kind of person do I want to be while I ask for it?" When you are angry, the outlet is usually more obvious than the outcome. The body wants to speak, type, leave, accuse, prove, punish, or force recognition. Outcome requires a wider field. It requires enough space to remember that the point is not merely to express anger, but to use its information well.

This is why suppression is not the answer. Suppression tells anger, "You are not allowed to exist." It may keep the room polite for a while, but it rarely creates real calm. The unsaid thing remains active. It leaks into tone, distance, sarcasm, coldness, resentment, headaches, fatigue, private arguments, or sudden disproportionate reactions later. Suppressed anger does not vanish; it waits for a less convenient doorway.

Unfiltered expression is not the answer either. It tells anger, "You are in charge." That may feel powerful, especially for someone who has spent years swallowing their needs. But being dominated by anger is not freedom. It is another form of being controlled. The person who explodes is no more free than the person who collapses into silence if neither can choose what happens after the feeling rises.

The mature middle is containment.

Containment is often misunderstood as restraint for the sake of appearances. It is deeper than that. To contain anger is to hold its energy without letting it decide the whole method of communication. It means the anger is present, acknowledged, and taken seriously, but not allowed to become reckless. Containment says, "This feeling is real, and I am responsible for how it leaves me."

That responsibility is not a punishment. It is power.

When anger and action are fused, you have fewer choices. You feel the heat and you speak. You feel the insult and you attack. You feel the pressure and you send. You feel the boundary being crossed and you slam the door. Everything happens in one line, as if the emotion has a direct wire to behaviour. Separating anger and action cuts that wire. It does not remove the electricity. It places a switch between charge and consequence.

The switch is the pause.

Not a long, serene pause. Not the kind of pause that looks graceful in a staged conversation. Often it is rough and internal: a breath caught before it becomes a sentence, a hand moved away from the phone, a jaw unclenched before the first word, a decision to say one sentence instead of six. The pause may feel awkward. It may feel hot. It may feel as though everything in you is leaning against it. That does not mean it is failing. It means it is interrupting a well-rehearsed route.

The first skill is to notice the action urge as separate from the anger itself. This can be surprisingly difficult because anger often dresses the urge as justice. "I need to tell them exactly what they are." "I should make them understand." "I have to respond now." "I cannot let this stand." "They need to know how much they have hurt me." Sometimes a response is needed. Sometimes a boundary must be named. Sometimes silence would be dishonest. But the language of necessity deserves examination when the body is heated.

A useful question is: "What is anger asking me to do?"

This question creates distance. It turns the impulse into an object you can look at rather than a command you must obey. Anger may be asking you to interrupt. It may be asking you to accuse. It may be asking you to send a long message. It may be asking you to withdraw affection. It may be asking you to agree coldly and punish later. It may be asking you to raise your voice, repeat yourself, or drag old evidence into the present. Once the request is visible, you can decide whether it deserves to be followed.

The next question is: "What is anger trying to protect?"

This is where the feeling becomes useful. Beneath the push, there is often a value. Respect. Fairness. Safety. Honesty. Time. Effort. Autonomy. Care. Recognition. Rest. Anger may be clumsy, but it is rarely empty. When you identify what it is protecting, you can speak more accurately. Instead of "You never care," the real message may be, "I need my time to be treated as important." Instead of "You are so selfish," the real message may be, "I am not willing to keep absorbing last-minute changes." Instead of "Fine, do whatever you want," the real message may be, "I am angry, and I need a minute before I can discuss this properly."

Accuracy is the reward for pausing.

Anger without pause often exaggerates. It widens the accusation beyond the present facts. It turns one behaviour into a character judgement. It turns disappointment into prosecution. It reaches backwards and forwards, pulling in old wounds and future predictions until the original issue disappears under the weight. A pause helps you return to the cleanest version of the truth. What happened? What mattered? What do I need now? What is the smallest clear statement that protects the boundary without adding unnecessary harm?

This is not about sounding pleasant. It is about staying proportionate.

Proportion is one of the first things anger disturbs. The body may react to a small present event with the force of a long history. A partner forgets a task, and the anger is not only about the task; it is about every time you felt alone with responsibility. A colleague interrupts you, and the anger is not only about the interruption; it is about every time your competence felt questioned. A friend replies dismissively, and the anger is not only about the reply; it is about the fear of not mattering. The current moment may deserve attention, but it may not deserve the whole archive.

Separating anger and action allows you to ask, "How much of this belongs here?"

That question does not invalidate the old wounds. It protects the current conversation from being crushed by them. There may be a later time to address the pattern, the history, the deeper resentment. But in the first surge, bringing everything at once often creates too much force for anything to be understood. Anger wants total expression. Repair usually requires sequence.

There is also a difference between firmness and attack. Firmness names reality clearly. Attack tries to make the other person feel the force of your distress. Firmness can say, "I am not available for this conversation while you are raising your voice." Attack says, "You are impossible to talk to." Firmness says, "I need you to follow through when you agree to something." Attack says, "You never do anything properly." Firmness says, "That comment was not acceptable." Attack says, "You are rude and selfish."

The difference is not weakness. It is precision.

Precision gives anger a better chance of being heard. Reactive anger often invites argument about your tone, your exaggeration, your timing, or your fairness. The other person may then avoid the central issue by focusing on the way you delivered it. This can be frustrating, especially when the issue is real. But it also reveals why delivery matters. If the truth arrives wrapped in avoidable injury, the injury may become the new problem.

A pause protects the truth from being dismissed because of the damage around it.

There are, of course, moments when anger must lead to swift action. If someone is being unsafe, threatening, abusive, or violating a clear limit, leaving, seeking help, or setting an immediate boundary may be necessary. Separating anger and action does not mean staying in harmful situations to prove composure. It means making the action cleaner. Even urgent action can be chosen more wisely when it is not fused with the rawest impulse.

The principle is not "do nothing." The principle is "do not let the first surge write the whole response."

Sometimes the right action is to speak. Sometimes it is to stop speaking. Sometimes it is to leave. Sometimes it is to refuse. Sometimes it is to say, "I will not continue this at this volume." Sometimes it is to delay the conversation. Sometimes it is to write down what you want to say and decide later whether it should be sent. Separating anger and action does not remove action from the table. It improves the quality of action available.

The body can help. Anger often needs a physical interruption because thought alone may not be enough. Unclench the hands. Put both feet on the floor. Let the exhale lengthen. Relax the tongue from the roof of the mouth. Lower the volume before you lower the point. Move the phone out of reach. Feel the table under your palm. These are not attempts to become peaceful. They are ways of telling the body, "We are not acting at full speed."

This body-first approach matters because anger can make reasoning feel insulting. The heated mind may reject careful thought as delay, weakness, or self-betrayal. A physical pause does not require agreement with a calming idea. It simply changes the conditions. Once the body has slowed by even a small amount, the mind can ask better questions.

One useful practice is to separate the sentence into three parts: feeling, meaning, and action urge. The feeling might be anger. The meaning might be, "I am being dismissed." The action urge might be, "Interrupt and prove them wrong." Seeing these as separate parts changes the whole moment. The meaning may need checking. The action urge may need delaying. The feeling may simply need acknowledging. Without separation, they collapse into one command: "I am angry, therefore I must interrupt."

Another practice is to ask, "What would I say if I had to keep my dignity and theirs?"

This is not always easy. Sometimes the other person's behaviour has been poor. Sometimes they have not protected your dignity. But your standard should not be entirely dependent on their state. Keeping their dignity does not mean excusing them. It means refusing to make humiliation your method. You can be firm without degrading. You can be clear without contempt. You can end a conversation without cruelty. You can protect yourself without turning the moment into a punishment.

Anger often argues against this. It says the other person does not deserve restraint. Perhaps they do not. But restraint is not only a gift to them. It is a commitment to your own standards. It means you do not hand your behaviour over to someone else's provocation. It means you remain the author of your conduct, even when someone else has contributed to your state.

That is the deeper freedom: not never feeling anger, but not being governed by it.

Self-respect after anger is built in these small decisions. The message not sent. The insult not used. The pause taken. The boundary named cleanly. The room left without a slammed door. The apology offered later for the sharpness, without surrendering the valid point. Each of these moments teaches the body that anger can be survived without being discharged destructively.

This is important because many people fear their own anger. They worry that if they let themselves feel it, it will become too much. They may have seen anger used harmfully. They may have used it harmfully themselves. They may have learned that anger causes abandonment, punishment, ridicule, or shame. Separating anger from action helps rebuild trust. It shows that feeling anger does not mean becoming dangerous. The feeling can rise, peak, and move without being allowed to choose every behaviour.

For others, the lesson is different. They may trust anger too much. They may see it as authenticity, strength, or protection. They may believe that anything less than immediate expression is dishonesty. Separating anger from action teaches a harder truth: not every unfiltered expression is honest in the deepest sense. Sometimes it is merely immediate. Sometimes the first angry sentence is not the most truthful sentence, but the most pressurised one.

Truth improves when pressure lowers.

This does not mean you should wait until anger has disappeared before speaking. That would be unrealistic and sometimes unnecessary. The goal is not emotionless communication. The goal is chosen communication. You may speak while still angry, but with enough separation to avoid excess. You may say, "I am angry, and I want to be careful." You may say, "This is not okay with me." You may say, "I need a pause because I do not want to turn this into an attack." Such statements honour the feeling while refusing to be overrun by it.

The cleanest anger often has fewer words.

This is worth remembering. A surge wants to elaborate. It wants to add examples, motives, verdicts, history, predictions, and moral commentary. A disciplined anger chooses the sentence that matters most. "Do not speak to me like that." "I need you to stop." "I disagree." "I am not ready to answer." "This needs to change." Short sentences are not automatically kind, but they are often safer than long, heated speeches. They leave less room for the surge to smuggle in damage.

After the pause, action may still be needed. The issue may still require a conversation, decision, boundary, consequence, or repair. Separating anger and action is not the end of responsibility; it is the beginning of better responsibility. Once the surge has slowed, you can decide what the anger is asking you to protect and how to protect it without unnecessary harm.

That is the real promise of this skill. You do not become less strong. You become less hijacked. Anger remains available as information, energy, and moral signal, but it no longer has unchecked access to your voice, hands, phone, feet, or silence. It has to pass through choice.

The next time anger rises, do not start by asking whether the feeling is allowed. It is already here. Ask instead: what is the signal, and what is the impulse?

Then keep them apart long enough to decide which one deserves your loyalty.

Scripts for safe pauses

A pause is only useful if you can take it without making the moment worse.

This is where many people struggle. They understand the value of not reacting immediately. They know, at least in theory, that a short delay can prevent a damaging sentence, a rushed promise, a sarcastic reply, or a message sent from heat. But when anger is rising, silence can feel dangerous. It can feel as though the other person will misunderstand it, exploit it, mock it, or fill it with their own version of events. The body wants to respond, not because a response is ready, but because pressure demands movement.

That is why a safe pause needs words.

Not many words. Not a speech. Not an emotional essay explaining why you are pausing, what childhood pattern is being activated, how hard you are trying, or why the other person should appreciate your restraint. During anger, too many words often become another form of escalation. A safe pause uses language as a small bridge: enough to stop the old reaction, enough to tell the other person you have not disappeared, and enough to protect the next minute from becoming damage.

The aim is not to sound perfectly calm. That is an unrealistic standard and, in some situations, an irritating one. People can usually sense when calm is being performed with clenched teeth. The better aim is to sound responsible. Responsible language does not deny anger. It does not pretend the issue is small. It does not grovel. It does not threaten. It says, in effect, "Something in me is heated, and I am going to handle that before I continue."

That is a strong move.

A safe pause must do three things at once. It must buy time, reduce heat, and preserve connection where connection is appropriate. If it only buys time, it may sound evasive. If it only reduces heat, it may erase the issue. If it only preserves connection, it may slide into pleasing. The best pause scripts are short because they have a narrow job. They are not there to resolve the conflict. They are there to stop the conflict from being hijacked by the first surge.

A useful script often begins with intention. This helps the other person understand that the pause is not contempt, punishment, or avoidance. "I want to answer well." "I want to be fair." "I want to hear you properly." "I do not want to say this badly." These sentences are powerful because they frame the pause as care rather than escape. They also remind you of your own standard at the exact moment your body wants to abandon it.

"I want to answer well - give me a minute."

This is one of the cleanest pause scripts because it is both warm and firm. It does not over-apologise. It does not invite a debate about whether you deserve a minute. It does not accuse the other person of causing your state. It simply names a better intention and asks for the space needed to meet it. The phrase works because it keeps dignity on both sides. You are not saying, "You are making me angry." You are saying, "I am choosing not to answer from the roughest part of my anger."

Another useful script is: "I am too heated to discuss this well right now."

This is direct, and directness matters. Many people try to disguise anger because they fear it will sound aggressive. The disguise often leaks. A tight smile, a cold "fine," a clipped tone, a sudden helpfulness, or an unnatural calm can create more confusion than a clean admission. Saying "I am too heated" is not an attack. It is a state report. It tells the truth without turning the other person into the villain of the sentence.

The phrase "to discuss this well" is important. It does not say the issue is unimportant. It does not say the conversation is over. It says the quality of the conversation matters. This shifts the pause from avoidance to protection. You are not refusing the issue. You are refusing to handle the issue badly.

For moments when anger is rising but you can remain present, a softer script may be better: "Give me a second. I am listening."

This is useful when the other person is speaking and your body has begun preparing a counterattack. It prevents the pause from sounding like withdrawal. It also gives your attention a job. You are not merely holding back words; you are trying to listen. That distinction is essential in conflict. Many people stop listening long before they stop speaking.

They hear just enough to defend themselves. A script that includes "I am listening" can interrupt the internal courtroom and bring you back to the actual conversation.

When the issue is sharp and a boundary is needed, the pause script should not become too soft. Some moments require firmness. "I need a minute before I respond to that." This sentence is clean. It does not explain. It does not perform gentleness. It does not apologise for needing time. It is especially useful when someone says something provocative, dismissive, or unfair. The phrase protects you from firing back, but it also signals that the comment has landed and will not simply be absorbed.

There is a difference between a safe pause and a disappearing act. A safe pause gives a return point where possible. "I am going to step away for ten minutes, then come back." "I need a short break. I will come back to this after I have cooled down." "I cannot do this well while I am this angry. I will return to it later." These phrases matter because unexplained withdrawal can injure trust. The person leaving may feel they are preventing escalation. The person left behind may feel abandoned, punished, or shut out.

A return point changes the meaning of space.

It says, "I am not vanishing. I am containing myself." In relationships where withdrawal has caused harm before, this distinction is not cosmetic; it is central. If you need to leave the room, leave with enough clarity that the other person does not have to invent the story. You may still be angry. You may still need distance. But the distance has a frame.

The frame must be realistic. Do not promise to return in a few minutes if you know you will need longer. Do not say "later" if later usually means never. A pause becomes unsafe when it is used to avoid the conversation indefinitely. If you are not ready to continue, say so plainly and set a more honest return point.

"I cannot talk about this well tonight. I will come back to it tomorrow morning." That is better than a vague retreat that leaves the issue suspended in the room.

Digital anger needs its own scripts because the pause is often invisible. If someone sends a message that provokes you, silence may be wise, but sometimes silence may also be misread. A short holding reply can prevent both escalation and abandonment. "I have seen this. I want to think before I reply." "I am not ignoring you. I need time to answer properly." "I do not want to respond quickly and make this worse." These are not elaborate. They create a barrier between reading and reacting.

The key is not to smuggle the argument into the holding reply. A holding reply should not include your evidence, your irritation, your judgement of their tone, or a preview of your counterattack. "I will reply when I can do it properly" is a pause. "I will reply when I can do it properly, because right now I cannot believe how unfair you are being" is the conflict arriving through the side door. Keep the holding message clean.

Some pause scripts are unsafe because they sound calm while carrying contempt. "Whatever." "I am done." "Calm down." "You are being ridiculous." "I cannot deal with you." "Fine, have it your way." These may create distance, but they do not create safety. They often function as disguised attacks. The body gets the relief of withdrawing or punishing while the words pretend to be a boundary. A safe pause should reduce heat, not merely relocate it.

Other scripts fail because they over-explain. "I am feeling really triggered because this reminds me of several previous situations and I am trying not to respond from a place of dysregulation, so I need to take a pause to process all of this." There may be truth in that sentence, but in a heated moment it is often too much. It asks the other person to process your process while the original issue is still active. It can sound clinical, evasive, or self-focused. Save the deeper explanation for later, if it is needed at all.

In the surge itself, plain language is stronger.

"I need a minute."

"I want to answer well."

"I am too angry to do this carefully."

"I hear you. I need a moment before I respond."

"I am going to pause so I do not make this worse."

These scripts work because they are short enough to remember when the body is hot. The best script is not the most elegant one. It is the one you can actually say before the old move takes over.

Tone matters as much as wording. A good script can be damaged by a punishing tone. "I need a minute" can sound mature, or it can sound like a slammed door in sentence form. The aim is not to sound sweet. It is to lower the force. Slow the pace by a fraction. Keep the volume steady. Let the sentence end cleanly instead of adding a muttered insult, a sigh of contempt, or a final "because clearly this is pointless." The pause should not carry hidden shrapnel.

Body language matters too. If you say you need a minute while pointing, crowding, glaring, or typing furiously, the body contradicts the words. A safer pause is supported by a small physical shift: hands unclenched, phone lowered, eyes not fixed aggressively on the other person, feet steady, breath slightly slower. Again, this is not performance. It is alignment. The body and the words should be giving the same message: not now, not like this, not from the peak of heat.

There is also a relational skill in choosing the right script for the person and situation. At work, you may need something contained: "Let me take a moment before I answer that." With a partner, something warmer may serve better: "I care about this, and I do not want to answer badly." With a child or younger person, reassurance may be needed: "I am upset, but I am not leaving you. I need a minute to calm my voice." With someone who pushes boundaries, the script may need firmness: "I am taking a pause. I will not continue while this is escalating."

A safe pause should fit the setting without betraying the purpose.

One mistake is asking for a pause as though you are asking permission to regulate yourself. "Is it okay if maybe I take a minute?" may be appropriate in some gentle conversations, but in heated dynamics it can become too tentative. You do not need to seek approval for not escalating. A steadier version is: "I am going to take a minute." This is not rude. It is clear. When the body is heated, clarity is kinder than vague politeness.

Another mistake is using a pause to control the other person. "I will talk when you can be reasonable." "Come back when you are ready to apologise." "I am not discussing this until you admit what you did." These statements may contain a boundary, but they also contain judgement and pressure. A cleaner version focuses on your participation: "I am willing to continue when we can both speak respectfully." "I am going to pause because this is getting too heated." "I will talk about this when I can stay steady." You are naming the conditions for your involvement, not trying to dominate the other person's state.

The safest scripts use "I" without becoming self-absorbed. "I need a minute." "I want to answer well." "I am too heated to continue carefully." This keeps responsibility where it belongs. It does not say, "You made me like this." It does not say, "Your tone is the only problem." It does not surrender the issue either. It simply says, "My state needs managing before my response can be trusted."

That is emotional accountability in its most practical form.

Practising pause scripts matters because anger does not reward improvisation. When the body is heated, the most familiar language wins. If the only phrases you have rehearsed are defensive, sarcastic, apologetic, or final, those are the phrases most likely to appear. A safe pause script must become familiar before it is needed. Say it aloud when you are calm. Write it somewhere. Test whether it sounds like you. Adjust it until it is natural enough to survive pressure.

A script that does not sound like you will fail when you most need it. If you are direct, choose a direct phrase. If you are warm, choose a warm phrase. If you become wordy under stress, choose a phrase so short it interrupts the wordiness. If you become silent, choose a phrase that keeps connection. If you become sharp, choose a phrase that slows the edge. The script should meet your default move, not someone else's idea of what calm sounds like.

For the person who attacks, the script must slow speech.

For the person who withdraws, the script must promise return.

For the person who pleases, the script must protect truth.

For the person who over-explains, the script must stay brief.

For the person who performs competence, the script must admit state without collapse.

This is how a pause becomes personal rather than decorative.

Safe pauses also require follow-through. If you say you need a minute, take the minute. Do not stand there continuing the argument in a quieter voice. If you say you will come back, come back. If you say you want to answer well, use the pause to reduce heat, not to rehearse a more polished attack. The credibility of a pause is built over time. People learn whether your pauses mean repair is coming or whether they mean the issue has been buried.

After the pause, return with a smaller, clearer sentence. This is where many people lose the benefit. They calm slightly, then re-enter with a full prosecution. The pause is not a loading bay for a bigger argument. It is an opportunity to choose the next safe move. Perhaps that move is a boundary. Perhaps it is a question. Perhaps it is an apology for tone. Perhaps it is a request to continue later. Perhaps it is one honest sentence: "I was angry because I felt dismissed, and I want to talk about that without attacking you."

The pause does not have to solve everything. It has done its first job if it prevents the surge from choosing the most damaging version of you.

There will be times when the other person does not respect the pause. They may keep talking, follow you, send more messages, accuse you of avoiding, or demand an immediate answer. This is where the script may need repetition rather than expansion. "I am taking a minute." "I will respond when I can do it properly." "I am not continuing while this is escalating." Repeat the core sentence without adding fuel. Longer explanations often give the conflict more material to grab.

Repetition is not weakness. It is structure.

Of course, safe pauses are not a substitute for safety. If a situation is threatening, coercive, or emotionally unsafe in a serious way, a pause script is not the whole answer. You may need distance, support, or a more substantial boundary. The tools here are for the ordinary but combustible moments where anger can turn a manageable conflict into lasting fallout. A pause is not meant to keep you trapped in harm. It is meant to keep you from adding harm of your own.

The beauty of a safe pause is that it honours two truths at once. The feeling matters. The delivery matters. You are allowed to be angry, and you are responsible for how anger enters the room. You are allowed to need time, and you are responsible for making that time as clear as possible. You are allowed to protect yourself, and you are responsible for not disguising punishment as space.

The next time anger rises and the first sentence comes armed, do not wait for perfect calm. Use the words that hold the line.

"I want to answer well."

"I need a minute."

"I am too heated to do this carefully."

"I will come back to this."

A safe pause is not empty silence. It is a small act of leadership in a heated moment. It tells the surge, the other person, and yourself: this matters too much to handle badly.

Chapter 6
Panic tools for real moments

The cafe is ordinary until it is not. The cup is on the table, the door is visible, the conversation nearby is unremarkable, and nothing in the room appears to justify alarm. Then the body changes. The heart begins to race. The breath feels strange, as though it cannot quite complete itself. The hands feel unsteady. The room seems slightly distant, as if a thin pane of glass has dropped between you and everything else. Nobody else reacts, which somehow makes the experience more frightening.

The mind rushes to explain the body. Perhaps you are about to faint. Perhaps something is seriously wrong. Perhaps you need to leave immediately before the feeling becomes unbearable. The more alarming the interpretation, the more the body accelerates; the more the body accelerates, the more convincing the interpretation becomes. Panic has a brutal talent for making its own evidence.

In that moment, reassurance alone may not reach you. The calm facts that would make sense from a distance can feel too small for the size of the sensations. You may know, somewhere, that this has happened before and passed before, yet the current wave still feels fresh, urgent, and absolute. Panic does not merely ask, "What if?" It asks with a racing body, a narrowed field, and a demand for immediate certainty.

The central tension is recognition without recklessness. Panic must be taken seriously as an experience, but not automatically believed as an interpretation. That distinction is delicate. Dismissing panic with "it is nothing" can make a person feel more alone inside the surge. Treating every sensation as proof of danger can feed the spiral. The useful middle is steadier: something powerful is happening in the body, and the meaning of that event still needs careful handling.

The stakes are high because panic often creates a second problem on top of the first. The sensations are uncomfortable enough, but the fear of the sensations can become the engine. A racing heart becomes a threat. Unreality becomes a sign that you are losing control. Shaking becomes evidence that something is wrong. A tight breath becomes a test you keep failing. The body is already activated; then interpretation adds fuel. What began as a spike becomes a loop.

The aftermath matters too. A panic moment may pass, but the body can remain sensitised. The mind may start reviewing, checking, researching, seeking reassurance, avoiding places, or punishing itself for having reacted. These responses are understandable, but they can teach the body that panic was more dangerous than it was. A person may survive the wave and then accidentally train fear around the memory of the wave. Calm after panic is therefore not only about getting through the peak; it is about not building a shrine to it afterwards.

The path begins by learning to recognise panic patterns without turning recognition into self-diagnosis. From there, the fear spiral can be interrupted by reducing frightening meanings rather than demanding instant disappearance of sensations. When the world feels unreal or distant, grounding must become firmer and more physical, using texture, temperature, voice, feet, and hands to re-enter the present. Once the spike has moved through, recovery depends on steady aftercare: less checking, less self-attack, and a clear return to the day.

This is not a promise that panic will become pleasant. It will not. Nor is it a suggestion that every frightening symptom should be waved away; new, severe, unusual, or medically concerning symptoms deserve appropriate care. But many panic spikes become worse because the mind treats discomfort as proof, urgency as instruction, and uncertainty as danger. The practical skill is to meet the body firmly enough to stay present, gently enough not to start a fight with it.

So when panic rises and the room begins to feel less real than the alarm inside you, the question is not, "How do I make this vanish immediately?" That question usually tightens the trap. The sharper question is: can you recognise the pattern before the story becomes the master?

Recognising panic patterns

Panic is frightening partly because it feels so physical. It does not arrive as a neat thought that can be examined from a distance. It arrives as a body event: heart racing, breath changing, hands shaking, stomach turning, chest tightening, skin prickling, legs feeling weak, the room seeming strange, the mind suddenly searching for danger. The experience can feel so immediate and convincing that the first interpretation is rarely calm. The body shouts, and the mind tries to explain the shouting.

That explanation is often the beginning of the second wave.

A panic spike can be understood as an intense alarm response that has become attached to catastrophic meaning. The body produces sensations of activation, and the mind reads those sensations as proof that something is seriously wrong. This does not mean the sensations are imaginary. They are real. The heart may truly be pounding. The breath may truly feel tight. The hands may truly tremble. The world may truly feel distant or unreal. What needs careful handling is the meaning placed on those sensations while the body is already alarmed.

Recognition is the first act of steadiness. Not diagnosis. Not dismissal. Recognition.

There is a vital difference between saying, "This is panic, therefore nothing matters," and saying, "This may be a panic pattern, so I should be careful about the story my mind is adding." The first is careless. The second is skilful. Panic tools should never be used to ignore symptoms that are new, severe, unusual, or medically concerning. If something genuinely feels medically unsafe, appropriate help matters. But many panic spikes have a familiar pattern: sudden bodily activation, intense fear of the sensations, catastrophic interpretation, urgent checking or escape, then more fear because the body remains activated.

The pattern is what gives you leverage.

Ordinary stress usually has a visible object. A deadline, an argument, a crowded schedule, a difficult message, a financial concern, a family demand, an exam, a work problem. The body may feel tense, rushed, irritated, or overloaded, but the distress is often connected to an identifiable pressure. Panic can certainly be triggered by stress, but it frequently feels more alarming because the body itself becomes the object of fear. The question shifts from "How do I deal with this situation?" to "What is happening to me?"

That shift is important. When stress becomes panic, attention often turns inward with unusual force. The breath is checked. The heartbeat is checked. The steadiness of the legs is checked. The feeling of reality is checked. The body becomes a screen on which the mind keeps looking for signs of danger. The more intensely it looks, the more noticeable every sensation becomes. The body feels louder because attention has moved closer.

Common panic cues include a racing or pounding heart, trembling, sweating, hot or cold flushes, tightness in the chest, nausea, dizziness, tingling, breath discomfort, unreality, fear of losing control, and a sudden urge to escape. These cues can appear in different combinations. Some people feel panic mostly in the chest and breath. Others feel it in the stomach, head, skin, or legs. Some become restless and urgent. Others become frozen and quiet. Panic does not need to look dramatic from the outside to be intense on the inside.

One of the most unsettling panic cues is derealisation, the sense that the world feels unreal, distant, flat, dreamlike, or strangely separate from you. This can be deeply disturbing, especially the first time it happens. The panic story may say, "Something is seriously wrong with my mind," or "I am not safe because everything feels strange." Yet unreality can also be part of the body's alarm state. It is frightening, but the fear attached to it often makes it larger. Recognition allows a different response: "This is a panic cue. I need contact with the present, not a frightening theory."

Another common cue is the fear of fainting. A person may feel light-headed, shaky, hot, weak, or unreal and conclude, "I am going to faint." That thought can intensify the surge immediately. The fear creates more alarm, the alarm creates more sensations, and the sensations appear to support the fear. In many panic moments, "I am going to faint" is not a careful conclusion; it is a panic story layered onto adrenaline and discomfort. The body feels dramatic, so the mind creates a dramatic explanation.

This does not mean you should argue aggressively with the thought. Panic often strengthens when it is fought too hard. A better response is to name the category: "This is a panic prediction." That wording is useful because it neither believes the thought completely nor tries to crush it. It places the thought where it belongs: inside a state of alarm. The prediction may feel urgent, but feeling urgent is not the same as being accurate.

Panic patterns often include a demand for certainty. "Am I okay?" "Will this stop?" "What if I cannot cope?" "What if people notice?" "What if it gets worse?" "What if this means something terrible?" The questions multiply because panic does not want ordinary reassurance; it wants impossible certainty. Even when reassurance arrives, it may only settle the body briefly before the next question appears. This is why recognition must focus less on answering every fear and more on seeing the loop itself.

The loop is usually simple: sensation, scary meaning, more fear, more sensation.

A tight chest becomes "I cannot breathe properly." A racing heart becomes "Something is wrong." A strange feeling becomes "I am losing control." A moment of dizziness becomes "I need to escape." The meaning increases fear, and fear increases the body's alarm. Once this pattern is recognised, the task changes. You are no longer trying to solve every "What if?" You are trying to reduce the fuel being added to the body's alarm.

Recognition helps because it creates a gap between sensation and interpretation. Without recognition, the body sensation and the panic story appear fused. Chest tightness means danger. Dizziness means collapse. Unreality means loss of control. With recognition, the sentence changes: "My chest feels tight, and panic is adding a danger story." "My body feels unreal, and panic is making that feel threatening." "My heart is racing, and my mind is searching for a catastrophic explanation." These sentences are not soft. They are precise.

Precision matters because panic thrives on vague terror. "Something is wrong" is more frightening than "My hands are trembling and my breath feels tight." "I cannot cope" is more overwhelming than "I am having a panic spike and my body is activated." "I am losing it" is more frightening than "The room feels strange and I need grounding." Plain description lowers the drama of the interpretation. It does not remove discomfort, but it reduces the fear layered on top of discomfort.

This is the purpose of distinguishing panic from ordinary stress. Not to create a label for its own sake, but to choose the right response. Stress may require planning, prioritising, asking for help, resting, or setting limits. Panic requires interrupting the fear of bodily sensations. Stress often says, "There is too much to handle." Panic often says, "My body feels dangerous." Those are different problems. Treating panic as if it were merely a planning issue may miss the point. Treating ordinary stress as if every tension is panic can also make life smaller than it needs to be.

Panic also needs to be distinguished from genuine medical concern with humility. No self-help tool should encourage someone to dismiss symptoms that are new, severe, unusual, or worrying. If there is uncertainty about physical health, especially with symptoms that feel significantly different from previous experiences, seeking appropriate medical advice is sensible. The skill is not to become reckless. The skill is to avoid treating familiar panic sensations as fresh emergencies every time they appear.

For people who experience repeated panic spikes, familiarity can become an asset. You begin to know your personal pattern. Perhaps it starts with a tight chest, then a thought about breathing, then checking, then an urge to leave. Perhaps it starts with dizziness, then fear of fainting, then scanning for exits. Perhaps it starts with unreality, then fear of losing control, then repeated reassurance-seeking. Your pattern is not a life sentence. It is a map.

The map might sound like this: "When panic rises, my heart races, my breath feels unsatisfying, I think I am not safe, and I want to escape immediately." Or: "When panic starts, the room feels unreal, I check whether I feel normal, and the checking makes it worse." Or: "When I feel light-headed, my mind predicts fainting, and I begin searching for reassurance." These sentences are useful because they join body cue, story, and default move. Once joined, they can be interrupted.

The interruption begins with a shift in question. Panic asks, "What if?" It asks this with frightening creativity. What if this gets worse? What if I faint? What if I cannot leave? What if I embarrass myself? What if this means something serious? What if I never feel normal again? Trying to answer every "What if?" is exhausting because panic can always generate another one. A better question is: "What is happening right now in my body?"

Right now, my heart is racing.

Right now, my hands are shaky.

Right now, my breath feels tight.

Right now, my mind is predicting danger.

Right now, my feet are on the floor.

This shift is not a cure, and it should not be sold as one. It is a reduction of interpretation. "What if?" projects into a feared future. "What is happening right now?" returns attention to the present body. Panic may still be present, but it has less room to build a catastrophic world around the sensation.

Recognition also reduces secondary fear. Secondary fear is the fear of panic itself: "Oh no, it is happening again." "I cannot have this here." "I must stop this immediately." "This is unbearable." This second layer can make the spike feel larger than the original sensations. A person is no longer only experiencing panic; they are panicking about panic. Clear recognition changes the tone: "This is the pattern. I know this route. I do not need to add terror to it."

That does not mean you will feel brave. Often you will not. The body may still be loud, and the mind may still be tempted by catastrophic interpretations. Recognition is not the absence of fear. It is the presence of enough clarity to stop feeding fear automatically.

A useful recognition phrase is: "This is a panic spike, not a command."

The word "spike" matters because it suggests movement. A spike rises. A spike can feel intense. A spike is not the whole day, the whole body, or the whole self. The phrase "not a command" matters because panic often issues instructions: leave now, check now, ask now, search now, escape now, breathe harder now. Some actions may be appropriate, but panic should not be allowed to dictate them unexamined. The feeling can be real without being in charge.

Another useful phrase is: "My body is alarmed, and my mind is adding a story."

This phrase separates the two parts of the event. The body alarm is one thing. The story is another. You do not have to decide everything in the first second. You do not have to solve the sensation. You do not have to find perfect certainty. You only need to prevent the story from pouring fuel onto the alarm.

Recognition should remain brief. Panic loves excessive analysis. If you spend too long examining why panic is happening, whether it is definitely panic, what caused it, what every sensation means, and how long it might last, the analysis can become another form of checking. The aim is not to study the spike while it is happening. The aim is to name it well enough to choose the next stabilising move.

That move may be grounding, soft breathing, sitting down, loosening your grip, naming objects, feeling your feet, using a cold drink, speaking one plain sentence, or stepping to a quieter place with intention rather than panic. The specific tool comes next. Recognition simply tells you which road you are on.

The value of recognising panic patterns is that it stops the moment from feeling entirely new each time. Panic often pretends to be unprecedented. It says, "This time is different," even when the sequence is familiar. Sometimes, of course, new or severe symptoms should be taken seriously. But when the pattern is known, recognition can prevent panic from resetting your memory. You can say, "This is the familiar loop: sensation, scary meaning, fear, more sensation. I do not have to complete the loop."

That sentence is a quiet act of authority.

Panic may still rise. The body may still tremble. The breath may still feel odd. The room may still seem distant. But when the pattern is recognised, the experience becomes less mysterious. Less mysterious does not mean easy. It means workable. You are no longer only the person being hit by the wave. You are also the person who can name the shape of the wave.

The next time panic begins, the first task is not to win an argument with every sensation. It is to recognise the pattern before the frightening story becomes the master. Notice the cue. Name the spike. Separate the sensation from the meaning. Return to what is happening now.

Panic may be loud.

Recognition is the first quieter voice that does not have to obey it.

Stopping the fear spiral

Panic is not only the sensations. It is the meaning attached to the sensations.

This is why a panic spike can grow so quickly. A sensation appears in the body: the heart races, the chest tightens, the breath feels strange, the hands tremble, the head feels light, the room seems unreal. The sensation may be uncomfortable, even frightening, but the real acceleration often begins a moment later, when the mind adds its interpretation. "What if something is wrong?" "What if I faint?" "What if I cannot get out?" "What if people notice?" "What if this never stops?"

That interpretation is not a neutral thought. It is fuel.

Once the mind gives the sensation a frightening meaning, the body receives the message that danger is present. More alarm follows. The heart may beat faster. The breath may feel tighter. The room may seem even stranger. The mind then points to these increased sensations as further evidence that the original fear was correct. Panic begins to feed itself. Sensation creates scary meaning; scary meaning creates more fear; fear creates more sensation; sensation appears to confirm the scary meaning. Around it goes.

This is the fear spiral.

It is important to understand the spiral without becoming lost in analysis. During panic, you do not need a grand theory of why this is happening. You do not need to review every stressor, every memory, every previous episode, every possible cause. That kind of investigation may have value later, in the right setting, with enough steadiness. At the peak of panic, too much analysis can become another form of checking. The first task is simpler: stop adding frightening meaning to an already activated body.

The aim is not to remove sensations on command.

That expectation is one of panic's traps. A person feels the heart racing and thinks, "I must make it slow down." The heart does not slow immediately, so the fear rises. A person feels breath discomfort and thinks, "I must get a perfect breath." The breath still feels imperfect, so the fear rises. A person feels unreal and thinks, "I must feel normal right now." The strangeness remains, so the fear rises. The demand for instant relief becomes another source of alarm.

A better target is reducing interpretation.

Instead of asking, "How do I make this stop?" ask, "What meaning am I adding?" This question changes the work. You are no longer trying to control every sensation in the body. You are trying to interrupt the story that turns those sensations into catastrophe. The body may still be loud, but the mind does not have to shout with it.

Panic often begins its spiral with "What if?" This phrase deserves close attention because it sounds like problem-solving while often functioning as threat rehearsal. "What if I collapse?" "What if I cannot breathe?" "What if I lose control?" "What if I embarrass myself?" "What if I need help and cannot get it?" Each question may appear to be seeking safety, but under panic it often creates more danger imagery. The mind tries to prepare for every feared outcome and accidentally convinces the body that all of those outcomes are near.

The antidote is not a forced positive thought. Telling yourself, "Everything is fine," may not feel believable when the body is activated. Panic can reject reassurance quickly, especially if the sensations remain. The more useful move is to replace "What if?" with "What is happening right now in my body?" This is not a soft question. It is precise. It pulls attention away from imagined disaster and back towards present description.

"What is happening right now?" has plain answers.

"My heart is beating fast."

"My chest feels tight."

"My hands are shaking."

"My breath feels unsatisfying."

"My mind is predicting danger."

"My feet are on the floor."

"I am having a surge of fear."

These descriptions do not make the body instantly comfortable. They do something more strategic: they reduce the amount of story attached to the discomfort. "My heart is beating fast" is not the same as "Something terrible is happening." "My breath feels tight" is not the same as "I cannot cope." "The room feels unreal" is not the same as "I am losing control." Description gives the mind a smaller, more accurate job.

The fear spiral weakens when sensation and meaning are separated.

This separation can be done in one sentence: "This is a sensation, and panic is adding a story." Use that sentence gently. Do not use it as a weapon against yourself. The point is not to scold the mind for producing fear. The mind is trying, clumsily, to protect you. The point is to stop treating its most frightening interpretation as a verified fact. Panic predictions are not commands. They are thoughts generated inside alarm.

Another useful sentence is: "My body is alarmed; I do not need to escalate the alarm."

This sentence respects the body without obeying the spiral. It does not say the sensations are fake. It does not say you should be calm. It says that the alarm is already present, and your next job is not to add more alarm through checking, catastrophic thinking, or frantic attempts to make the body behave normally.

Checking is one of the most common ways the spiral continues. You check whether your heart is still racing. You check whether your breath feels normal. You check whether your hands are steady. You check whether the unreality has gone. You check whether you feel safe yet. Each check seems sensible because it promises certainty. But checking keeps attention locked onto threat. It asks the body, again and again, "Are we in danger?" The body often responds by staying activated.

Reassurance can work the same way when it becomes repetitive. Asking once for support may be wise and human. Asking again and again whether you are okay, whether this will stop, whether you look strange, whether something is wrong, or whether you should be afraid can train the mind to rely on external certainty that never lasts. The relief fades, the question returns, and the spiral continues.

Stopping the fear spiral does not mean refusing all support. It means noticing when support has turned into fuel. There is a difference between saying, "I am having a panic spike; please sit with me for a moment," and repeatedly asking, "Am I definitely okay? Are you sure? What if this time is different?" The first request brings steadiness. The second keeps the fear question alive.

Escape can also feed the spiral if it is driven by panic rather than choice. Leaving a place is sometimes appropriate. A quieter environment, fresh air, sitting down, or stepping away from a crowd may help. But if every panic sensation is followed by urgent escape, the body may learn that the place was dangerous and escape was the only reason you survived it. The next time, the alarm may rise sooner. The point is not to force yourself to stay anywhere unbearable. The point is to make movement deliberate rather than panicked.

A useful distinction is: "Am I choosing to move, or am I obeying the alarm?"

Choosing has steadiness in it, even if fear remains. Obeying has a frantic, compulsory quality. Choosing might sound like, "I am going to step outside slowly and ground myself." Obeying sounds like, "I have to get out now or something terrible will happen." The outward action may look similar. The internal training is different.

Breath can help interrupt the spiral, but only when it is not turned into a test. During panic, many people try to breathe in a way that proves they are safe. They take a big inhale and immediately check whether relief has arrived. If it has not, they become more frightened. This turns breathing into a pass-or-fail examination. A steadier approach is to let the breath be small, soft, and ordinary. The aim is not to produce a perfect breath. The aim is to stop fighting the breath.

Try this kind of inner instruction: "Small inhale. Soft exhale. No test."

The words "no test" matter. You are not checking whether panic has vanished. You are giving the body a rhythm without demanding proof. A few ordinary breaths, paired with grounded attention, can reduce the spiral more effectively than one dramatic breath followed by anxious inspection.

Grounding helps because panic pulls attention inward. The more you stare at sensations, the larger they may feel. Bringing attention to the physical environment interrupts that inward collapse. Feet on the floor. Hands on a surface. Eyes open to the room. One neutral object named plainly. One sound noticed. One texture felt. This is not distraction in the shallow sense. It is rebalancing attention so the body is not the entire world.

The phrase "I am here" can be useful if it is paired with contact. Alone, it may feel too abstract. With contact, it becomes physical: "I am here, feet on the floor." "I am here, hand on the table." "I am here, looking at the blue cup." Panic says, "Something is happening to me." Grounding answers, "Something is happening in me, and I am also here in this room."

The word "also" is powerful.

It allows both realities to exist. I feel dizzy, and I am sitting down. My heart is racing, and my hands are touching the chair. The room feels strange, and I can name the door, the table, the cup. My breath feels tight, and air is still moving. Panic tries to make one sensation total. "Also" widens the field.

Stopping the fear spiral also requires changing how you speak to yourself. Panic is already threatening. Harsh inner language adds threat. "Stop this." "You are being ridiculous." "You cannot cope." "Not again." "What is wrong with you?" These sentences may feel like attempts to regain control, but they often create shame and urgency. The body hears danger from outside and inside. It has no reason to settle.

A better tone is firm and plain. Not sugary. Not falsely cheerful. Firm.

"This is panic rising."

"My body is activated."

"I do not need to answer every what-if."

"I can describe what is happening now."

"I can stop checking for a moment."

"I can take the next small action."

These sentences are useful because they give direction without drama. Panic does not need a motivational speech. It needs fewer frightening meanings and a clearer next step.

The next small action should be simple enough to do while afraid. Sit down if standing feels unsteady. Put both feet on the floor. Hold a cool drink. Loosen your grip on the phone. Look at a neutral object. Let the exhale soften. Say one sentence aloud if that helps: "This is a panic spike." The action should not be chosen to make panic disappear instantly. It should be chosen to stop feeding the spiral.

This is an important standard. A tool can be working even while panic is still present. If you stop checking for ten seconds, that is progress. If you describe sensations rather than catastrophising them, that is progress. If you move more slowly instead of bolting, that is progress. If you let one breath happen without testing it, that is progress. If you ask for support without demanding repeated certainty, that is progress. Panic may still be uncomfortable, but it has less control over the sequence.

Many people abandon tools because they expect comfort too soon. They use grounding and still feel unreal. They soften the breath and still feel tightness. They name the spiral and still feel fear. Then they decide nothing works. But the first measure is not whether the sensation has gone. The first measure is whether you have stopped making it worse. In a panic spike, not making it worse is a serious achievement.

There is also a timing issue. The earlier the spiral is interrupted, the less it has to unwind. The first "What if?" is a cue. The first urge to check is a cue. The first thought that you must escape immediately is a cue. The first frightening interpretation is a cue. These are not signs that you have failed. They are opportunities to change the sequence before it gathers more force.

A simple sequence can be used in under a minute.

Name the pattern: "This is panic."

Describe the present: "My chest is tight and my heart is fast."

Reduce interpretation: "That does not mean I need to predict catastrophe."

Ground attention: "Feet on the floor, hand on the chair."

Choose one small action: "Soft exhale, no checking for the next few breaths."

This sequence is not meant to be performed perfectly. Panic does not require elegant technique. It requires a firm refusal to keep feeding the alarm. Even a messy version can help if it interrupts the loop.

The fear spiral weakens when you stop treating panic as a puzzle that must be solved immediately. Panic wants you to investigate, check, predict, escape, and seek certainty. Steadiness asks you to describe, ground, soften, and wait for the peak to pass without adding fresh fear. That is a different posture. It is less dramatic and more effective.

There will still be times when you need help, and there is no shame in that. If symptoms are new, severe, unusual, or medically worrying, seek appropriate medical advice. If panic is frequent, disruptive, or linked to trauma, professional support can be valuable. The 60-second tools are not a substitute for proper care. They are immediate skills for the moments when familiar panic begins to build a frightening story around bodily alarm.

The central move remains the same: stop adding terror to sensation.

A racing heart is uncomfortable. A racing heart plus "I am in danger" is more frightening. A tight breath is uncomfortable. A tight breath plus "I cannot cope" is more frightening. Unreality is uncomfortable. Unreality plus "I am losing control" is more frightening. The sensation may not be yours to remove instantly. The added meaning is where you can begin.

The next time panic asks, "What if?" do not enter the whole courtroom of fear. Return to the body, plainly and specifically. What is happening right now? What sensation is present? What story is being added? What contact point is available? What is the smallest action that does not feed the alarm?

Panic may still speak loudly.

You do not have to become its echo.

Grounding during derealisation

Derealisation can make the ordinary world feel strangely out of reach.

A cafe may still be there: the cup on the table, the chair under the body, the voices nearby, the door in sight, the light on the wall. Yet everything can feel altered. Distant. Flat. Dreamlike. Too bright or oddly muted. As though the world has become a scene being watched rather than a place being lived in. The mind, unsettled by this shift, may rush to frightening conclusions: "Something is wrong with me." "I am losing control." "I need to get out." "I will not feel normal again."

The strangeness is real as an experience. The frightening story attached to it is not automatically true.

That distinction matters because derealisation often becomes more frightening when it is examined too intensely. A person notices the world feels unreal, then checks whether it still feels unreal, then checks again, then begins comparing the present moment with how reality "should" feel. The checking keeps attention fixed on the altered sensation. The more attention narrows around it, the larger and more important it seems. Panic then adds its own pressure: fix this now, understand this now, make it stop now.

Grounding during derealisation must therefore be stronger, more physical, and more external than ordinary calming advice. Gentle reassurance may not be enough when the world itself feels distant. You need contact. Texture. Temperature. Weight. Movement. Voice. The aim is not to argue yourself back into feeling normal. The aim is to give the body repeated evidence of here.

Here is not a concept. It is physical.

Your feet pressing into the floor are here. Your hand around a cold glass is here. The rough seam of your sleeve is here. The sound of your own voice naming the table, the cup, the chair, and the door is here. The chair supporting your weight is here. The slow turn of your head from one side of the room to the other is here. Derealisation pulls experience into distance; grounding brings attention back through the senses.

The first mistake is trying to think your way out of derealisation. Thought may be too slippery in that moment. The mind can easily become a hall of mirrors: "Why does everything feel strange?" "Am I really here?" "What if this gets worse?" "How do I know I am okay?" These questions feel urgent, but they often deepen the unreality by keeping attention trapped inside interpretation. When the world feels unreal, you do not need more theory. You need more contact.

Start with the feet.

Press both feet into the ground with deliberate steadiness. Not violently. Not as a dramatic exercise. Just enough pressure to feel that the floor is meeting you. Notice the heels. Notice the toes. Notice the weight travelling down through the legs. If you are sitting, let the chair take more of your weight and feel the points of contact: thighs, back, feet. If you are standing, shift weight slowly from one foot to the other. The purpose is to remind the body that it has a location.

Location is stabilising. Derealisation can make you feel as though you are floating slightly outside the moment. Feet restore orientation. They say, without words, "The body is here. The ground is here. This is the place where the next breath is happening."

Hands come next because hands are excellent anchors. They can feel the world in detail. Place a hand on something with texture: a wooden table, fabric, a key, a bag strap, a mug, a wall, the edge of a chair. Do not merely touch it. Notice it. Smooth or rough. Warm or cool. Hard or soft. Still or moving. Let the fingers explore slowly enough to give the brain simple information from the outside world.

Texture is useful because it does not require belief. You do not have to convince yourself that the table is real in a grand philosophical sense. You only need to feel that it is hard, flat, and cooler than your hand. That is enough. In derealisation, the mind may want certainty about reality as a whole. Grounding gives it something smaller and sturdier: this surface, this pressure, this temperature, this contact.

Temperature can be especially effective. Hold a cold drink. Touch a cool glass. Run cool water over your hands if appropriate. Hold a warm mug and notice the heat through your fingers. Step into cooler air and feel it on the face. Temperature has a clean, immediate quality. It cuts through mental fog because it is difficult to turn into an abstract argument. Cold is cold. Warm is warm. The body receives the signal quickly.

A cold drink in a cafe can become a practical anchor. Hold the glass with both hands if that feels steadying. Notice the condensation, the weight, the firmness, the chill against the skin. Take a small sip and feel the temperature in the mouth and throat. Name it plainly: "Cold glass. Wet surface. My hand is holding it. My feet are on the floor." This is not childish language. It is emergency simplicity. A flooded mind needs plain facts.

Use your voice if the unreality feels strong.

Speaking brings the body into the room. It uses breath, throat, mouth, hearing, and attention all at once. You do not need to speak loudly. If you are in public, speak quietly or move your lips subtly if that feels safer. Name what is directly present: "I am sitting at a table. There is a cup in my hand. My feet are on the floor. I can see the door. I can hear voices. I am having a panic surge." Keep the language descriptive, not dramatic.

Voice works because derealisation often makes experience feel private and sealed off. Speaking, even softly, creates an outward bridge. It reminds the system that you are not only observing the world from a distance; you are participating in it. The sound of your own words becomes one more contact point.

Deliberate movement can help too. Not frantic movement. Not escape driven by panic. Slow, purposeful movement. Press the toes into the floor. Roll the shoulders once. Turn the head and name what you see on the left, then on the right. Open and close the hands. Stand up carefully if sitting makes the unreality worse. Walk slowly to a safer or quieter spot if needed, noticing each step. Movement should communicate steadiness, not alarm.

The difference between deliberate movement and panic movement is important. Panic movement says, "Get me out of this now." Deliberate movement says, "I am moving my body on purpose." One trains the alarm. The other trains agency. Even if you choose to leave a place, leave as deliberately as possible: feet on the floor, eyes open, one step, then the next. The aim is not to prove bravery by staying. The aim is to avoid teaching the body that derealisation is an emergency requiring frantic escape.

Eyes need careful handling during derealisation. Some people stare hard at objects, trying to make the world feel normal again. This can backfire because the staring becomes another test. "Does it look real now? What about now? Why does it still look strange?" Instead, use the eyes to gather simple external information. Look around slowly and name neutral objects: table, cup, chair, window, bag, light, door. Let the eyes move rather than fix.

Naming objects reduces the pull of interpretation. "The room feels unreal" may still be present, but now it is joined by direct description. "There is a wooden table. There is a blue cup. There is a square window. There is a black chair." The words are ordinary on purpose. Derealisation often feels eerie because the mind is flooded with meaning and fear. Neutral naming lowers the emotional temperature of perception.

A useful cafe example might look like this. You are sitting with a drink when the room suddenly feels distant. Your heart begins to race. Your hands feel strange. The thought appears: "I am not really here." Instead of chasing that thought, you put both feet on the floor. You wrap one hand around the cold drink. You feel the glass, the wetness, the temperature. You name three objects: "Table. Cup. Window." You take a small sip and feel the cold. You say quietly, "This is derealisation. It feels strange, and I am here." Then you turn your head slowly and notice the exit without rushing towards it.

The key is to stop asking the world to feel normal immediately.

That demand creates pressure. Derealisation often fades more easily when it is not constantly tested. The aim is to function gently while the feeling passes through. You can feel unreal and still keep your feet on the floor. You can feel distant and still hold a cup. You can feel strange and still describe the room. You can feel frightened and still choose not to feed the fear with catastrophic meanings.

Grounding does not always make derealisation vanish at once. This is crucial. If you expect instant normality, you may judge the tool as a failure and panic more. A grounding method succeeds when it reduces the struggle, widens attention, and helps you remain connected to the present. The unreality may linger for a while. The body may need time to settle. That does not mean you are doing anything wrong.

A good standard is: less checking, more contact.

Checking asks, "Do I feel real yet?" Contact says, "My hand is on the glass." Checking asks, "Is this going away?" Contact says, "My feet are pressing into the floor." Checking asks, "What if this means something terrible?" Contact says, "I can hear a chair moving." Checking pulls attention back into fear. Contact moves attention outward into reality as it is physically available.

This outward movement should be repeated, but not obsessively. Choose one or two anchors and stay with them briefly. Feet and cold drink. Hands and table. Voice and object naming. Movement and sound. Too many techniques can become frantic. The body does not need a complicated rescue operation. It needs firm, simple evidence of presence.

If derealisation happens around other people, you may not want to explain everything. That is understandable. A short phrase can be enough: "I feel a bit off; I am going to ground for a moment." Or simply, "Give me a second." You do not owe everyone a full description. But if you are with someone safe, a clear sentence can reduce fear: "Things feel unreal for a moment. I know this is a panic cue. Please just sit with me while I ground." The goal is support, not repeated reassurance.

Avoid making derealisation the main event after it passes. The mind may want to review it, analyse it, search for explanations, or check whether it could happen again. Some reflection may be useful later, but immediate rumination can sensitise the body. After grounding, return to an ordinary action as soon as you reasonably can. Drink water. Continue a simple task. Walk slowly. Wash your hands. Send the necessary message. Finish the conversation later if needed. The nervous system learns safety not only from calming down, but from rejoining life.

There is also an important safety note. Derealisation can occur with panic and stress, but if experiences are new, severe, persistent, linked with medical symptoms, substance use, or a sense that you cannot stay safe, appropriate professional or medical support matters. Grounding is a practical tool, not a substitute for care when care is needed. Taking the experience seriously does not mean believing every frightening story panic tells about it.

The skill is to meet derealisation with firmness rather than fear.

Firmness says, "This is strange, and I know what to do next." Fear says, "This is strange, so it must be dangerous." Firmness uses contact. Fear uses checking. Firmness names objects. Fear searches for catastrophic meaning. Firmness moves slowly. Fear bolts. Firmness returns to the present in pieces. Fear demands that the whole world feel normal before anything can continue.

Return in pieces.

Feet first. Hands next. Eyes open. Voice if needed. Temperature if available. One slow movement. One neutral object. One ordinary action. You do not need to recover the entire world in a single breath. You only need enough contact to stop the unreality from becoming the ruler of the moment.

Derealisation may feel like distance, but distance is not disappearance. The room is still there. The body is still there. The cup, floor, wall, chair, sound, and air are still offering points of return. Panic may make them feel remote for a while, but grounding gives you a way back through the senses.

The next time the world feels unreal, do not start a debate with the feeling. Touch something. Name something. Press your feet down. Use your voice. Let temperature, texture, weight, and movement do what thought cannot do quickly.

Come back through contact.

Aftercare after panic

The panic spike may pass before your body believes it is over.

This is one of the most confusing parts of panic. The peak begins to drop, the room becomes more ordinary again, the breath feels less urgent, the heart is no longer the whole story, and yet you do not feel fully restored. You may feel shaky, tired, embarrassed, watchful, or oddly fragile. The mind may begin circling back: "Why did that happen?" "What if it happens again?" "Did anyone notice?" "Was that really panic?" "Should I check something?" The alarm has lowered, but the system is still listening for danger.

Aftercare is the way you handle this vulnerable period without accidentally creating a second wave.

The first wave is the panic itself: sensations, fear, urgency, interpretation, grounding, waiting, riding it through. The second wave often comes afterwards, when the person starts reviewing the event as though it must be solved immediately.

Checking the body, replaying each sensation, searching for certainty, asking repeatedly for reassurance, avoiding the place where it happened, or attacking yourself for having panicked can all keep the nervous system sensitised. The spike may be over, but the mind keeps tapping the alarm.

A calm recovery does not begin with analysis. It begins with signalling safety.

This matters because the body after panic is often not ready for a full investigation. It may still be carrying leftover activation. Muscles may remain tense. The stomach may feel unsettled. The breath may still be slightly guarded. The mind may feel both exhausted and restless. If you use that state to interrogate yourself, you are asking a recovering system to become a detective at the scene of its own alarm. The result is rarely clarity. More often, it is rumination dressed as responsibility.

The first aftercare principle is simple: do not punish the body for having had a panic response.

Many people turn harsh immediately afterwards. "That was pathetic." "I cannot believe this happened again." "I should be over this." "I ruined the day." "What is wrong with me?" This may sound like self-discipline, but it is usually another threat signal. Panic has already made the body feel unsafe; self-attack teaches it that even recovery is unsafe. A frightened body does not settle faster because it is insulted. It settles through steadiness, repetition, and ordinary evidence that life can continue.

A more useful response is plain and kind without becoming sentimental: "That was a panic spike. It was uncomfortable. It is passing. I am returning to the day."

That sentence gives the event a boundary. It does not make panic your identity. It does not make the episode mysterious or catastrophic. It names what happened, acknowledges discomfort, recognises movement, and points attention forward. Panic often feels endless while it is happening. Aftercare teaches the body that it can have a beginning, a peak, and an ending.

The second principle is to avoid immediate body-checking. This is difficult because checking feels sensible. After panic, you may want to test whether your heart is normal, whether your breathing feels right, whether the unreality has fully gone, whether your hands are steady, whether you feel "back to yourself" yet. One check can become five. Five can become a private surveillance routine. The body becomes an object of suspicion.

Checking promises certainty, but it often trains alarm.

Each check asks, "Are we safe now?" If the body is still slightly activated, the answer may feel uncertain, which prompts more checking. The attention narrows again. Sensations become louder again. The mind begins attaching meanings again. In this way, the recovery period can become the doorway back into panic. The aim is not to ignore the body completely. The aim is to stop monitoring it as though every remaining sensation is a problem to solve.

A useful aftercare phrase is: "No checking, just settling."

Settling is different from proving. Proving demands evidence that panic has vanished. Settling allows the body to come down at its own pace. You may still feel a little shaky. You may still feel tired. You may still feel cautious. These are not signs that the episode has failed to end. They are signs that the body has been through activation and is returning gradually. Let gradually be acceptable.

The third principle is to reduce reassurance loops. Human support can be valuable after panic. It may help to tell someone safe, "I had a panic spike. I am okay, but I need a steady moment." That is different from asking repeatedly, "Am I okay? Are you sure? Did I look strange? Do you think it will happen again? What if it means something?" Reassurance may soothe briefly, but if repeated too often, it can teach the mind that safety must be confirmed externally again and again.

A steadier request for support is specific and time-limited. "Please sit with me for a minute while I ground." "Can we talk about something ordinary while I settle?" "I do not need reassurance; I just need company." These sentences are quietly powerful. They allow connection without handing panic the microphone.

The fourth principle is to return to ordinary action as soon as reasonably possible.

Not heroic action. Not a dramatic act of bravery. Ordinary action. Wash a cup. Step outside for air. Reply to a simple message. Finish the drink. Fold a jumper. Walk slowly to another room. Continue the errand if that feels manageable. Eat something gentle if you need it. Put your feet on the floor and look at the next small task. Panic narrows life around the alarm. Ordinary action widens life again.

This does not mean forcing yourself harshly. If you are exhausted, rest. If you need a quieter space, take it. If symptoms are new, severe, unusual, or medically concerning, seek appropriate care rather than trying to regulate your way through uncertainty. But when the episode is familiar panic and the peak has passed, returning to a small ordinary action helps teach the body that panic is not a full stop. It is an event you can move through.

A short recovery sequence can be useful because the post-panic mind may be too tired to improvise.

Begin with contact. Feel your feet, hands, chair, cup, or clothing. Let the body know where it is.

Take one or two soft exhales, not as a test, but as a signal that the emergency pace is no longer required.

Name the event plainly: "That was panic. It is passing."

Choose one ordinary next action: drink water, stand slowly, wash your hands, step outside, continue a simple task, or rejoin the conversation gently.

Then do not review the episode immediately unless there is a genuine practical need.

The final step is often the hardest. Panic wants a post-match analysis. It wants to know why it happened, whether it could have been prevented, whether it means something, whether it will return, whether you handled it well enough. Some reflection can be helpful later, especially if patterns repeat. But immediate analysis often happens while the body is still sensitised, which means the analysis is not neutral. It is fear trying to become intellectual.

Delay the review.

You might say, "I will think about this later if needed, not while my body is still coming down." This is not avoidance. It is good timing. A settled mind can learn from panic. A freshly alarmed mind tends to magnify it. Later, if useful, you can briefly note what happened: the cue, the story, the tool used, what helped, what to try next time. Keep it short. The purpose is learning, not building a case against yourself.

Aftercare also means resisting the urge to make panic the headline of the day. A spike may have been unpleasant, but it does not need to become the defining event. The mind may want to keep announcing it internally: "I had panic there. That was awful. What if it comes back?" Each announcement refreshes the alarm. A calmer approach is to acknowledge once, then redirect: "Panic happened. Now I am making tea." "Panic happened. Now I am walking home." "Panic happened. Now I am answering this one email." The word "now" matters. It brings the day forward.

Avoidance is another post-panic trap. If panic happened in a cafe, queue, meeting, car, shop, or conversation, you may feel tempted to mark that setting as unsafe. This is understandable. The mind links panic with the place where it occurred, even when the place was not the true danger. Sometimes taking a break is wise. But permanently shrinking life around panic can strengthen fear. The body learns, "I survived because I avoided." Aftercare should gently preserve contact with life where it is safe to do so.

This does not require dramatic exposure or forcing. It may simply mean not making a sweeping decision from the aftermath. Do not decide, while still shaky, "I can never go there again." Do not decide, "I cannot handle meetings." Do not decide, "I must avoid queues." A better sentence is: "I will decide later, when I am steadier." Panic is a poor architect for your future.

There is also relational aftercare. If someone witnessed the panic, you may feel embarrassed or exposed. You may want to over-explain, apologise excessively, or pretend nothing happened. Keep it simple. "I had a panic spike. It has passed. Thank you for giving me a moment." Or, "I felt overwhelmed for a bit, but I am settling now." You do not owe a full explanation to everyone. You also do not need to cover the experience with shame. Plain language protects dignity.

If panic affected another person, perhaps you snapped, withdrew, left suddenly, or asked for repeated reassurance, a small repair may be appropriate once you are steadier. Repair should not become self-erasure. "I am sorry I left abruptly. I was panicking and should have said I needed a minute." This takes responsibility without turning the episode into a character trial. The goal is to restore trust, not punish yourself in front of someone else.

Aftercare also includes the body's basic needs. Panic consumes energy. Afterwards, the body may need water, food, warmth, movement, quiet, or rest. These are not glamorous interventions, but they matter. A person who tries to process panic while hungry, exhausted, overstimulated, and dehydrated is making recovery harder than it needs to be. Meet the simple needs before demanding deep insight.

Movement can be useful if it is gentle and deliberate. A slow walk, stretching the hands, rolling the shoulders, tidying one small area, or moving from one room to another can help the body discharge leftover activation. Avoid turning movement into frantic escape or punishment. You are not trying to outrun panic. You are helping the body complete the shift from alarm back into ordinary function.

Breath after panic should remain soft. This is not the time to force a rigid breathing pattern in order to prove you are calm. Let the exhale lengthen slightly if it feels comfortable. Allow the next inhale to arrive without chasing it. Pair breath with contact: feet on the floor, hand on a cup, eyes on a neutral object. Again, the goal is not to test whether panic has fully gone. The goal is to communicate steadiness.

Sleep and rest may also be affected. If panic happened late in the day, the mind may want to replay it at bedtime. Set a boundary with the review: "Not now. I have already noted what happened." Keep the body routine simple. Dim the environment if possible, reduce stimulation, do something ordinary and repetitive, and avoid feeding the mind with alarming searches or long internal debates. The nervous system needs cues of normality, not a courtroom session in the dark.

One of the most powerful aftercare decisions is to refuse the identity story. Panic may say, "This means I am fragile." "This means I cannot trust myself." "This means I am going backwards." "This means I will always be like this." These are not conclusions. They are post-panic interpretations. A more accurate sentence is: "I had a panic spike, and I am practising recovery." That sentence keeps the episode in proportion.

Progress after panic is often measured by what you do not do.

You do not spend the next hour checking symptoms. You do not ask for reassurance ten times. You do not search for frightening explanations. You do not punish yourself. You do not make a permanent avoidance rule from a temporary state. You do not treat lingering shakiness as failure. You do not make panic the centre of the day once the peak has passed.

This kind of progress can feel quiet. It may not produce a dramatic sense of victory. But it is deeply important because it changes what the body learns after the spike. Instead of learning, "That was dangerous; we must watch for it forever," the body begins to learn, "That was uncomfortable; we returned."

Returned is the key word.

Returned to the room. Returned to the body. Returned to the conversation. Returned to the errand. Returned to the day. Returned imperfectly, perhaps. Returned shakily. Returned with tenderness and some frustration. But returned.

A panic spike does not end only when the sensations reduce. It ends more fully when you stop organising the rest of the day around it. Aftercare is how you help that ending happen. It is the quiet discipline of not feeding the second wave, not building fear around the memory, and not letting one surge become a verdict on your capacity.

The next time panic passes and leaves you shaky in its wake, do not rush to analyse the ruins. There may be no ruins. There may simply be a body coming down from alarm.

Give it contact. Give it water if needed. Give it ordinary movement. Give it kinder language. Give it fewer checks. Give it a next small action.

Then let the day become larger than the spike.

Chapter 7
What to avoid during escalation

What if the thing you reach for to calm down is quietly keeping the surge alive?

That is one of the more uncomfortable truths of emotional pressure. Not every coping move is actually calming. Some are threat responses wearing respectable clothes. A forced deep breath may look like regulation while the body experiences it as strain. A long explanation may sound responsible while it feeds defensiveness. A demand for certainty may feel like self-protection while it teaches panic to ask again. A repeated scan of symptoms may seem sensible while it trains attention to keep searching for danger.

The trap is that these moves often bring a flicker of relief. Sending the message reduces the pressure of not sending it. Explaining yourself at length reduces the fear of being misunderstood for a few seconds. Checking the body gives a brief answer. Replaying the argument creates the illusion of control. The problem is not that these behaviours are foolish. The problem is that they are persuasive. They seem useful at the exact moment your judgement is least equipped to test them.

This is the central tension of escalation: the body wants relief, but relief is not the same as recovery. Relief asks, "What will make this pressure drop right now?" Recovery asks, "What will reduce harm and restore choice?" Those two questions can lead in opposite directions. A sharp reply may relieve anger and damage trust. A frantic apology may relieve fear and erase a valid boundary. A dramatic decision may relieve uncertainty and create consequences your steadier self must later repair. A familiar "solution" can become another way of serving the surge.

The stakes are practical because escalation rewards speed. It pushes towards actions that cannot easily be unsaid, unseen, unread, or undone. A sentence spoken in heat may become the centre of the conflict. A message sent from panic may travel farther than the feeling that produced it. A decision made from humiliation may reshape a relationship, a job, or a plan that needed steadier consideration. The first task, then, is not always to find the perfect calming technique. Sometimes the fastest win is simply to avoid feeding the fire.

This matters after the moment too. Surges often leave residue: replay, analysis, imagined comebacks, self-criticism, and the private trial in which you argue both sides long after everyone else has left the room. Rumination can feel productive because the mind is busy. It produces phrases, evidence, motives, verdicts, and alternative endings. Yet busyness is not the same as resolution. A mind that keeps returning to the threat may keep the body activated, even when the original event is over.

The danger is subtle: you may believe you are trying to understand yourself, when you are actually rehearsing the surge. You may believe you are preparing for next time, when you are keeping the body in a state of unfinished defence. You may believe you are seeking clarity, when you are demanding certainty from a moment that cannot provide it. Emotional skill requires a sharper standard. A practice is only useful if it returns you to choice. If it narrows attention, increases urgency, or pushes irreversible action, it may not be a tool at all.

The path begins by identifying the common calming mistakes that add pressure while pretending to reduce it. From there, the emphasis shifts to delaying high-impact decisions and messages so the first surge does not gain permanent form. After the immediate danger has passed, attention turns to the mind's habit of replaying, rebuilding, and rearguing the moment, and to the need for a clean way to close the loop without pretending nothing happened.

There is relief in this approach because it lowers the burden. You do not have to become perfectly calm in order to make progress. You do not have to untangle every feeling, solve every relationship pattern, or produce the ideal response while your body is still hot. You only have to stop doing the thing that reliably makes the state worse. Put down the match. Leave the draft unsent. Stop checking the sensation for one more answer. Refuse the imaginary courtroom when it opens again in your head.

So the question now is not, "What should I do to feel better immediately?" That question is too easily hijacked by the surge. The more useful question is stricter: when pressure rises, which of your favourite solutions is secretly part of the problem?

Common calming mistakes

Not every attempt to calm down is actually calming.

This is a hard truth because most people do not escalate only through obvious reactions. They also escalate through respectable ones. They breathe too forcefully because they are trying to regulate. They explain too much because they are trying to be understood. They ask for certainty because they are trying to feel safe. They scan their body because they are trying to be responsible. They rehearse the conversation because they are trying to prepare. From the outside, these behaviours can look sensible. From the inside, they can feel necessary.

Yet during a surge, necessity is not always trustworthy.

A threat response will often disguise itself as a solution. It borrows the language of care, clarity, planning, honesty, or self-protection, then quietly keeps the system activated. The body wants relief, and the mind finds an action that promises it. The problem is that relief and regulation are not the same.

Relief may reduce pressure for a moment while teaching the nervous system to repeat the pattern next time. Regulation reduces the authority of the surge over your next move.

The difference can be subtle. A calming move usually makes the body a little steadier, the attention a little wider, and the next action a little safer. A threat response usually makes the body more urgent, the attention more narrowed, and the next action more compulsive. The question is not, "Does this make me feel better for five seconds?" The better question is, "Does this return me to choice, or does it make the surge more important?"

One of the most common mistakes is forcing deep breaths.

Breathing can help, but force is rarely the friend of a frightened or angry body. When people hear "take a deep breath," they often pull air in aggressively, lift the chest, tighten the shoulders, and try to inhale their way into control. If the body is already braced, this can increase discomfort. If panic is present, it can make breathing feel like a test. If anger is hot, it can feel like an imposed act of politeness rather than a real reset.

The mistake is believing that bigger means calmer.

During escalation, the body often needs less drama, not more. A useful breath does not have to be huge. It does not have to impress anyone. It does not have to prove that you are in control. For many surges, especially panic, a smaller inhale and a softer, longer exhale are more helpful than a grand breath dragged into a tight chest. The breath should lower pressure, not become another task that the body has to perform under scrutiny.

Another mistake is checking whether the breath is working while you are doing it. You breathe once, then ask, "Am I calm now?" You breathe again, then inspect the chest, the throat, the heart, the head, the level of fear. This turns breath into surveillance. Instead of receiving a signal of steadiness, the body receives repeated questions about danger. The tool has been converted into a test, and tests create pressure.

A second common mistake is over-explaining.

Over-explaining often feels like responsibility. You want the other person to understand your intention, your context, your stress, your history, your reasons, your innocence, your effort, your meaning, and the exact sequence that led to this moment. You may believe that if you can only explain it fully enough, the pressure will drop. Misunderstanding feels unsafe, so words become your attempt to secure safety.

The trouble is that over-explaining during escalation often carries more anxiety than clarity. It is not only communication; it is a bid for relief. The body keeps adding details because it has not yet felt safe. Each extra sentence promises to close the gap, but often widens it. The listener may become overwhelmed, defensive, impatient, or less able to hear the central point. You then feel more misunderstood and explain harder. The loop tightens.

A clear explanation has a destination. Over-explaining has a hunger.

You can feel the difference in the body. A clear explanation steadies as it speaks. Over-explaining speeds up. It adds clauses, examples, qualifications, justifications, and emotional footnotes. It tries to make the other person's possible judgement impossible. But no explanation can fully control another person's interpretation, especially in a heated moment. At some point, more words stop increasing understanding and start increasing pressure.

A useful test is whether the explanation is serving the conversation or serving your fear. If you have already stated the essential truth and are still adding material because silence feels unbearable, the surge may be using language to avoid discomfort. In that moment, the calmer move may be fewer words. One sentence. A pause. A return later. A willingness to be temporarily not fully understood rather than compulsively understood badly.

A third mistake is demanding certainty.

Certainty is seductive during stress and panic because uncertainty feels like danger. You want to know whether everything is fine, whether the relationship is safe, whether the message means what you fear, whether the sensation is harmless, whether the decision is correct, whether the other person is angry, whether you have made a mistake, whether this will happen again. The mind insists that if it can secure the answer, the body will settle.

Sometimes information is genuinely useful. But under escalation, the demand for certainty can become endless. One answer leads to another question. One reassurance fades and needs replacing. One checked symptom becomes the start of a new scan. The body is not really asking for information; it is asking for the impossible condition of never having to tolerate doubt.

Panic is especially skilled at this. It asks, "Am I okay?" and for a moment reassurance helps. Then it asks, "But am I definitely okay?" Then, "What if this time is different?" Then, "What if I missed something?" Each question appears reasonable in isolation. Together, they form a loop. The nervous system learns that uncertainty must be resolved immediately, and because life cannot provide perfect certainty, the alarm stays alive.

The calmer move is not to answer every fear. It is to recognise the demand for certainty as part of the surge. "I want certainty right now" is a state cue, not a command. It tells you that your body is uncomfortable with not knowing. That discomfort may be real, but it does not mean the next action should be reassurance-seeking, checking, confessing, accusing, or demanding an immediate response from someone else.

A fourth mistake is scanning symptoms obsessively.

This often begins with sensible concern. You notice a tight chest, a racing heart, dizziness, trembling, breath discomfort, or unreality. You check the sensation. Has it changed? Is it worse? Is it still there? What does it mean? Does it feel normal? What about now? The more you check, the more important the sensation becomes. Attention acts like a magnifying glass. The body becomes louder because you are listening for danger.

There is a difference between noticing and scanning.

Noticing is brief and practical: "My chest feels tight. I will ground and soften the exhale." Scanning is repetitive and fear-driven: "Is my chest still tight? Why is it tight? Is this normal? What if it gets worse? Has it changed since a second ago?" Noticing gives you information. Scanning keeps you trapped inside the question.

This mistake is common because scanning feels responsible. Nobody wants to ignore the body. And to be clear, new, severe, unusual, or medically concerning symptoms deserve appropriate care. Emotional regulation should never be used to dismiss real health concerns. But familiar panic sensations often become worse when treated as fresh evidence of danger every few seconds. The skill is to respond to the cue without turning the body into a courtroom.

Another common mistake is trying to solve the whole problem while still escalated.

The mind says, "We need to deal with this now." It wants to settle the relationship, define the future, make the decision, write the reply, prove the point, extract the apology, explain the pattern, understand the cause, and secure the outcome. It wants the entire knot untied while the body is still pulling it tighter. This is poor timing. A surge reduces the very capacities that complex problem-solving requires: flexibility, proportion, patience, perspective, and careful speech.

Some problems need serious attention. But serious attention is not the same as immediate attention. In fact, many serious matters deserve the respect of being handled after the first wave has passed. A hard conversation may still need to happen. A boundary may still need to be set. A reply may still need to be sent. A decision may still need to be made. The mistake is letting the most activated version of you chair the meeting.

A related mistake is using emotional honesty as permission for emotional dumping.

There is nothing wrong with naming what you feel. Honest language can reduce confusion and support connection. But under escalation, "I am just being honest" can become a licence to unload. The person may say everything with full force, full detail, and no concern for timing, impact, or proportion. The truth becomes mixed with punishment. The result is not intimacy. It is pressure transferred from one nervous system to another.

Real honesty is not merely unfiltered expression. It is accurate expression.

Accuracy asks: what is the cleanest truth here? What belongs to this moment? What am I adding from heat, fear, shame, or old history? What can be said now, and what needs waiting? Emotional dumping often says too much because the body wants relief. Accurate honesty says what is needed in a way that the steadier self can stand behind later.

Another mistake is mistaking rumination for reflection.

After a tense moment, the mind may replay the exchange again and again. It imagines better replies, sharper arguments, alternative endings, hidden motives, future confrontations, and what should have been said. This can feel productive because the mind is active. It appears to be learning. But many rumination loops do not produce learning; they keep the body rehearsing threat.

Reflection has a yield. It leads to a clearer next step, a lesson, a repair, a boundary, or a decision to let the matter rest. Rumination circles without landing. It keeps reopening the moment in search of emotional completion, but the reopening itself prevents completion. You may feel as if you are preparing for next time, when actually you are keeping your nervous system inside last time.

This is especially dangerous after conflict. The body may already be activated. Rumination adds fresh arguments and imaginary confrontations, which can reignite anger long after the other person has gone. It can also intensify shame: the mind replays your mistake, then attacks you for it, then replays the attack as proof that something is wrong with you. Either way, the loop keeps the surge alive.

A further mistake is seeking the perfect inner state before taking a wise action.

People often think they must feel calm before they can behave calmly, feel certain before they can delay a decision, feel forgiving before they can repair, feel confident before they can set a boundary, feel normal before they can continue after panic. This gives the surge too much power. It makes behaviour dependent on emotional comfort. But the 60-second calm is built on a different standard: can you choose one safer action while still uncomfortable?

Waiting to feel fully calm may mean waiting too long. You can put the phone down while still angry. You can say, "I need a minute," while still heated. You can stop checking symptoms while still afraid. You can postpone a decision while still uncertain. You can ground while still unreal. The feeling does not have to disappear before the next move improves.

Another hidden mistake is turning calming into self-criticism.

You notice the surge and immediately judge yourself for having it. You think, "I should be better at this by now." "Why am I like this?" "I am so dramatic." "I always ruin things." This may look like accountability, but it is usually escalation turned inward. The body is already in threat, and now the self has become another threat. Shame narrows attention, increases urgency, and often pushes people back into their default moves: defending, pleasing, withdrawing, over-explaining, checking, or collapsing.

A better response is more exact and less cruel: "A surge is here. What would reduce harm in the next minute?" That sentence does not excuse behaviour. It does not flatter you. It gives you a job. Self-attack gives you a verdict. A job is more useful.

The common thread in these mistakes is pressure.

Forced breathing adds pressure to the body. Over-explaining adds pressure to the conversation. Certainty-seeking adds pressure to uncertainty. Symptom scanning adds pressure to sensation. Immediate problem-solving adds pressure to judgement. Emotional dumping adds pressure to the other person. Rumination adds pressure after the moment has passed. Self-criticism adds pressure to the self. Each move promises relief, but each can keep the system in threat.

The way out is to ask a sharper question: "Is this move widening or narrowing me?"

If it widens attention, lowers urgency, softens the body slightly, protects the next action, and restores some choice, it may be useful. If it narrows attention, increases checking, speeds up speech, demands immediate certainty, or pushes irreversible action, it may be the surge in disguise. This question is simple enough to use under pressure and honest enough to cut through many false solutions.

Another useful question is: "Would I recommend this move to someone I cared about in the same state?"

Would you tell them to send the furious email immediately? Would you tell them to keep checking their breathing every few seconds? Would you tell them to explain for another ten minutes to someone who is no longer listening? Would you tell them to make a permanent decision from a temporary surge? Often, compassion for someone else reveals the standard you need for yourself.

Avoiding the wrong move is a fast win because it reduces damage immediately. You may not know the perfect response yet. You may not feel calm. You may not understand the whole pattern. But you can stop feeding the surge in one specific way. Do not force the breath. Do not send the message. Do not ask for reassurance again. Do not scan the body for another answer. Do not keep explaining past the point of clarity. Do not let the imaginary courtroom reopen without limit.

This is not passivity. It is containment.

Containment means you are holding the moment safely while judgement returns. You are not ignoring the issue. You are not pretending the feeling does not matter. You are not allowing someone else to behave badly without consequence. You are simply refusing to let a threat response choose the method. The issue can still be addressed. The boundary can still be set. The decision can still be made. The difference is timing and state.

There is dignity in not adding fuel. It may not feel dramatic, but it is often the hinge on which the whole outcome turns. The message left unsent. The breath made softer rather than larger. The explanation shortened. The reassurance loop interrupted. The symptom scan stopped. The rumination postponed. These are invisible victories, but they are not small.

A surge does not always need a heroic intervention. Sometimes it needs subtraction.

Less force.

Fewer words.

Less checking.

Less certainty-seeking.

Fewer irreversible actions.

Less rehearsal of the threat.

The next time you reach for a familiar calming move, pause long enough to examine its effect. Does it make the body steadier, or does it make the alarm more central? Does it create choice, or does it create compulsion? Does it reduce harm, or merely reduce discomfort for a moment?

Some solutions are only the surge asking for a better disguise.

Delaying decisions and messages

A surge loves a permanent action.

That is one of its most dangerous qualities. Stress, anger, panic, shame, and fear do not merely create uncomfortable feelings;

they create pressure to *do something*. Send the email. End the conversation. Quit. Confess. Accuse. Agree. Apologise. Demand an answer. Make a declaration. Delete the thread. Walk out. Say the sentence that has been building pressure behind your teeth. The body wants relief, and irreversible action can look like relief with a door handle.

The trouble is that the surge is rarely interested in tomorrow. It is interested in release. It wants the pressure out of the body, out of the phone, out of the room, out of the mind. A message sent in anger may bring a sharp, satisfying drop in tension for a few seconds. A dramatic decision may feel clean because uncertainty has ended. A confession made from panic may seem honest because it reduces the unbearable feeling of holding something inside. But relief is not the same as wisdom. Sometimes it is simply the body rewarding you for obeying urgency.

This is why delaying high-impact action is one of the fastest ways to prevent emotional fallout. Delay does not mean avoidance. It does not mean cowardice, passivity, dishonesty, or weakness. Delay means recognising that a heightened state is a poor place from which to make moves that cannot easily be reversed. It means giving your steadier self the right to review what your activated self wants to do.

The principle is simple: when the action has lasting consequences, do not let a temporary state be the only author.

This applies most obviously to messages. Digital communication is beautifully convenient and emotionally dangerous because it removes natural friction. You can feel wounded, compose a reply, press send, and create a record of your surge before your body has even begun to settle. The screen makes reaction feel tidy. The words look neat. The grammar may even be excellent. But a polished message can still be written from panic, resentment, defensiveness, or humiliation.

The send button is not a calming tool.

It can feel like one because it ends the pressure of holding back. Once the message is sent, the body may experience a moment of release: there, done, now they know, now I have acted. But the action has travelled beyond you. It can be read in a different tone, reread later, forwarded, screenshotted, replied to, ignored, misunderstood, or used as the new centre of the conflict. Your state may pass quickly. The message may remain.

A useful rule is to separate writing from sending.

Writing can be helpful. It gives the surge somewhere to place its language without immediately giving that language to another person. You can write the furious reply in a notes app, on paper, or in a draft with the recipient removed. You can let the first version be too sharp, too long, too needy, too defensive, too grand, too wounded. That first version is not communication. It is extraction. It gets the pressure out where you can look at it.

Sending is different. Sending is publication. Sending is relationship. Sending is consequence.

Once those two acts are separated, choice returns. The activated self may write. The steadier self decides what, if anything, should be sent. This single barrier changes everything. It allows the surge to speak without letting it act. It gives you the information inside the emotion without handing the emotion the keys to your relationships.

A simple practice is the unsent draft. When a message provokes you, do not reply in the thread. Open a blank note. Write the reply you want to send, exactly as it appears in the first surge. Then stop. Do not edit immediately while still hot. Do not move it into the message box. Do not send a softened version just to relieve pressure. Let the draft sit until your body has dropped enough for judgement to return.

Even a short delay can change the quality of the response. A message that felt urgent at the peak may look excessive a little later. The phrase that seemed necessary may reveal itself as punishment. The explanation may be too long. The apology may be too self-erasing. The accusation may be built on an assumption. The real point may be hiding under three paragraphs of emotional smoke.

Postponing a tense reply for twenty minutes can be enough to protect the moment. Not because twenty minutes is magic, but because it creates distance between state and action. During that time, do something physical and ordinary. Put the phone down. Walk to another room. Drink water. Feel your feet. Let the exhale lengthen. Look away from the screen. The aim is not to become perfectly calm before replying. The aim is to stop replying from the peak.

Some messages should wait longer. Anything involving a relationship rupture, resignation, accusation, financial decision, legal issue, public statement, complaint, confession, boundary, or apology that changes the future deserves more than a surge. These communications carry weight. They may still need to be sent. They may even need to be firm. But firmness improves when it is not fused with alarm.

A second useful rule is to remove the immediate route to action.

If you know you send reactive messages, do not rely on virtue alone. Make the reactive move harder. Put the phone in another room. Turn the screen face down. Remove the recipient before drafting. Switch to pen and paper. Save the email as a draft and close the app. Ask yourself to wait until after a walk, a meal, a shower, or a specific time marker. Friction is not childish. It is design.

A surge will argue against friction. It will say, "This cannot wait." "I need to say it now." "If I do not reply, they will think they have won." "If I delay, I am being fake." "If I do not explain, they will misunderstand me." These statements may feel convincing because they are carried by bodily pressure. Treat them as state cues, not facts. The more urgent the body feels, the more valuable a barrier becomes.

There is a useful question for digital moments: "Will I still stand behind this when my body is calmer?"

If the answer is uncertain, delay. If the message contains insults, mind-reading, sweeping claims, dramatic finality, excessive apology, desperate reassurance-seeking, or a need to make the other person feel what you feel, delay. If you are writing to reduce the discomfort of not writing, delay. If you are hoping the message will force certainty from someone else, delay. If you are secretly waiting for the impact of the message to regulate you, delay.

Delaying decisions follows the same logic.

Surges love decisions because decisions create the illusion of control. Quitting, ending, confessing, agreeing, buying, cancelling, promising, threatening, blocking, announcing, or cutting someone off can feel clean in a messy emotional state. The mind says, "At least now something is settled." But many surge decisions are not true choices; they are exits from discomfort. The body is trying to end uncertainty, shame, anger, or fear by turning it into action.

Some decisions are genuinely urgent. Safety, care, and immediate responsibility may require action. But many decisions only feel urgent because the state is urgent. A useful distinction is: "Is this time-sensitive, or is my body activated?" Those are not the same. A deadline may be real. A danger may be real. A boundary may need to be set. But the body's demand for instant resolution is not, by itself, proof that the decision belongs to this minute.

A good rule is to delay any high-impact decision until the surge has visibly changed.

Not necessarily vanished. Changed.

Your breathing is less trapped. Your jaw is softer. You can imagine more than one option. You can state the other person's position without caricature. You can describe the decision without using absolute language. You can tolerate waiting a little longer. You can ask, "What will this cost?" as well as "What will this relieve?" These are signs that judgement is returning.

Until then, choose a temporary holding action. Instead of quitting, write down what needs to change. Instead of ending the relationship in the heat of a row, say the conversation cannot continue safely right now. Instead of confessing from panic, decide when and how the truth should be handled with steadiness. Instead of accusing, ask for time. Instead of agreeing to escape tension, say, "I need to think before I answer." Instead of making a sweeping promise, make a short pause.

A holding action protects both urgency and wisdom. It says, "This may matter, and I will not decide it from the worst state." That sentence is not avoidance. It is respect for consequence.

Accusations deserve particular delay because they often arrive with certainty before evidence has caught up. Under stress, the mind can mistake a fear for a fact. "You did that on purpose." "You do not care." "You are trying to make me look bad." "You never wanted this to work." Such statements may feel clarifying in the moment, but they often escalate quickly because they define another person's motives rather than describing observable behaviour. Once accused, people usually defend. The issue then shifts from what happened to whether your interpretation is fair.

Delay gives you time to convert accusation into description. "You ignored me" may become "When I did not hear back, I felt dismissed and I want to understand what happened." "You are trying to embarrass me" may become "That comment landed badly in front of everyone." "You never support me" may become "I needed support today and did not feel I had it." The delayed version may still be difficult. It is also more accurate.

Confession can also be surge-driven. This may sound strange because confession is often associated with honesty. But panic can push people to disclose in order to reduce immediate anxiety, not because the timing, setting, or form is wise. A person may confess too much, too abruptly, to the wrong person, or in a way that burdens someone else with their unprocessed alarm. Honesty matters. But honest communication deserves steadiness. The question is not only "Is this true?" but "Is this the right way, time, and context to say it?"

The same caution applies to apology. A sincere apology can repair. A panic apology can erase. When you apologise too quickly from fear, you may accept responsibility you have not considered, promise changes you cannot sustain, or use self-blame to make the other person reassure you. Delay helps you apologise for the right thing. "I am sorry I spoke sharply" is cleaner than "I am sorry, everything is my fault, please do not be upset." The first repairs behaviour. The second asks the other person to regulate your panic.

Boundaries also benefit from delay when possible. A boundary delivered from heat can become a threat. A boundary delivered from panic can become a plea. A boundary delivered after a pause is usually clearer. It names what you will do, not what the other person must feel. It has fewer insults attached.

It is less likely to become a dramatic announcement and more likely to become a usable limit.

The delay itself should be spoken clearly when another person is involved. Silence without explanation can escalate. A safe delay sounds like: "I need time before I answer." "I have read this and will reply later." "I am too heated to respond well right now." "This matters, and I do not want to rush it." "I need to think before I decide." These sentences do not solve the issue. They protect the issue from being handled at the wrong speed.

Do not over-explain the delay. The more you justify it, the more likely you are to slide back into the argument. A delay sentence should be short, clean, and repeatable. If the other person presses, repeat the boundary around timing: "I will respond when I can do it properly." This is especially important with digital pressure, where repeated messages can make your body feel chased. You are allowed to refuse the pace of someone else's urgency.

There is also a private delay phrase: "Not from this state."

Use it when the body is hot, frightened, ashamed, rushed, or overly certain. "Not from this state" does not mean never. It means not yet. Not the email. Not the resignation. Not the accusation. Not the confession. Not the promise. Not the final verdict. The phrase is useful because it honours the possibility that action may be needed later. It simply refuses to let the current state be the sole authority.

Delay should be active, not vague. Passive delay says, "I will deal with it sometime," and often becomes avoidance. Active delay says, "I will return to this after twenty minutes," or "I will reread this before sending," or "I will decide tomorrow morning," or "I will speak after I have eaten and walked." The specific return point matters because it reassures the steadier self that the issue is not being buried. It is being scheduled for better conditions.

After the delay, review the intended action through three questions.

Is it true enough?

Is it necessary now?

Is it proportionate to the present moment?

"True enough" asks whether you are stating what you actually know rather than what your surge suspects. "Necessary now" asks whether the timing is genuinely required or merely demanded by discomfort. "Proportionate" asks whether the size, tone, and consequence of the action fit the situation rather than the intensity of your state. These questions slow the move without making it endlessly complicated.

For messages, add one more question: "What do I want this message to do?"

If the honest answer is "make them feel bad," delay longer. If it is "make them reassure me," consider whether a direct request would be healthier. If it is "prove I am right," the message may become a courtroom. If it is "state a boundary," shorten it. If it is "repair," remove the self-punishment and focus on behaviour. If it is "clarify," make it easier to answer. A message should have a job. The surge will try to give it several.

A delayed reply might be much shorter than the original. The first draft says: "I cannot believe you would send that after everything I have done. You clearly do not understand how hard this has been for me, and I am tired of always being the one who has to explain basic respect."

After delay, the steadier version may be: "Your message landed badly with me. I want to talk about it, but I need to do that later when I can respond properly."

This version does less, which is why it does more. It names the impact, avoids accusation, delays escalation, and preserves the possibility of a better conversation. It may not satisfy the surge. It serves the outcome.

Delay does not guarantee the perfect response. You may still send something imperfect. You may still decide firmly. You may still need to say a hard thing. The purpose is not to sand every edge off your communication. The purpose is to ensure that the edge belongs to the message, not merely to the state.

This distinction is crucial. Some messages should be direct. Some decisions should be decisive. Some boundaries should be firm. Some truths should be spoken. Delay is not a strategy for becoming endlessly agreeable. It is a strategy for making sure that strength is not confused with reactivity. The delayed action may still be strong, but it will be cleaner.

There will be times when delaying feels unbearable. That is usually a sign that delay is needed. The body may protest because it has learned to regulate through action: send, say, decide, fix, confess, escape. To delay is to sit briefly with unspent pressure. This is uncomfortable. It is also where freedom grows. Every time you survive the urge without obeying it immediately, the urge loses a little authority.

The point is not to become slow about everything. It is to become slower where speed has been harming you.

Some actions are low-impact and reversible. Choose the meal, move the chair, take the walk, drink the water, step into another room. Other actions shape trust, reputation, safety, money, work, family, and self-respect. These deserve a barrier. The barrier may be a draft, a timer, a pause phrase, a walk, a night of sleep, a second read, or a conversation held outside the peak. The exact form matters less than the principle: consequence deserves steadiness.

The next time a surge says, "Do it now," listen carefully for what kind of action it wants. Is it asking for relief, or for wisdom? Is it trying to protect a value, or merely discharge pressure? Is the next move reversible, or will it live beyond the feeling?

Delay is not doing nothing.

It is giving your future self a vote.

Managing rumination loops

Rumination often arrives dressed as responsibility.

After a tense message, a sharp exchange, a panic spike, or a moment you wish you had handled differently, the mind begins its private replay. It reviews the words. It tests the tone. It imagines what the other person meant. It builds a better answer. It drafts the message you should have sent, then improves it, then sharpens it, then adds the line that would finally make them understand. The body may be sitting quietly in a chair, but internally the argument is still happening.

This can feel productive. That is why rumination is so persuasive. It looks like reflection. It sounds like preparation. It promises clarity, justice, safety, repair, or protection from being caught off guard next time. The mind says, "I am just trying to understand." Sometimes that is true. But often, rumination is not understanding. It is reactivation.

The difference matters.

Reflection moves towards a useful end. It may help you notice what triggered you, what you did next, what needs repair, what boundary is required, or what you want to practise differently. Reflection has a yield. It gives you one next step, then lets the nervous system come down. Rumination circles. It repeats the same material with slightly different wording. It produces heat without resolution. It keeps the body ready for a conversation that is no longer happening.

A rumination loop often begins with an unfinished feeling. Anger wants recognition. Shame wants reversal. Panic wants certainty. Fear wants reassurance. Regret wants a second chance. The mind tries to complete the moment by replaying it. It imagines saying the perfect thing, receiving the apology, proving the point, catching the danger early, or undoing the mistake. For a few seconds, this may feel satisfying. Then the loop opens again because imagined completion is not real completion.

That is the trap. Rumination offers the feeling of action without the effect of action.

You can spend an hour constructing a brilliant argument and still have done nothing to repair the relationship, protect the boundary, calm the body, or choose the next step. You can replay a panic spike repeatedly and still not become safer. You can review your mistake with forensic cruelty and still not learn more than you would have learnt from one honest sentence: "I was activated, and I need a different pause next time." The mind may be busy, but busyness is not wisdom.

Rumination keeps the body activated because the body does not always distinguish sharply between the original event and the rehearsed event. If you vividly replay the criticism, your body may tighten again. If you imagine the confrontation, your jaw may clench again. If you review the panic sensations, your chest may become a threat target again. If you rehearse the unfairness, anger may rise again as though the moment has returned. In this way, the mind reopens the file and the body reloads the state.

That is why rumination can feel exhausting. You are not merely thinking. You are repeatedly asking the body to prepare.

The signs are usually recognisable. You keep returning to the same sentence. You imagine what you should have said. You argue with someone who is not there. You search for the hidden meaning behind their tone. You replay your own behaviour and wince. You ask, "Why did I do that?" without moving towards a practical answer. You predict future conflict. You check whether you are still upset. You try to force emotional closure by thinking harder. The loop promises one more review will settle it. It rarely does.

A useful question is: "Is this thought leading to a next step, or is it keeping me in the surge?"

This question cuts through the disguise. Rumination often insists it is necessary. It says, "I need to think about this." Perhaps you do. But thinking should eventually change something. It should clarify a repair, a boundary, a lesson, a decision, or a need for rest. If the thought only produces more heat, more shame, more certainty, more imaginary dialogue, or more checking, it is not helping. It is extending the escalation.

The aim is not to ban thought. That would be unrealistic and unnecessary. The aim is to close the loop before it becomes a second emotional event. Closing the loop does not mean pretending nothing happened. It means giving the mind a clear, brief process so it does not keep reopening the moment in search of completion.

A close-the-loop practice begins with naming the replay.

"This is rumination."

"This is the argument continuing in my head."

"This is panic reviewing itself."

"This is shame replaying the scene."

"This is my mind trying to get certainty."

The naming should be plain, not dramatic. You are not scolding yourself. You are identifying the process. Once the process is named, it loses a little of its authority. It is no longer "the truth I must keep examining." It is a loop.

Next, extract the useful information in one or two sentences. This is the part rumination pretends to be doing, so do it deliberately and briefly. Ask: what is the actual lesson or next step? Not the whole moral trial. Not the complete psychological history. One clean point.

"I need to apologise for my tone."

"I need to delay replies when I feel accused."

"I need to ask for clarification instead of assuming motive."

"I need to stop checking symptoms after panic passes."

"I need to set a boundary, but not from anger heat."

"I need rest before I decide anything."

This step is important because the mind resists closure when it feels ignored. If you simply say, "Stop thinking," the unfinished part may protest. If you harvest the useful message, the mind has less reason to keep circling. You are not dismissing the event. You are taking what can be used and refusing to keep burning energy on the rest.

Then choose whether action is needed now, later, or not at all.

Now means there is a small practical repair or safety step that should not be delayed: sending a brief apology, writing a reminder, stepping away from a trigger, drinking water after panic, or putting the phone down. Later means the issue matters, but the body is not settled enough yet: a conversation, decision, boundary, or longer reflection. Not at all means the loop is asking for impossible certainty, perfect hindsight, or an argument with the past. That category is often the hardest to accept and the most freeing.

If action is needed later, give it a container. "I will write three notes about this after dinner." "I will reply tomorrow morning." "I will raise this when I am calmer." "I will decide after I have slept." Without a container, the mind may keep returning out of fear that the issue will be forgotten. A container reassures the responsible part of you that the matter has been placed somewhere. It does not need to keep shouting.

The final step is to re-enter the present through the body. Rumination is largely mental, but it has physical fuel. Close the loop with contact. Feet on the floor. Hands on a surface. A soft exhale. Look at the room. Name one ordinary task. Stand up. Wash a cup. Step outside. Move slowly. The body needs evidence that the replay is over. Thought alone may not be enough.

A close-the-loop sequence might sound like this: "This is rumination. The useful point is that I need to apologise for interrupting. I will do that after lunch when I am steadier. For now, I am putting the phone down and making tea."

That is not avoidance. It is completion.

The tea matters more than it sounds. Ordinary action helps end the false emergency. Rumination keeps the body oriented towards the event; ordinary action orients the body towards the present. Make the bed. Wash your hands. Open a window. Walk to the end of the street. Return to the work in front of you. Fold laundry. Feed the pet. Reply to an uncomplicated message. These actions are not glamorous, but they teach the nervous system that the moment has passed.

Some rumination loops are anger loops. They replay unfairness and add sharper arguments each time. The mind imagines confrontation, evidence, exposure, victory. Anger rumination often feels energising at first, then draining. The useful question is: "What boundary or request is hidden inside this argument?" If there is one, write it in a single sentence. If there is not, the loop may be feeding outrage without direction. A boundary can be acted on. An imaginary prosecution usually cannot.

Some loops are shame loops. They replay your mistake and use it as evidence against your character. Shame says, "How could you?" "You always do this." "Everyone noticed." "You are impossible." Shame rumination can pretend to be accountability, but real accountability produces repair. Shame produces collapse. The useful question is: "What behaviour needs repair, and what self-attack can be dropped?" Keep the behaviour. Drop the verdict.

Some loops are panic loops. They replay sensations, places, symptoms, and what-ifs. Panic asks, "What if it happens again?" "What if that sensation meant something?" "What if I cannot cope next time?" The useful question is: "What helped me reduce the spiral, and what checking made it worse?" The answer should be short. Panic does not need a lengthy investigation immediately after the event. It needs steady aftercare and a return to life.

Some loops are preparation loops. These are particularly deceptive. You tell yourself you are getting ready for a future conversation. You rehearse what you will say. You improve the wording. You predict their response. You prepare your counter-response. Soon you are not preparing; you are living through a conflict that has not happened. The useful question is: "What are the three points I actually need to remember?" Write them down. Then stop rehearsing. Preparation that cannot end is anxiety with a notebook.

A strong way to interrupt rumination is to set a thinking boundary. Not forever. For now. "I am not reopening this until tomorrow." "I have already taken the lesson." "I am not holding a trial in my head." "I will not solve this while activated." These phrases may feel blunt, but the mind sometimes needs a firm edge. Rumination thrives in vague permission. It enters through "just one more thought." A boundary closes the door.

The body may resist. You may feel a pull to return to the loop. That pull does not mean the loop is useful. It means the loop is familiar. The mind has learnt to treat replay as protection. Stopping may feel exposed at first, as though you are leaving something unfinished. This is why the close-the-loop practice includes extracting the lesson and setting a return point where needed. You are not abandoning responsibility. You are refusing compulsion.

There is also a digital dimension. Phones are perfect tools for rumination because they offer endless ways to reopen the moment. Reread the message. Check whether they are online. Draft a reply. Delete it. Search for advice. Screenshot the exchange. Ask a friend what they think. Revisit the thread. Watch for a reply. Each action refreshes the emotional charge. If the loop is digital, the interruption must often be physical. Put the phone in another room. Turn it face down. Disable the immediate route back into the thread. Let your hands do something else.

Rumination is not always solved by insight. Sometimes it is solved by friction.

Make the loop harder to continue. Stand up. Change rooms. Begin a task that requires both hands. Write the single useful point on paper and close the notebook. Take a short walk without composing messages in your head. If the mind resumes the argument, say, "The loop is open again," and return to contact. This may need repetition. Repetition is not failure. It is training.

A common fear is that stopping rumination will mean losing the lesson. In reality, rumination often buries the lesson under noise. The real lesson is usually simple and repeatable. I need to pause before replying. I need to ask, not assume. I need to repair my tone. I need to stop checking. I need to rest before deciding. I need to set a boundary earlier. Once the lesson has been named, continuing to replay the event may be less about learning and more about trying to change what has already happened.

You cannot edit the past by rehearsing it.

That sentence may sound severe, but it is merciful. The mind often suffers because it keeps trying to obtain a different ending from an event that has already ended. It imagines the perfect reply, the better exit, the calmer breath, the wiser choice. There may be grief in accepting that the moment cannot be redone. But there is also freedom. The next moment can still be handled.

This is where choice returns. Rumination keeps you facing backwards while calling it preparation. Closing the loop turns you forward. Not with denial. Not with forced cheerfulness. With one usable lesson and one next action.

The practice can be very short:

Name the loop.

Take the lesson.

Choose now, later, or not at all.

Return through the body.

Rejoin the day.

The brevity is part of its strength. Rumination loves complexity. It loves long internal hearings, elaborate motives, moral verdicts, and imagined scenes. A brief practice refuses to feed it. It says, "Enough has been extracted. The rest is heat."

There will be moments when deeper reflection is genuinely needed. Some conflicts reveal patterns. Some panic episodes suggest that more support would help. Some reactions point to exhaustion, grief, trauma, resentment, or a boundary that has been ignored too long. Closing a rumination loop does not mean refusing deeper work. It means choosing the right time and state for that work. Deep reflection belongs to steadier ground, not to the hot replay immediately after escalation.

A useful later review is calm, timed, and written. It asks a few direct questions: what was the trigger, what did I feel in the body, what story did I add, what did I do, what helped, what is one adjustment for next time? Then it ends. This is reflection. It has structure and a finish line. Without a finish line, review can slide back into rumination.

The aim is to regain choice.

Choice over where attention goes. Choice over whether a message is sent. Choice over whether the body stays activated by an argument that is no longer happening. Choice over whether panic becomes the centre of the day. Choice over whether shame becomes identity. Choice over whether an event becomes a lesson or a loop.

The next time your mind reopens a finished moment and calls it useful, listen carefully. Is it leading somewhere, or merely circling the same heat? Is it producing a next step, or producing more pressure? Is it helping you repair, decide, learn, or rest? Or is it keeping the surge alive because the body has not yet accepted that the moment has passed?

Close the loop.

Not because it did not matter.

Because it matters too much to keep living inside it.

Chapter 8
Fast recovery after conflict

Conflict does not end the moment the words stop.

A difficult call finishes, a door closes, a message thread goes quiet, or the other person leaves the room, yet the body may still be arguing. The heart remains quick. The jaw stays tight. The shoulders hold their defensive shape. The mind keeps producing sentences that were not said, points that should have been made, accusations that might still be justified, apologies that may or may not be enough. Outwardly, the event is over. Inwardly, the system is still mobilised.

This is where many people create a second conflict. Not necessarily with the other person, but inside themselves. They replay the conversation until anger returns. They punish themselves for snapping. They imagine how they were perceived. They rush into an apology that erases their own valid point. They seek reassurance, send another message, or try to force immediate emotional closure because the residue of conflict feels intolerable. The original impact may have passed, but the aftershock begins making new decisions.

Fast recovery is not pretending nothing happened. It is not sweeping the issue away, performing cheerfulness, or becoming the person who always "moves on" before anything has been understood. That kind of speed is often avoidance in polished clothes. Real recovery is different. It helps the body come down from activation so that whatever needs to happen next can happen from steadier ground. Sometimes that next step is repair. Sometimes it is rest. Sometimes it is a boundary. Sometimes it is simply not carrying the conflict into the next room, the next task, or the next person.

This matters because unresolved adrenaline looks for somewhere to go. If it is not discharged safely, it may turn into rumination, irritability, coldness, over-apology, fresh accusation, or a sudden need to fix everything immediately. A person can leave a tense work call and bring the same sharpness into family life. They can finish an argument with a partner and then pick a fight with themselves. They can handle the visible conflict reasonably well and still lose the hour afterwards to inner prosecution. Recovery is the skill that prevents one hard moment from spreading.

The work begins with downshifting after impact. The body needs a way to complete the stress response without choosing a new target. Movement, breath, contact, and attention can help clear the charge without turning it into another argument. This is not dramatic self-care; it is practical emotional hygiene. After conflict, the system must be shown that the danger phase has ended, even if the issue itself remains unfinished.

Repair then becomes possible without self-erasure. This distinction is crucial. Many people confuse apology with collapse. They apologise for having needs, for being upset, for setting a boundary, for taking space, for making another person uncomfortable. Others avoid apology because they fear it will weaken their position or invite blame. Neither route is good enough. Mature repair names behaviour clearly without surrendering the truth of what mattered.

A clean repair does not grovel, explain for ten minutes, or demand instant forgiveness. It does not make the other person responsible for soothing your shame. It also does not hide behind pride. It says, in plain terms, what you did, what you intended or failed to handle well, and what you will do next. "I spoke sharply. I was angry, but I do not want to speak to you that way. I still want to talk about the issue when we are both steadier." That kind of repair keeps accountability and dignity in the same room.

The challenge is timing. Repair offered while the body is still flooded often becomes panic in polite language. Recovery attempted without repair can become avoidance. The skill is to downshift enough that repair, if needed, comes from steadiness rather than fear. Conflict may disturb the relationship, but the aftermath decides whether the disturbance becomes a wound, a lesson, or another layer of distance.

So the question after conflict is not simply, "Who was right?" That may matter later, but it is not the first recovery question. The sharper question is: can you bring your body down before it drags the conflict into the next moment, and can you repair what is yours without disappearing from your own side of the truth?

Downshifting after impact

A conflict can end on the outside while the body continues to fight it.

The call has finished. The message has been sent, or deliberately not sent. The other person has left the room. The meeting has moved on. Nothing more is being said. Yet inside, the system remains armed. The jaw is still tight. The breath is still shallow. The hands still want to move. The shoulders remain lifted, as if preparing for another blow. The mind keeps supplying the sentence that would have landed better, the accusation that would have proved the point, the apology that might fix the discomfort, the imagined reply that may still arrive.

This is the after-impact state. It is not the conflict itself, but it is still shaped by conflict. The body has mobilised energy to defend, explain, escape, endure, or repair, and that energy does not vanish simply because the conversation has stopped. If it is not given a safe route down, it often searches for a new route out. That is when people pick a secondary fight, send a follow-up message they do not need to send, become sharp with someone uninvolved, over-apologise, collapse into shame, or spend the next hour arguing in their head.

Downshifting is the skill of helping the body leave the conflict state before the conflict state chooses the next part of your day.

This is not the same as "getting over it." That phrase is far too crude for what happens after emotional impact. A hard exchange may matter. A boundary may still need to be set. A repair may still be required. A pattern may need attention. Downshifting does not erase the significance of what happened. It simply recognises that a body still carrying the force of conflict is not yet the best place from which to decide what the conflict means.

After impact, the body often wants completion. It wants the last word, the clean explanation, the apology received, the point understood, the threat removed, the shame dissolved, the uncertainty ended. These wants are human. They are also dangerous if obeyed too quickly. The system may confuse completion with discharge. It may push you towards any action that releases pressure, even if that action extends the conflict.

A follow-up message can feel like completion.

So can a sarcastic remark in another room.

So can replaying the argument until you win it privately.

So can apologising for everything just to stop feeling exposed.

So can deciding that the other person is entirely wrong and you are entirely safe from reflection.

None of these is true recovery. They may reduce discomfort for a moment, but they keep the nervous system organised around the conflict. Real downshifting changes the body's state before it tries to change the story.

Start by recognising the residue. Residue is what remains after the visible conflict has ended: heat, trembling, tightness, restless energy, heaviness, numbness, a buzzing mind, an urge to speak again, or a sudden drop into exhaustion. These sensations are not proof that the conflict is still happening. They are signs that your body has not yet fully received the message that the impact phase is over.

The first move is physical contact.

Place both feet on the floor. Let the weight settle down through the legs. If you are sitting, feel the chair supporting you. If you are standing, feel the pressure through the soles of your feet. If your hands are clenched, open them slowly. Rest one hand on a surface, a table, a wall, the kitchen counter, the arm of a chair. Let the body touch something that is not part of the argument.

Contact is simple, but it is not trivial. Conflict pulls attention into threat and interpretation. Contact returns attention to location. It says, without drama, "I am here. The conversation is not my whole environment. There is a surface under my hand. There is ground under my feet." The body needs such ordinary evidence. It has been preparing for impact; it now needs proof of support.

The second move is to release the breath without forcing it.

Do not perform a large calming breath as though you are trying to erase the event. Let the inhale be ordinary. Let the exhale be a little longer, a little softer. The exhale is a signal that the body does not need to keep holding everything at battle speed. If anger is still hot, the exhale may stop the next sentence from forming too quickly. If shame is rising, it may soften the collapse. If panic is present, it may reduce the urge to check, confess, or seek certainty immediately.

Use the breath as a brake, not a verdict. You are not deciding that everything is fine. You are deciding not to let the body keep accelerating.

The third move is deliberate movement. Conflict energy needs somewhere to go, but not into another person. A short walk around the room. Washing your hands. Putting a cup away. Stretching the fingers. Rolling the shoulders. Going outside for a few minutes. Walking slowly down a corridor. Tidying one small area. These actions help discharge energy without turning it into fresh words.

The movement should be purposeful, not frantic. There is a difference between pacing while rehearsing the argument and walking to downshift the body. One keeps the conflict alive; the other helps the body complete the stress cycle. If your mind continues arguing while you move, bring attention back to the physical details: feet lifting and landing, water on the hands, shoulder blades moving, air on the face, the weight of an object being placed down.

A useful phrase is: "No new target."

After conflict, the body may look for someone or something else to receive the leftover charge. The next person who asks a question may get the tone that belonged to the argument. A small inconvenience may receive the force of a much larger frustration. A harmless message may become the place where the nervous system dumps pressure. "No new target" is a clear internal boundary. It says, "This energy is real, but it will not be handed to the next available person."

This matters especially when moving from one setting into another. After a difficult work call, do not walk straight into family life carrying the same clenched state if you can avoid it.

After an argument at home, do not immediately answer an unrelated message from heat. After a tense exchange in public, do not drive, decide, or speak sharply before checking your state. Even a brief transition can protect the next environment from the previous impact.

Transitions are recovery spaces.

A doorway, a bathroom sink, a parked car, a staircase, a short walk to the kitchen, the moment before opening the next email: these are places where downshifting can happen quickly. You do not need a perfect setting. You need a pause long enough to tell the body, "That moment has ended. This is the next one."

The fourth move is to widen attention. Conflict narrows the field around what was said, what was meant, who was wrong, and what might happen next. After impact, the mind often keeps staring at the emotional injury. Widening interrupts that stare. Look around. Name a few neutral objects. Notice the space beside you and behind you. Listen for one sound that has nothing to do with the conflict. Feel the temperature of the room.

This does not trivialise the issue. It restores proportion. The conflict is part of the day, not the whole day. The sentence was part of the relationship, not the whole relationship. The mistake was part of your behaviour, not the whole of your character. Widening does not solve the meaning of the event; it stops the event from occupying every inch of your attention.

The fifth move is to delay interpretation.

This may be the hardest step because the mind wants a verdict. It wants to know who was right, whether the relationship is damaged, whether you handled it badly, whether you should apologise, whether they are unreasonable, whether you should send another message, whether this always happens, whether it means something larger. Some of those questions may deserve attention. But immediately after impact, the body's state can distort the answers.

A downshifting phrase can help: "I will interpret this later."

Not ignore it. Not excuse it. Later.

Later is a powerful word after conflict. It protects serious thinking from the heat of immediate activation. It gives your steadier mind a chance to return before you build a full meaning around the event. Many people make the conflict worse not during the conflict itself, but in the interpretation that follows. They decide too quickly that they were attacked, abandoned, exposed, trapped, humiliated, or unforgivable. A delayed interpretation is often a more accurate one.

This is not avoidance if you make the delay clean. You might say, "I will decide what repair is needed after I have calmed." Or, "I will not send anything for twenty minutes." Or, "I will write down the issue later, not while my body is still heated." The point is to contain the meaning-making until the body is less charged.

A short reset sequence can be used after almost any conflict.

Feet on the floor.

One soft exhale.

Hands unclenched.

One small movement.

Look around the room.

No new target.

No interpretation yet.

This sequence is intentionally plain. After conflict, the mind does not need another complicated demand. It needs a reliable exit route from activation. Even if you do only two parts of the sequence, you have interrupted the carry-over.

Downshifting after impact is especially important when you handled the conflict reasonably well. This may sound surprising, but even a good response can leave adrenaline behind. You may have paused instead of snapping, listened instead of attacking, set a boundary without cruelty, or delayed a message instead of sending it. That is excellent. It is also effortful. The body may still be charged from holding the line. If you do not recover afterwards, you may resent the effort, replay the moment, or discharge the held-back energy elsewhere.

A calm-looking response is not always a calm body.

Give yourself recovery even when you behaved well. Perhaps especially then. A few minutes of downshifting teaches the body that restraint will not mean endless internal pressure. It shows your system that choosing not to escalate does not trap the energy inside you forever. The energy can move through safely.

There is also a form of downshifting needed after you did not handle the conflict well. Perhaps you snapped, withdrew, over-apologised, or sent the message. The temptation may be to rush into repair immediately because shame feels unbearable. Repair matters, but shame is a poor repair manager. If you apologise from panic, you may apologise for too much, demand reassurance, or make the other person responsible for easing your guilt. Downshift first. Then repair what is yours.

A downshift before repair might be as simple as washing your hands slowly, taking a short walk, breathing out, and saying, "I need to apologise for my tone, not for having a concern." That sentence already protects you from self-erasure. It separates behaviour from the underlying issue. It helps you repair cleanly rather than collapse.

The same principle applies if the other person behaved badly. Downshifting does not mean forgiving them instantly, minimising the issue, or pretending you are unaffected. It means giving yourself enough steadiness to decide what the next boundary should be. A boundary made from a steadier body is often stronger than one made from the first burn of anger. It is clearer, shorter, and less likely to be dismissed as a reaction.

Recovery after conflict therefore serves both relationship and self-respect. It protects others from your leftover activation, and it protects you from decisions made while still inside the impact. It prevents a hard moment from spreading into the next conversation, the next room, the next hour, or the next version of yourself.

One practical recovery method is the "reset before re-entry" rule. Before you re-enter normal life after conflict, take one minute to shift state. Before returning to work, reset. Before speaking to a child, reset. Before driving, reset. Before opening another message, reset. Before deciding what the conflict means, reset. The pause does not need to be visible or dramatic. It only needs to be real.

A reset before re-entry might look like standing at the kitchen sink after a tense call, feeling warm water over your hands, exhaling slowly, naming three neutral objects, and deciding not to think about the call until you have made a cup of tea. It might look like sitting in the car after a difficult appointment, both hands resting on your thighs, breathing out, and waiting until your shoulders drop before starting the engine. It might look like closing the laptop after a heated email, standing up, walking to the window, and looking at the farthest thing you can see.

These are small acts of closure. Not emotional closure in the grand sense. Physiological closure. They tell the body that the impact has happened and that the next moment does not have to carry the same charge.

Do not confuse recovery with numbness. Some people downshift by disconnecting completely. They go blank, distract themselves aggressively, scroll, eat without tasting, work without pausing, or declare themselves "fine" while the body remains unsettled underneath. Numbing may reduce awareness, but it does not necessarily complete the stress response. Downshifting keeps enough contact with the body to help it settle. Numbing cuts contact.

The difference is felt afterwards. Downshifting tends to leave you clearer, steadier, and more able to choose the next action. Numbing often leaves you distant, irritable, fatigued, or vulnerable to a later surge. The aim is not to feel nothing. The aim is to feel the body move from mobilisation towards steadiness.

There is no need to analyse every conflict immediately. In fact, immediate analysis is often the enemy of recovery. A better rhythm is: downshift, re-enter, review later if needed. This rhythm respects both the body and the issue. It gives the nervous system time to come down, then gives the mind a chance to reflect without being flooded.

Later review can be brief. What happened? What did I do well? What needs repair? What boundary or request remains? What should I practise next time? Then stop. If the review becomes a replay, return to the loop-closing skills. Recovery is not an invitation to hold a private court case all evening.

Downshifting after impact is a modest practice with large consequences. It will not make conflict pleasant. It will not guarantee that others behave well. It will not remove the need for hard conversations. But it can stop one difficult moment from becoming three. It can prevent the second message, the unnecessary snap, the shame spiral, the displaced irritation, the rumination marathon, the apology that erases your own truth.

The next time a conflict ends, do not assume your body has ended with it. Check the residue. Feel the feet. Let the exhale lengthen. Move deliberately. Widen the room. Refuse a new target. Delay the verdict.

The conflict may be over.

Now help your body leave it.

Repairing without self-erasure

Repair is not the same as surrender.

This distinction matters because many people enter the aftermath of conflict with only two familiar options. They either defend themselves so completely that no repair can reach them, or they apologise so completely that they disappear from their own side of the truth. One protects the ego and neglects the relationship. The other protects the relationship and neglects the self. Neither is good enough.

After conflict, especially if you snapped, shut down, interrupted, accused, became cold, sent a reactive message, or left badly, the body may push towards urgent repair. Shame rises. The stomach drops. The mind starts searching for a sentence that will make everything safe again. "I am so sorry." "It was all my fault." "I am terrible." "Please do not be upset." "Forget I said anything." The apology becomes less about accountability and more about escaping the unbearable feeling of being the person who caused impact.

That kind of apology may sound humble, but it often carries panic. It asks the other person to reassure you before they have had space to register what happened. It may put them in the strange position of comforting the person who hurt, dismissed, or overwhelmed them. It may also erase the issue that started the conflict. If you apologise for everything, you may never address the one thing that actually needs to change.

Self-erasing repair is especially common in people who fear disconnection. The moment tension appears, they rush to restore closeness, even if closeness comes at the cost of accuracy. They apologise for being upset, for having a boundary, for asking a question, for needing time, for reacting to something that genuinely mattered. They may call this being mature, but often it is fear in polished clothing. The body is not repairing; it is trying to stop the threat of distance.

Real repair is cleaner.

It does not require you to become the villain of the whole story. It does not require you to give up your concern, swallow your boundary, or pretend the other person's behaviour was fine. It requires you to name your behaviour clearly, acknowledge its impact where appropriate, and state what you will do differently next. That is all. Repair is precise. Self-erasure is excessive.

A useful repair begins with the behaviour, not the identity. "I spoke sharply." "I interrupted you." "I left without saying when I would come back." "I sent that message while I was angry." "I went quiet instead of telling you I needed a pause." These sentences are strong because they are specific. They do not collapse into "I am awful," and they do not dodge behind "I was just stressed." They name what happened in observable terms.

This is important because identity-based apologies often become emotionally messy. "I am a terrible person" may sound remorseful, but it shifts attention away from the behaviour and towards your self-image. The other person may feel pressured to say, "No, you are not," which means they are now soothing you instead of receiving accountability. Behaviour-based repair keeps the focus where it belongs. You did something. That thing had an effect. You can respond to it.

The second part of repair is intention, handled carefully. Intention can clarify, but it should not be used as a shield. "I did not mean to hurt you" may be true, but if said too early or too defensively, it can sound like an attempt to cancel the impact. Better repair places intention after accountability, not before it. "I spoke sharply. I was trying to explain myself, but it came out as an attack." This sentence keeps both truths in view: the intention was not harm, and the delivery still caused harm.

Impact matters because people live with what happened, not only with what you meant. You may have meant to take space, but the other person experienced you vanishing. You may have meant to be honest, but the words landed as contempt. You may have meant to defend yourself, but your tone made listening harder. A mature repair can hold that difference without collapsing. It can say, "That was not what I intended, and I can see that it affected you."

The word "and" is doing important work there.

Defensiveness says, "That was not what I intended, so you should not feel hurt." Self-erasure says, "You felt hurt, so my intention does not matter and I am completely wrong." Repair says, "My intention and your experience both belong in the room." This is the posture that allows accountability without distortion.

The third part of repair is the next step. An apology without a next step can become emotional theatre. It may soothe the moment, but it gives the other person little reason to trust change. The next step does not have to be grand. In fact, grand promises made from shame are often unreliable. A good next step is small, specific, and connected to the behaviour.

"I will take a pause before replying when I feel that heated."

"Next time I need space, I will say when I am coming back."

"I will not continue the conversation by text when I am angry."

"I will slow down and let you finish before I answer."

"I still want to discuss the issue, but I will do it without raising my voice."

These sentences are useful because they turn remorse into structure. They show that repair is not simply a feeling; it is a plan for the next pressure moment.

Notice that a clean repair can still preserve the original concern. This is where many people lose themselves. They think that if they apologise for tone, they must withdraw the boundary. If they apologise for snapping, they must concede the whole disagreement. If they apologise for shutting down, they must accept the other person's version of events. Not so. You can repair the way you handled something while still standing by the thing that mattered.

"I am sorry I raised my voice. I still need us to talk about how decisions are being made."

"I apologise for the message I sent last night. The concern underneath it is still real, but I should not have sent it that way."

"I should not have walked out without saying anything. I did need space, and I should have taken it more clearly."

"I am sorry for interrupting. I felt defensive, but I want to hear the rest before I respond."

This is repair without self-erasure. It separates behaviour from message. It takes responsibility for the impact of the behaviour while keeping the valid issue alive. That separation is essential for mature conflict. Without it, every apology becomes a surrender document, and every boundary becomes contaminated by the fear that accountability will cost you your position.

Some people avoid repair because they fear exactly that. They believe that apologising will be used against them. They worry that any admission will become proof that they were wrong about everything. In some dynamics, that fear may be based on experience. If another person consistently weaponises your accountability, larger boundaries may be needed. But in healthy or workable relationships, repair usually strengthens authority rather than weakens it. A person who can own their behaviour cleanly is harder to dismiss, not easier.

Defensive non-repair has its own cost. When you refuse to acknowledge the way you handled something, the other person may stop trusting your good intentions. They may begin to expect attack, withdrawal, coldness, or overreaction. The issue itself may become secondary to the pattern of how conflict unfolds. Over time, unrepaired moments accumulate. They do not always look dramatic, but they create distance.

Repair clears the debris.

It does not rebuild the whole relationship in one sentence. It does not guarantee forgiveness. It does not require the other person to respond warmly. It simply removes what is yours from the middle of the room so the real issue can be seen again. If you spoke harshly, repair the harshness. If you disappeared, repair the disappearance. If you over-apologised and erased your own truth, repair that too: "I apologised for too much because I was anxious. I do want to own my tone, but I do not want to pretend the issue does not matter."

That last form of repair is particularly powerful. Sometimes the self-erasing apology itself needs correction. You may realise later that you said sorry for having needs, for being upset, or for naming a problem. A steadier follow-up can restore accuracy. "I have thought about what I said earlier. I am sorry for snapping, but I am not sorry for raising the concern. I want to talk about it more calmly." This kind of sentence may feel uncomfortable, but it teaches both you and the relationship that accountability does not require disappearance.

Repair also needs timing. Too soon, and it may be panic. Too late, and it may allow distance to harden. The right time is usually after enough downshifting that you can speak without begging, attacking, or performing. You do not need perfect calm. You do need enough steadiness to avoid making the apology another demand. If you are still desperate for the other person to reassure you immediately, pause longer. If you are still building a defence while apologising, pause longer. If you can name your part simply, you are closer.

The body can tell you. In panic repair, the voice rushes, the apology multiplies, and the eyes search for relief. In defensive repair, the jaw tightens, the explanation expands, and the apology is surrounded by reasons. In clean repair, the body may still be uncomfortable, but the sentence is shorter. It does not chase. It does not prosecute. It stands.

A strong repair can be built with a simple shape: behaviour, impact or acknowledgement, next step.

"I interrupted you earlier. That made it harder for you to finish what you were saying. I will slow down and let you complete the point before I respond."

"I went silent after your comment. I can see that may have felt like I was shutting you out. Next time I will say I need a pause rather than disappearing."

"I sent that reply while I was angry. It was sharper than it needed to be. I am going to wait before responding to messages when I feel that heated."

"I raised my voice. That is not how I want to speak to you. I still want to address the issue, but I want to do it more carefully."

These repairs are brief because repair should not become a performance. The more words you add, the more likely you are to drift into defence, self-punishment, or pressure. Brevity protects sincerity. It gives the other person room to receive the apology without being buried under your emotional process.

There are also phrases that weaken repair and are best avoided when possible. "I am sorry you feel that way" often sounds like distance rather than ownership. "I am sorry, but..." usually announces that defence is about to take over. "I guess I am just a terrible person" asks to be rescued. "I only did that because you..." shifts responsibility away too quickly. "Fine, I am sorry" carries resentment more than repair. These phrases may appear when you feel cornered, ashamed, or misunderstood, but they rarely help.

Cleaner alternatives are available.

"I am sorry I spoke that way."

"I can see why that landed badly."

"I want to take responsibility for my part."

"I do not want to excuse it."

"I also want us to come back to the issue itself."

The last sentence is important because repair should not always close the conversation. Sometimes it reopens the right conversation. Once the tone, timing, or behaviour has been repaired, the underlying matter may still need attention. If repair is used to avoid the issue, resentment will return. If the issue is used to avoid repair, defensiveness will remain. Mature conflict often requires both: repair the process, then address the problem.

This is especially true in close relationships. The person you hurt may need to know that you understand the impact. You may need to know that your original concern has not been erased. Both needs can coexist. A repair that preserves connection while leaving room for the issue might sound like, "I am sorry I became sarcastic. That was not fair. I was angry because I felt dismissed, and I would like us to talk about that when we are both steadier."

This sentence does not grovel. It does not accuse. It does not pretend the sarcasm was acceptable. It also does not throw away the feeling underneath. That balance is the heart of repair without self-erasure.

At work, repair may need to be more contained. "I was abrupt in that meeting. I apologise. I will follow up more clearly by email." Or, "I pushed back too sharply earlier. I still have concerns about the proposal, but I should have raised them in a more constructive way." Professional repair does not require emotional overexposure. It requires clarity, ownership, and a better next step.

With children or younger people, repair has another layer. Adults sometimes fear that apologising will reduce authority. In reality, clean repair often teaches emotional responsibility.

"I raised my voice. That was my job to manage. I was frustrated, and I should have paused." This does not mean removing the boundary or consequence. It means showing that authority and accountability can exist together. That lesson is more powerful than pretending adults never misstep.

Repair also includes repairing with yourself.

After conflict, especially if you feel ashamed, you may become brutal internally. You replay your mistake, attack your character, and promise never to do it again with a kind of desperate intensity. This is not repair. It is self-punishment. Internal repair sounds different: "I did not handle that well. I can take responsibility. I can repair what is mine. I can learn the earlier cue." This tone keeps you engaged with change rather than buried under shame.

Self-repair is not letting yourself off the hook. It is keeping yourself available for responsibility. A person drowning in self-attack often becomes less capable of clean repair, not more. They may avoid the other person, over-apologise, collapse, or become defensive because shame is too painful to hold. A steadier internal stance allows for better external repair.

Sometimes repair will not be received. The other person may still be hurt, angry, distant, or unwilling to continue. A clean repair does not control their response. This is difficult to accept, especially for people who use apology to restore immediate safety. Once you have repaired sincerely and proportionately, the next task is to tolerate the space that remains. You cannot force another person to be ready. You can remain accountable without chasing.

Chasing turns repair into pressure. "Are we okay?" "Do you forgive me?" "Please tell me you are not angry." "I said sorry, why are you still upset?" These questions may come from fear, but they can crowd the other person's process. A better follow-up is, "I understand you may need time." Then actually give time. This is where repair becomes mature: not only in the apology, but in your willingness not to demand instant emotional relief from it.

There are situations where repeated repair is not enough because the same behaviour continues. If you apologise for snapping every week but do nothing to change the conditions that lead to snapping, the apology begins to lose meaning. Repair must eventually connect to practice: noticing body cues earlier, taking safe pauses, delaying messages, downshifting after conflict, sleeping, eating, setting boundaries, asking for support, or changing the structure around known triggers. An apology points backwards. A practice points forwards.

The strongest repair, then, is not the most dramatic apology. It is the one supported by different behaviour next time.

This is why the next step in a repair should be realistic. Do not promise never to be angry again. Do not promise that you will always respond perfectly. Do not promise that the pattern is gone forever because you feel ashamed in this moment. Make a promise the body can learn. "I will pause before replying." "I will say I need space instead of going silent." "I will not continue by text when I am heated." "I will come back after I cool down." Small promises kept rebuild trust better than grand promises made from panic.

Repair without self-erasure is an act of emotional adulthood. It refuses the childish extremes of blame and collapse. It says, "I am responsible for what I did, and I am still allowed to have a point." It says, "Your experience matters, and so does accuracy." It says, "I can apologise without handing over my whole dignity." It says, "I can stay present after impact."

The next time you know you have handled something badly, resist the urge to either defend the whole thing or apologise yourself out of existence. Slow down. Name the behaviour.

Acknowledge the impact. State the next step. Keep the valid issue separate from the harmful delivery.

Repair what is yours.

Do not erase what is true.

Chapter 9
Daily practice for pressure moments

Why do the tools you understand so clearly in calm moments sometimes vanish when you need them most?

You know the principle. Pause before replying. Exhale before speaking. Feel your feet. Widen your field. Do not send the message from heat. Name the panic pattern. Delay the decision. These ideas may make perfect sense while reading, reflecting, or advising someone else. Then pressure rises, the body accelerates, and the old route appears before the new one has even reached for its shoes. The theory is still there somewhere, but it is not close enough to the hand.

This is not because you are careless. It is because pressure rewards what has been rehearsed. The nervous system does not reach for the most elegant idea; it reaches for the most familiar pathway. If your most familiar pathway is defending, disappearing, pleasing, checking, over-explaining, sending, or replaying, that is what will appear first under load. Insight alone is often too slow. Practice makes a tool reachable at the speed of a surge.

The central tension is therefore not knowledge versus ignorance. It is availability. A calming tool can be excellent and still fail you if it has only ever lived as a concept. The question is not whether the method is impressive on paper, but whether it can be found while the kettle boils over, the phone lights up, the meeting turns tense, the car door closes after a hard day, or the body begins its first private signal of alarm. Calm has to be trained in the places where life actually asks for it.

This matters because pressure moments are rarely generous. They do not give you a quiet room, a prepared mind, and a full hour to become regulated. They arrive while you are walking between tasks, trying to sleep, reading a message, entering a meeting, waiting for a lift, stepping through a doorway, or sitting in the car before going inside. If practice only happens in ideal conditions, it may remain trapped there. A skill practised only when you are already calm may not travel well into heat, speed, embarrassment, conflict, or panic.

The good news is that daily practice does not need to be long, solemn, or elaborate. In fact, it should not be. Long practice can become another project to avoid, another standard to fail, another arena for self-improvement theatre. Pressure skills are built through brief, repeated transitions: tension to breath, tunnel to wide, urge to pause, heat to one clean sentence, panic story to present description. Consistency beats intensity because the body learns through return. The kettle, the doorway, the notification, the car seat, the meeting room, the bedtime routine: these ordinary cues can become training grounds.

Practice also protects you from relying on motivation. Motivation is unreliable under stress. You may not feel like using a tool when anger is hot, when panic is loud, or when shame wants to hide. That is why automatic cues matter. A cue does some of the remembering for you. Sitting in the car can become the signal for a short exhale reset before re-entering home life. A notification can become the signal to feel the feet before reading. A doorway can become the signal to loosen the jaw. The aim is not to become more disciplined through force, but to design the day so the next helpful move is easier to find.

There is another kind of realism required: practice must eventually include mild stress. Not overwhelming stress. Not reckless exposure. Mild, safe friction. If every rehearsal happens when nothing is at stake, the skill may stay delicate. A small time pressure, a slightly awkward task, a mildly uncomfortable wait, a message you delay on purpose, a conversation in which you practise one breath before answering: these moments teach the body that regulation is possible while activation is present. The point is not to flood yourself. It is to train the shift within your window of tolerance, where learning can actually happen.

The path begins with one-minute rehearsal drills that fit into ordinary life rather than demanding a separate identity as a calm person. Then cues are attached to predictable moments so the body begins to associate specific triggers with specific tools. Practice becomes slightly more realistic through safe, manageable pressure, and finally the tools are refined through brief tracking: what state was present, what tool was used, what changed, and what context mattered. Over time, this becomes a personal playbook rather than a borrowed routine.

The real test of daily practice is not whether it makes you serene. It is whether, at the next pressure point, something familiar appears before the old pattern completes itself. A breath before the sentence. A wider gaze before the assumption. A pause before the message. A small delay before the decision. So the question now is practical and exact: what can you rehearse in one ordinary minute today that your future self will need in one difficult minute later?

One-minute rehearsal drills

Calm under pressure is not summoned. It is rehearsed.

This is an uncomfortable truth for people who prefer insight to repetition. Insight feels intelligent. Repetition can feel embarrassingly simple. You may understand exactly why a pause helps, why breath should come before speech, why attention needs widening, why a message should wait, and why panic should be named rather than chased. Yet under pressure, the body does not search its library of elegant ideas. It reaches for what has been practised.

That is why one-minute rehearsal drills matter. They are not grand acts of self-improvement. They are small rehearsals of the exact transitions you will need when the moment becomes heated: from tension to breath, from tunnel vision to wider attention, from urge to pause, from panic story to present fact, from immediate reply to deliberate delay. These transitions are the real skill. The tool itself is often simple. Remembering it at the right moment is the hard part.

A rehearsal drill is deliberately brief because pressure skills must fit into ordinary life. If a method requires a perfect setting, quiet music, a long uninterrupted stretch, and a mood of spiritual readiness, it will not help much when the kettle is boiling, the phone lights up, the meeting turns sharp, or someone says the sentence that catches you in the ribs. Real tools must be practised where real surges begin: in kitchens, cars, corridors, queues, desks, bathrooms, doorways, train platforms, and the small spaces between one demand and the next.

The first drill is the tension-to-breath drill.

Choose an ordinary moment when your body is mildly activated or simply moving quickly. Waiting for the kettle is ideal because the time is short and contained. Stand still. Notice one place where the body is holding effort: jaw, shoulders, hands, chest, stomach, forehead. Do not analyse it. Do not ask why it is there. Simply notice: "jaw tight," "hands gripping," "shoulders lifted." Then let one exhale become a little longer than the inhale. Keep it comfortable. Let the next breath be ordinary. Repeat once if it feels natural.

The purpose is not to become deeply calm beside a kettle. The purpose is to train the sequence: notice tension, soften breath, continue. Under pressure, this is exactly what you will need. The jaw tightens before a sharp reply. The chest tightens before panic adds a story. The shoulders lift before stress turns into hurry. Practising in low-stakes moments teaches the body that tension is not merely something to endure; it is a cue.

The second drill is the tunnel-to-wide drill.

Choose a neutral object in front of you: a mug, a door handle, a book, a screen, a chair. Look at it directly for a moment. Then soften your gaze and allow the surrounding space to come into awareness. Notice the edges of the room, the colours nearby, the space to the left and right, the light, the background. Do not turn this into a complex visual exercise. The shift is simple: from one point to the wider field.

This drill matters because emotional surges narrow attention. A difficult message becomes the whole world. A sensation becomes the whole body. A criticism becomes the whole relationship. By practising widening when nothing is wrong, you create familiarity with the movement of attention itself. Later, when the mind locks onto a threat target, the body has already learnt that attention can move.

The third drill is the urge-to-pause drill.

This is best practised with small, harmless urges. The urge to check your phone. The urge to interrupt a programme with another task. The urge to answer a non-urgent message immediately. The urge to fill a quiet moment with scrolling. When the urge appears, do not fight it dramatically. Simply insert one clean pause before acting. Feel your feet. Exhale once. Say silently, "Not yet." Then choose whether to continue with the action.

The power of this drill is that it separates urge from obedience. You may still check the phone. You may still send the message later. The victory is not in refusing every urge; it is in proving that an urge can be noticed before it becomes behaviour. This is the same muscle you will need when the urge is stronger: to accuse, confess, apologise too quickly, leave abruptly, send a heated reply, demand reassurance, or force a decision.

The fourth drill is the hands-off-send drill.

Open a blank note or an unsent draft. Write one sentence you might send when mildly irritated or rushed. It does not need to be serious. Then practise stopping before completion. Put the phone down. Let your hands leave the device. Take one exhale. Look away from the screen and name one neutral object nearby. Then return and decide whether anything needs sending at all.

This may sound too artificial, but it trains a vital barrier. Many people do not lose choice at the moment of deep reflection; they lose it at the moment their thumbs are already moving. The hands become the delivery system for the surge. Practising the physical act of stopping before sending makes delay more available when the emotional charge is real.

The fifth drill is the one-sentence pause drill.

Say aloud, in a normal voice, one phrase you can use when pressure rises: "I need a minute." "I want to answer well." "I am too heated to discuss this carefully." "Let me think before I respond." "I have read this, and I will reply later." The words should sound like you. If they feel stiff or theatrical, change them. A script that feels unnatural in practice will be unreachable in conflict.

Repeat the phrase once or twice during an ordinary transition: before entering a room, before starting work, before sitting in the car, before opening your laptop. The aim is not to create a performance. It is to make the phrase physically familiar. Under anger, panic, or stress, the mouth often reaches for its oldest language. Rehearsal gives it another option.

The sixth drill is the present-fact drill.

This is especially useful for panic-prone moments. At a neutral time, practise naming what is happening in direct, concrete language. "My feet are on the floor." "My hand is on the table." "The room is quiet." "My chest feels tight." "I am standing by the door." The key is to avoid interpretation. Do not move from "my chest feels tight" to "something is wrong." Do not move from "they have not replied" to "they are angry." Stay with the fact.

This drill trains the mind to describe before it predicts. Panic and stress often escalate because sensation becomes story too quickly. The body feels strange, and the mind declares danger. A message is delayed, and the mind declares rejection. Practising present facts when calm gives you a simpler route when the body is loud: describe what is happening now before believing what fear says it means.

The seventh drill is the recovery drill.

After any mild irritation, awkward moment, hurried task, or small disappointment, practise ending the state. Feel both feet. Exhale. Unclench the hands. Look around and name one ordinary next action: "wash the cup," "open the document," "walk to the car," "reply later," "make tea." This trains the body not to carry small surges forward. It is the daily version of downshifting after conflict.

Many people practise only the beginning of regulation and forget the ending. They notice stress, breathe, and then go straight back to mental replay. Recovery drills teach completion. The body learns that activation can rise, be met, and then release into the next ordinary action. That is not dramatic. It is exactly what pressure moments require.

The best rehearsal drills are attached to existing routines. Do not wait to feel inspired. Link the practice to something already happening: boiling the kettle, brushing your teeth, waiting for a lift, opening a laptop, sitting in the car, standing at a doorway, washing hands, putting on shoes, closing a front door, reading a notification. These small anchors make practice more likely because the cue does some of the remembering.

A kettle-boiling practice might be: notice tension, exhale slowly, widen the gaze to the whole kitchen.

A doorway practice might be: pause, feel feet, loosen jaw before entering.

A notification practice might be: exhale before opening, read once, do not reply until both feet are on the floor.

A car practice might be: sit before getting out, soften the exhale, let the day behind you stay behind you for one breath.

A lift-waiting practice might be: feel the soles of the feet, name one neutral object, release the hands.

These are not rituals for their own sake. They are rehearsals of state change.

Consistency beats intensity because the body trusts what it has met often. A single long practice session may feel satisfying, but it may not be as useful as several tiny repetitions woven through the day. Emotional pressure does not ask whether you once practised beautifully for half an hour. It asks whether, in this sharp second, your body recognises the next move.

Keep the drills small enough that you cannot easily fail them. This is important. Many people turn practice into another standard of perfection. They decide they must breathe exactly, ground deeply, widen fully, track thoroughly, and feel transformed. Then they avoid practice because it has become heavy. A one-minute drill should be almost too simple. One breath. One cue. One phrase. One widened gaze. One delayed reply. The modesty is the design.

The point is not to practise calm as a mood. The point is to practise transitions. You may begin tense and end only slightly less tense. That counts. You may begin rushed and end only slightly slower. That counts. You may begin irritated and still feel irritated, but with one less sharp sentence forming. That counts. The measure is not whether the feeling disappears. The measure is whether choice becomes a little more available.

There will be days when practice feels pointless. Do it anyway, gently. Not with grim discipline, but with respect for how humans learn. You are not trying to become a person who never surges. You are teaching your system to recognise the route back earlier. Rehearsal is how a tool moves from interesting idea to available action.

One warning: do not practise by overwhelming yourself. Low-stakes does not mean meaningless, but it does mean safe. Use mild tension, not full distress. Use ordinary irritation, not the biggest wound. Use a non-urgent message, not the most emotionally loaded one. The body learns best when there is enough activation to make the practice real and enough safety to make learning possible.

A useful question after any drill is: "What transition did I just practise?"

Not "Did I become calm?" Not "Was I good at this?" The question is more precise. Did I practise tension to breath? Tunnel to wide? Urge to pause? Story to fact? Impact to recovery? When you know the transition, practice becomes purposeful. You are no longer collecting random techniques. You are training the exact movements that interrupt escalation.

Over time, one-minute drills create a quiet confidence. Not the brittle confidence that says, "I will never react badly again." A better confidence: "I know the first move back." That is enough. Under pressure, you do not need the whole path immediately. You need the first move. Then the next.

The next time the kettle boils, the lift takes too long, the car engine stops, the phone lights up, or you reach a doorway, use the minute. Feel the cue. Practise the transition. Do it without ceremony.

The difficult moment later will not care how impressive your practice looked.

It will care whether your body remembers.

Building automatic cues

A tool is only useful if you can remember it while the surge is rising.

This is the weakness in many calming plans. They depend on a version of you who is already thoughtful enough to pause, organised enough to choose, and steady enough to recall the right technique at the right moment. But pressure does not usually meet you in that state. It meets you while your phone lights up, while you are halfway through a doorway, while someone is waiting for an answer, while you are tired in the car, while the meeting has turned awkward, while your body has already begun to accelerate.

In those moments, memory is not neutral. The mind does not politely open a menu of healthy options. It reaches for the path it knows best. If the familiar path is immediate reply, that is where the hand goes. If the familiar path is over-explaining, the mouth begins. If the familiar path is checking, the attention narrows. If the familiar path is withdrawal, the body disappears before the relationship knows where you have gone. Under pressure, familiarity often beats intention.

Automatic cues solve part of this problem by moving the remembering out of pure willpower and into the environment.

A cue is a small, predictable signal that tells the body what to do next. It can be a notification, a doorway, a seatbelt, a meeting link, a kettle, a bathroom mirror, a bedtime lamp, a front door key, a lift button, or the moment your hand touches the phone. The cue matters because it appears before the surge has fully taken over. Instead of waiting for emotional maturity to arrive in the heat of the moment, you build a link in advance: when this happens, I do that.

This is not mechanical living. It is intelligent design.

Most people already live by cues. A phone buzzes and the hand reaches. A certain tone of voice appears and the body defends. A meeting begins and the shoulders tighten. Bedtime comes and the mind starts reviewing the day. A car journey ends and the person carries work stress straight through the front door. These cue-response patterns are not chosen afresh each time. They are learned. The task is not to become free of cues, but to choose better ones and attach better responses.

The simplest structure is an if-then plan. If this cue appears, then I do this small tool. The power is in its plainness. If I see a notification from someone who activates me, then I feel both feet before opening it. If I sit in the car after work, then I take a twenty-second exhale reset before going inside. If I walk through the door into a meeting, then I loosen my jaw and widen my gaze. If I begin typing while angry, then I remove the recipient and draft elsewhere. If I get into bed and my mind starts replaying, then I name one next action for tomorrow and close the loop.

The cue does not need to be dramatic. In fact, the best cues are ordinary because they happen often enough to train the body. Doorways are excellent because life is full of thresholds. A doorway can become a reminder to pause before entering the next emotional space. Before walking into the kitchen after a hard call, breathe out. Before entering a meeting, soften the shoulders. Before returning to a difficult conversation, feel the floor. The doorway says, "Do not carry the last room unchanged into this one."

Notifications are another powerful cue because they so often trigger instant stories. A message arrives and the mind fills in tone, intention, urgency, threat, rejection, demand, or judgement before the text has even been read carefully. If your automatic cue is "notification equals immediate opening," you have already given the device control of your state. A better cue is: notification equals exhale first. Not reply first. Not interpret first. Exhale first.

This small barrier matters. It teaches the body that a message is not a summons. It may still need attention. It may even need a firm answer. But it does not deserve automatic access to your nervous system. A single breath before opening the message may be enough to reduce the speed of interpretation. A hand on the table before replying may be enough to prevent the thumbs from becoming the surge's delivery system.

Meetings need their own cues because work pressure often hides inside competence. You may appear composed while the body is braced, the breath high, the jaw tight, and the mind preparing defences before anyone has challenged you. A meeting cue might be the moment you click the link, sit down, open the notebook, or hear someone say your name. The linked action should be discreet: feet on the floor, one softer exhale, gaze widened to include the room, pen resting in the hand rather than gripped. Nothing theatrical. Nothing that announces itself. Just a private reset before status pressure begins choosing your tone.

Commuting and car moments are especially useful for cue-building because they sit between roles. The car, bus, train, walk, or short journey is often where one part of life leaks into another. Work irritation comes home. Family tension enters the school run. An argument follows you into errands. A car cue can become a boundary between states. When the engine stops, do not immediately get out. Sit for one short reset. Let the exhale lengthen. Unclench the hands from the wheel. Ask, "What state am I about to bring through the door?" Then choose one small adjustment before moving.

Bedtime cues matter because the mind often mistakes darkness and quiet for an invitation to reopen every unfinished file. The body is tired, defences are lower, and rumination can become strangely persuasive. A bedtime cue might be switching off the lamp, placing the phone away from the bed, brushing teeth, or touching the pillow. The linked response should not be a full life review. It should be brief closure: one sentence naming what is unfinished, one next step if needed, and a clear refusal to hold court at night. "This can wait until morning" is not avoidance when morning will think better.

The best automatic cues are tied to your actual escalation map. Generic cues are helpful, but personal cues are stronger. If you know that you over-explain when criticised, the cue might be hearing feedback begin. The response: exhale, listen to the full sentence, ask one question before defending. If you know that panic begins with breath-checking, the cue might be the first urge to test your breathing. The response: feet, soft exhale, eyes on the room. If you know that anger becomes digital, the cue might be the first draft of a long reply. The response: remove recipient, save, wait.

This is where automatic cues become more than habits. They become personalised interruption points.

The cue should appear as early as possible in the sequence. Many people choose cues that arrive too late: after they are already shouting, after the message is sent, after the panic loop is active, after the rumination has consumed an hour. Those later cues can still help, but early cues are more powerful. Look for the small hinge: hand touching phone, jaw tightening, opening the email app, stepping into the room, sitting in the driver's seat, hearing a certain phrase, noticing the first "what if." That is where the new pattern belongs.

The linked action must be tiny. This is non-negotiable. Under pressure, the body will not reliably perform an elaborate routine. It may perform one breath. One phrase. One grounding point. One delayed send. One widened gaze. One hand off the phone. One sentence: "I need a minute." If the action is too large, the surge will reject it. A cue works best when the response is so small that it can slip in before resistance has time to argue.

A useful automatic cue has three qualities: it is specific, frequent, and realistic.

Specific means you know exactly when it happens. "When I feel stressed" is too vague. "When I open my inbox" is clearer. "When I get angry" is too broad. "When I notice myself typing fast" is usable. "When I feel panic" may be too late. "When I first check my breath" is sharper.

Frequent means the cue appears often enough to train. A once-a-year crisis is not a good starting cue. Doorways, phones, meetings, meals, car seats, kettles, lifts, and bedtime are better because they repeat.

Realistic means the response fits the setting. You may not close your eyes and breathe visibly in a tense meeting, but you can soften your exhale while looking at your notes. You may not be able to leave a conversation immediately, but you can say, "Give me a second." You may not stop every notification, but you can stop replying from the first rush.

The goal is effortless recall. Not effortless calm. Recall.

There is a difference. You may still feel angry, anxious, rushed, ashamed, or panicked. The cue does not erase the state. It helps the next helpful move appear sooner. A notification arrives and the exhale happens before interpretation. A doorway appears and the jaw loosens before you enter. The car stops and you reset before carrying work inside. The meeting begins and the feet find the floor. These movements are small, but they interrupt the old automatic chain.

At first, the cue may feel artificial. That is normal. New patterns often feel staged before they feel natural. You may forget often. You may remember after the fact. You may think of the cue only once the message is already sent or the argument already underway. Do not turn this into another reason for self-criticism. Each late remembering is still data. It tells you where the cue needs to move earlier.

For example, if you keep remembering to pause only after you have opened a difficult message, move the cue back to the notification itself. If you remember only after replying sharply, move the cue back to the first tightness in the jaw or the first speed in the fingers. If you remember only after ruminating in bed, move the cue back to putting the phone on charge or turning off the light. Automatic cues are refined by honest observation, not by perfection.

There is also value in pairing cues with physical objects. A mug can become a reminder to exhale before speaking in the morning. A notebook can become a meeting anchor: hand on cover, feet on floor, listen before answering. A front door key can become a transition cue: before turning the key, release the day by one breath. A phone case can become a digital delay cue: feel the texture before opening a tense message. Objects help because they make the cue tangible.

Do not create too many cues at once. That is how practice becomes clutter. Choose two or three high-value cues connected to your most common pressure moments. Perhaps notifications, car stops, and bedtime. Or doorways, meetings, and the first urge to over-explain. Train those until they feel familiar. Then add more if needed. Reliability matters more than variety.

The strongest cue plans are written in plain language. "If I sit in the car after work, then I will do a twenty-second exhale reset before getting out." "If I receive a difficult message, then I will put both feet on the floor before replying." "If I feel the urge to explain more than once, then I will pause and ask, 'What is the main sentence?'" "If I enter a meeting, then I will widen my gaze before speaking." Plain language keeps the plan usable when the mind is crowded.

The twenty-second car reset is a good example because it is both short and meaningful. The cue is sitting in the car before transition. The action is one small downshift: hands resting, shoulders dropping, a comfortable exhale longer than the inhale, eyes noticing the space around you. The outcome is not instant peace. The outcome is that the next room receives a slightly less charged version of you. That is enough to matter.

Automatic cues also help with self-trust. Each time you follow a cue, even imperfectly, you teach yourself that you do not have to wait for crisis to practise. You become less dependent on last-minute heroics. The body begins to recognise certain moments as invitations to reset. Over time, the gap between cue and helpful action shortens. The old pattern may still appear, but it has competition.

This is how calm becomes more available: not through one impressive breakthrough, but through many small agreements kept with yourself.

A cue is a promise made in advance to a future pressured self. It says, "When you are busy, I will help you remember. When you are heated, I will not ask you to invent the whole plan. When you are frightened, I will give you one familiar next move." That is not weakness. It is respect for how pressure works.

The next step is simple. Choose one recurring moment in your day that often carries stress, speed, anger, panic, or rumination. Attach one small tool to it. Keep the cue clear. Keep the action tiny. Practise until the cue begins to do the remembering for you.

The surge will still speak.

But now, something else will answer before it finishes the sentence.

Practising with mild stress

Practice that only works when you are already calm is not enough.

This is where many people become confused. They practise a breath reset in a quiet room and it feels manageable. They widen their gaze while sitting alone and it makes sense. They rehearse a pause phrase when nobody is challenging them and the words sound clear. Then a real pressure moment arrives: a tense message, a sharp tone, a crowded queue, a deadline, a body sensation that feels alarming. The tool suddenly feels far away. It has not failed. It has simply not yet been trained under conditions that resemble the moment in which it is needed.

Calm skills need transfer. They must travel from the low-stakes world of practice into the higher-stakes world of life. That transfer does not happen through understanding alone. It happens when the body learns, through repeated experience, that it can shift state while some activation is present. Not overwhelming activation. Not panic at full volume. Not the most painful argument in your life. Mild, safe, controlled stress.

This matters because the body learns differently under pressure. A tool practised in perfect peace may become associated with perfect peace. That is pleasant, but limited.

The aim is to teach the nervous system a more useful lesson: I can feel a little rushed and still exhale. I can feel mildly embarrassed and still stay present. I can feel an urge to reply and still pause. I can feel discomfort in the body and still avoid turning it into a catastrophe. I can feel the beginning of heat and still choose the next move.

Mild stress is the training ground between theory and crisis.

The key word is *mild*. This is not about deliberately overwhelming yourself to prove strength. Overwhelming practice teaches the body overwhelm, not skill. If you push too far, the old patterns take over: fight, flight, freeze, please, check, explain, escape, collapse. Learning becomes harder because survival mode has taken the seat. The useful practice zone is uncomfortable enough to be real and safe enough that choice remains available.

Think of it as adding a small weight to a movement you already know. You are not trying to lift the heaviest thing in the room. You are training the transition. Under mild stress, the tool must do its real job: interrupt speed, widen attention, soften physical pressure, delay the impulse, and return you to one small safe action. If the stress is too low, the practice may not transfer. If the stress is too high, the body may not learn. The middle is where skill grows.

One simple way to practise is with gentle time pressure. Choose an ordinary task and give it a light boundary: tidying one surface before the kettle finishes boiling, replying to a simple message after taking one breath, organising a bag before leaving, choosing clothes without spiralling into unnecessary decisions. The aim is not to rush. The aim is to notice the first signs of hurry and practise slowing the body while continuing the task.

Time pressure reveals a great deal. The breath shortens. The hands move faster. The mind begins saying, "Come on, come on." The body mistakes speed for effectiveness. This is the moment to practise. Feel the feet. Let the exhale lengthen. Widen the gaze. Continue, but at a pace that still belongs to you. You are teaching the system that urgency does not automatically get to set the rhythm.

Another useful form of mild stress is awkwardness. Not humiliation. Not social risk that feels too large. Just ordinary awkwardness: asking a simple question in a shop, saying "I need a moment" before answering, letting a silence sit for a few seconds, making a small request, declining something minor, or admitting, "I will have to check and come back to you." Awkwardness is excellent practice because many surges are driven by the fear of how a moment feels socially.

A person who cannot tolerate mild awkwardness will often over-explain, agree too quickly, apologise excessively, or rush to fill silence. Practising with small awkward moments builds tolerance. You learn that discomfort can be present without needing immediate repair. You learn that a pause is survivable. You learn that not everyone has to be soothed instantly. You learn that your body may complain, but complaint is not command.

Gentle physical discomfort can also become practice, provided it is safe and sensible. Standing in a short queue without checking your phone. Waiting a few extra seconds before opening a notification. Sitting with a mild urge to fidget before moving. Taking a slow walk without filling every moment with audio. Holding a cool glass and noticing the sensation without turning it into a problem. These small discomforts help you practise staying present without needing instant escape.

The point is not to become tough in a harsh way. Toughness is often overrated. The better quality is steadiness. Steadiness says, "This is uncomfortable, and I can stay with it for a moment." That moment is the seed of the 60-second calm. Panic, anger, and stress all push towards immediate action.

Mild discomfort practice teaches the body that immediate action is not always required.

Digital triggers are particularly useful for mild stress practice because they happen often and they carry clear action urges. A notification appears. The hand wants to open it. A message lands. The mind wants to interpret tone. A thread goes quiet. The body wants to check again. Instead of waiting for the most charged message, practise with ordinary ones. See the notification. Exhale. Feel both feet. Wait a few seconds before opening. Read once. Do not reply until the body has settled into the chair.

This is not about becoming unavailable or artificially distant. It is about breaking the automatic chain between stimulus and response. If you practise delay with low-stakes messages, delay becomes more available when a high-stakes message arrives. The body recognises the sequence: notification, breath, feet, read, pause, choose. Without practice, the sequence may be: notification, story, surge, reply, regret.

Mild stress can also be added to conversation practice. Choose low-risk moments to rehearse one clean pause before speaking. When someone asks a question, take one breath before answering. When you disagree mildly, say so without padding the sentence with unnecessary apology. When you feel the urge to interrupt, let the other person finish one more sentence. When you feel the urge to explain in detail, give the shorter version first.

These practices may seem ordinary, but they target the exact muscles needed in conflict. Listening while activated. Pausing while a reply is ready. Staying with mild disagreement. Letting someone misunderstand briefly without flooding them with explanation. Speaking clearly without over-softening. These are not abstract emotional skills. They are behavioural rehearsals for pressure.

Another useful drill is the "controlled delay" practice. Choose a harmless desire and wait briefly before meeting it. Not as punishment. As training. Wait before checking the phone. Wait before correcting a small detail. Wait before opening another browser tab. Wait before asking for reassurance about something minor. While waiting, notice what happens in the body. Does urgency rise? Does irritation appear? Does the mind argue that the wait is pointless? Good. That is the practice.

The goal is not denial. You may still take the action. The learning is in the gap. You are proving to the nervous system that an urge can rise, remain present, and not immediately rule the body. This has direct relevance to stronger moments: the urge to accuse, the urge to flee, the urge to send, the urge to check symptoms, the urge to apologise yourself away, the urge to decide everything now.

Practice with mild stress should always include a recovery step. This is where many people get it wrong. They add challenge, then leave the body activated. A complete practice has a beginning, a stressor, a tool, and a downshift. After the mild stress, feel the feet, exhale, widen the room, and name the ordinary next action. This teaches the body that activation has an ending. Without recovery, practice can become agitation.

For example, if you practise waiting before opening a message, finish by placing the phone down and taking one soft exhale. If you practise speaking a small boundary, finish by noticing your hands and relaxing the jaw. If you practise standing in a queue without escaping into your phone, finish by naming one neutral object and moving on with the next task. The body needs the full pattern: rise, regulate, return.

The practice should stay inside your window of tolerance. This phrase simply means the zone where you are activated enough to learn but not so overwhelmed that you lose access to choice. You can recognise when you are inside it because you still have some awareness of the room, some ability to breathe, some capacity to choose, and some sense that the practice is difficult but manageable. You may feel discomfort, but not collapse. You may feel urgency, but not total compulsion.

When you are outside that zone, the signs are different. You may feel flooded, frozen, panicked, enraged, unreal, unable to think, or driven by an overwhelming need to escape, attack, confess, check, or shut down. That is not the time to intensify practice. That is the time to reduce demand, ground, seek support if needed, and return to safety. Good training respects limits. It does not glorify pushing through.

This is especially important for people with strong panic patterns. Practising with mild stress does not mean provoking panic deliberately or testing whether you can endure frightening sensations. It means working at the edge of manageable activation: a short wait, a small uncertainty, a gentle physical cue, a low-stakes public moment, a brief delay in reassurance. The aim is to build confidence without teaching the body that practice itself is dangerous.

For anger, mild stress practice may involve small frustrations: a slow-loading page, a minor interruption, a household task done imperfectly, a delayed reply, a plan changing slightly. These are moments where anger heat may flicker but not blaze. Practise the pause-breath. Practise unclenching the hands. Practise one clean sentence instead of a muttered complaint. Practise not turning a minor irritation into a character judgement.

For stress, mild practice may involve doing less while the body wants to do more. Leave a non-urgent task unfinished for a short, planned period. Take a breath before switching tasks. Stop midway through rushing and deliberately slow the next movement. Say, "Not everything at once." The body may protest because stress often equates speed with control. The practice teaches a different association: steadiness can also be effective.

For shame or social discomfort, mild practice may involve allowing a small imperfection to remain visible. Sending a brief message without over-editing. Asking someone to repeat themselves. Admitting you do not know something. Letting a pause exist. These moments train the body not to treat embarrassment as emergency. They are small acts of freedom.

The practice must remain humane. You are not designing traps for yourself. You are not trying to prove that you can tolerate anything. You are not trying to become immune to discomfort. You are training recoverable discomfort. That phrase is important. Recoverable discomfort is the kind you can enter, meet with a tool, and come down from afterwards. It leaves you more confident, not more sensitised.

A useful rule is to finish practice feeling steadier than you began, or at least not more threatened. If you finish agitated, ashamed, or flooded, the stress was too much or the recovery step was missing. Make it smaller next time. Smaller is not failure. Smaller is intelligent adjustment. The nervous system does not learn well from being bullied.

Practising with mild stress also reveals which tools actually work for you. Some people discover that breath helps with anger but not with panic unless paired with grounding. Some discover that widening attention works better than self-talk. Some discover that digital delay is their strongest intervention. Some discover that scripts matter more than body techniques in conflict. Practice turns theory into evidence.

That evidence should guide your personal plan. Do not keep using a tool simply because it sounds impressive. Use what changes your state or protects your next action. If a technique makes you tense, simplify it. If a cue is too late, move it earlier.

If a stressor overwhelms you, reduce it. If a practice works in private but not in public, adapt it until it fits real settings. The body is not interested in elegance. It is interested in what is repeatable.

One small weekly pattern can be enough: choose a mild stressor, choose one tool, practise for one minute, recover, and note what happened. That is all. The aim is not to create a demanding programme. The aim is to keep training the gap between activation and action. Over time, the gap becomes more familiar. Under real pressure, familiar matters.

The deepest benefit of mild stress practice is that it changes your relationship with activation. Instead of treating every rise in the body as a problem, you begin to recognise it as a training cue. A little hurry. A little heat. A little awkwardness. A little uncertainty. A little urge. These are not failures of calm. They are opportunities to practise returning to choice before the stakes are high.

That shift is powerful.

The next time you feel mild stress, do not waste it. Do not wait for the perfect calm moment to practise calm. Use the small rise. Notice the cue. Apply one tool. Downshift afterwards. Let the body learn the truth it will need later: activation can be present, and choice can still remain.

Tracking what actually works

A calming tool earns its place by what it does in a real moment, not by how good it sounds in theory.

This is where many people lose time. They collect techniques as if a larger toolkit automatically means a calmer life. One breath pattern, three grounding methods, a handful of scripts, a digital delay rule, a panic phrase, a recovery sequence, a journalling habit, a posture reset, a visualisation, a walking practice. The list becomes impressive. Then pressure rises, and the person still does not know which tool to use, when to use it, or whether it has ever helped in the moments that matter most.

A toolkit is only useful when it becomes personal.

Not every method fits every nervous system. Not every tool fits every context. A breathing technique that works beautifully for anger may feel unhelpful during panic. A grounding method that helps in public may do very little during a late-night rumination loop. A pause script that works with a colleague may sound too formal with a partner. A delay rule that protects you from reactive emails may not help if your main pattern is shutting down and avoiding repair. Calm becomes more reliable when you stop asking, "What is the best tool?" and begin asking, "What actually works for me, in this state, in this setting?"

Tracking is the way you answer that question without guesswork.

This does not mean turning your emotional life into a spreadsheet of self-improvement. It does not require long entries, elaborate mood ratings, or an evening audit of every breath you took badly. Over-tracking can become another form of pressure, and pressure is exactly what this work is trying to reduce. The best tracking is brief, practical, and almost plain enough to feel unimpressive. It records what happened, what you tried, what changed, and what you might adjust next time.

The purpose is pattern recognition.

During a surge, the mind often becomes dramatic. Afterwards, memory can become equally unreliable. You may decide that nothing helped because you still felt uncomfortable. You may decide that a tool failed because it did not make the feeling disappear. You may overlook small progress because the old regret is louder. Or you may keep using a familiar strategy because it feels natural, even though it consistently leaves you more activated. Tracking cuts through these distortions. It gives you evidence.

The first thing to record is the state. Not the full story. The state.

Was it anger heat, panic, stress rush, shame collapse, shutdown, rumination, digital urgency, social awkwardness, or post-conflict residue? Use ordinary words. "Angry after message." "Panic in shop." "Rushed before meeting." "Replay after argument." "Tense after call." The label should be short enough that you would actually write it. You are not creating a psychological report. You are naming the weather.

The second thing to record is the cue. What told you the surge had begun?

This may be a body cue: jaw tight, chest tight, face hot, breath held, hands restless, stomach drop, shoulders lifted. It may be an attention cue: staring at the message, replaying one sentence, scanning symptoms, imagining worst-case outcomes. It may be an impulse cue: reply now, leave, apologise, accuse, check, explain, confess, fix, decide. The cue matters because it shows you where the intervention could begin earlier next time.

The third thing to record is the tool you used.

Be specific. "Breathing" is too vague. "Longer exhale before replying" is better. "Grounding" is too broad. "Feet on floor, named three objects" is clearer. "Paused" is useful, but "said, 'I need a minute'" is stronger. "Delayed message" becomes more useful as "drafted in notes, waited twenty minutes, then shortened reply." Specific tracking shows which version of a tool actually helped.

The fourth thing to record is the outcome.

This is where the standard must be humane. The question is not, "Did I become calm?" That is too high and too crude. Better questions are: did the intensity drop at all? Did I avoid making it worse? Did I delay the action? Did I speak more cleanly? Did I stop checking? Did I recover faster? Did I repair without collapsing? Did I keep the message unsent until I could review it? Did I return to the day sooner than usual?

A tool can work even when discomfort remains.

This is one of the most important lessons tracking can teach. If you were angry and still angry afterwards, but you did not send the damaging reply, that tool worked. If you were panicked and still uncomfortable, but you stopped chasing the perfect breath and grounded through your hands, that tool worked. If you were ashamed and still uneasy, but you repaired one behaviour without apologising for your entire existence, that tool worked. Calm is not always the disappearance of feeling. Sometimes it is the weakening of the feeling's control over behaviour.

The fifth thing to record is context.

Context explains why a tool worked in one situation and not another. Were you tired, hungry, overstimulated, alone, in public, under time pressure, with a particular person, late at night, after several difficult moments, or already holding stress from elsewhere? Context prevents self-blame. A tool that usually helps may struggle when you are exhausted. A pause script may be harder with someone who presses for immediate answers. A breath reset may need grounding alongside it when panic is strong. Context lets you adjust intelligently instead of declaring yourself hopeless.

A simple tracking line might look like this: "State: anger after text. Cue: hot face, typing fast. Tool: wrote in notes, phone down, waited. Outcome: still annoyed, but sent shorter reply later. Context: tired after work."

That is enough.

Another might be: "State: panic in queue. Cue: chest tight, urge to leave. Tool: feet, cold bottle, named objects. Outcome: fear stayed but did not bolt. Context: crowded, hungry."

Or: "State: rumination after call. Cue: replaying same sentence. Tool: named lesson, scheduled reply tomorrow, washed cup. Outcome: loop returned twice, but shorter. Context: late evening."

This kind of tracking creates a personal playbook. Over time, patterns become visible. You may learn that exhale resets help with anger but not panic unless paired with texture. You may discover that you need a digital delay rule after work because tiredness makes messages feel more threatening. You may notice that rumination is worse at bedtime and needs a strict "review tomorrow" cue. You may find that safe pause scripts work only if you practise them aloud beforehand. You may realise that your best tool is not the most elegant one, but the one you actually use early.

Tracking also exposes tools that are not helping.

This is just as valuable. Perhaps "taking space" often becomes withdrawal because you do not return. Perhaps "explaining" becomes over-explaining and leaves you more activated. Perhaps "checking in" with someone becomes repeated reassurance-seeking. Perhaps "deep breathing" makes panic more intense because you start monitoring your breath. Perhaps "processing" becomes rumination. Tracking shows when a supposed solution is really the surge in a smarter outfit.

The honest question is: what happens after I use this?

If the answer is more urgency, more checking, more heat, more shame, more words, more compulsion, or more distance, the tool may need changing. Not because you failed it, but because it is not doing the job in that state. A good calming plan is not loyal to methods. It is loyal to outcomes.

Tracking should also notice partial wins.

Partial wins are the foundation of real change. You noticed the cue later than you wanted, but earlier than last time. You still snapped, but repaired sooner. You still checked your symptoms, but stopped after one round instead of ten. You still wrote the angry message, but did not send it. You still ruminated, but closed the loop after several minutes instead of losing the evening. These are not tiny scraps. They are evidence that the sequence is becoming more interruptible.

The old perfection standard says, "If I still reacted, I failed."

The better standard says, "Where did choice return?"

That question changes the whole tone of review. It keeps you looking for leverage rather than verdicts. Maybe choice returned after the first sharp sentence. Maybe after the message was drafted but before it was sent. Maybe after ten minutes of panic. Maybe after the conflict, when you chose repair. Wherever choice returned, that is a place to strengthen.

A useful weekly review can be very short. Look at a few tracking notes and ask: what state appeared most often? Which cue showed up earliest? Which tool helped most reliably? Which tool did I avoid using? What context made surges stronger? What is one adjustment for next week? Then stop. The stopping matters. Review should produce a next step, not an endless investigation into your flaws.

One adjustment is enough.

Perhaps the adjustment is: "When I receive a difficult message after work, I will not reply for twenty minutes." Or: "When panic starts with breath checking, I will use feet and hands before breath." Or: "When I need space in conflict, I will give a return time." Or: "When I ruminate at night, I will write one lesson and postpone the rest." Small adjustments are easier to practise and easier to evaluate. A vague promise to "handle things better" is not a plan. A specific cue-tool pairing is.

Tracking must remain compassionate, but not vague.

Compassion without precision becomes sentimental. Precision without compassion becomes self-attack. You need both. "I was exhausted and snapped" is compassionate but incomplete if it stops there. "I snapped because I did not pause when my jaw tightened" is precise, but could become harsh if used as evidence against yourself. A balanced note sounds like: "I was exhausted, jaw tight, snapped. Next time I need a pause phrase before continuing." This gives context, responsibility, and a forward path.

There is no need to track every surge forever. The aim is not lifelong emotional bookkeeping. Tracking is most useful while you are building your personal plan, testing tools, or working through a repeated pattern. Once a tool becomes reliable, you may not need to record it often. Return to tracking when something stops working, when a new trigger appears, or when you keep getting the same regret.

A good tracking practice should make you feel more informed, not more watched.

If it starts to feel like surveillance, shrink it. Use three words. Record only strong surges. Track only one pattern for a week. Write notes on paper rather than in an app if the phone triggers checking. Use plain marks: state, tool, result. The practice should serve you. It should not become another authority to please.

The strongest tracking is done after the body has downshifted. If you write while still heated, the note may become accusation. If you write while still panicked, it may become checking. If you write while ashamed, it may become punishment. Wait until there is enough steadiness to observe. This may be ten minutes later, an hour later, or the next day. Delayed reflection is often more accurate than immediate analysis.

A simple prompt can keep the review clean: "What helped, what harmed, what next?"

What helped might be one breath, one pause phrase, one delay, one grounding point, one moment of not sending. What harmed might be over-explaining, checking, replaying, forcing breath, demanding certainty, staying in the thread too long. What next should be one small adjustment. This keeps the review practical. It stops the mind turning the event into a moral trial.

Tracking also helps you respect context-specific tools. You may need one plan for work, another for home, another for panic in public, another for digital triggers, another for bedtime rumination. This is not inconsistency. It is realism. Human beings are not the same in every setting. A tool that fits a meeting may not fit an argument in a kitchen. A tool that fits panic in a cafe may not fit stress before sleep. Your playbook should match your life, not a tidy theory of calm.

For work pressure, tracking might reveal that your earliest cue is gripping a pen before answering. Your tool becomes: pen down, exhale, ask one clarifying question.

For family conflict, tracking might reveal that your default move is over-explaining. Your tool becomes: one sentence, then pause.

For panic, tracking might reveal that breath focus alone makes you monitor symptoms. Your tool becomes: feet, cold object, eyes open, then soft exhale.

For bedtime rumination, tracking might reveal that trying to solve the issue keeps you awake. Your tool becomes: write one next step, close the notebook, return to body contact.

This is how the personal playbook is built: not from ideals, but from repeated evidence.

The playbook should be small. Under pressure, you do not need a catalogue. You need a few trusted moves. One breath reset. One grounding anchor. One pause phrase. One digital delay. One panic recognition line. One recovery sequence. Tracking helps you choose those tools by performance, not preference. It shows which tools survive contact with real life.

There will be tools you like in theory that do little in practice. Let them go. There will be tools that seem almost too simple but work repeatedly. Keep them. There will be tools that work only when used early. Move the cue earlier. There will be tools that work only when paired: breath plus feet, pause phrase plus return time, draft plus delay, grounding plus cold temperature. Refine without drama.

This is the quiet craft of self-regulation.

Not collecting more. Not blaming yourself harder. Not chasing the perfect technique. Watching carefully. Testing gently. Keeping what helps. Removing what adds pressure. Adjusting for context. Returning to practice.

The next time a pressure moment passes, resist the urge to ask only, "Was I calm?" Ask a better question: "What actually changed the next move?"

That answer is gold.

Write it down before the lesson disappears into the day.

Chapter 10
Calming with other people present

The hardest place to stay calm is often in front of another person.

Alone, you may remember the tools. You can breathe, ground, widen your field, delay the message, or let the first wave pass without having to manage anyone else's expression. But add another person and the pressure changes. Their face becomes part of the surge. Their tone becomes evidence. Their silence becomes a question. Their next sentence seems to arrive before you have recovered from the last one. You are no longer only regulating a body; you are regulating a body in relationship.

This is why conflict can accelerate so quickly. While someone else is speaking, you may stop listening and begin preparing. A counterargument forms. A defence gathers. A correction waits at the edge of your mouth. You hear one phrase, perhaps not even the whole sentence, and your attention locks onto it. The body braces, the mind builds its case, and listening quietly turns into waiting for your turn to strike. It may look like conversation from the outside, but inside it has become a contest for safety.

The central tension is that other people can both activate and steady us. A voice can sharpen the body, but a steady voice can also slow it. A boundary can raise heat, but a clean boundary can reduce confusion. A disagreement can feel threatening, but a well-held pause can keep the relationship from becoming the battleground. Calm with others present is therefore not private serenity transported into public life. It is a relational skill: the ability to remain connected enough to hear, clear enough to speak, and firm enough not to be pulled into the other person's pace.

The stakes are high because most regrettable moments do not happen in isolation. They happen across tables, in meetings, in family kitchens, at service counters, in corridors, on calls, and in the charged space between one person's nervous system and another's. A sentence spoken too quickly can invite a sharper sentence back. A boundary delivered as a lecture can become a provocation. A pause without explanation can feel like rejection. A frantic attempt to de-escalate can sound like surrender. Other people do not merely witness our surges; they are often affected by the way our surges enter the room.

This does not mean you are responsible for managing everyone else's emotions. That would be an exhausting and dishonest standard. You cannot make another person reasonable, kind, calm, receptive, or fair. You cannot breathe on their behalf. You cannot listen them into accountability if they refuse it. But you can take responsibility for the part of the exchange that travels through you: your pace, your tone, your first sentence, your willingness to pause, your refusal to escalate unnecessarily, your ability to set a limit without turning it into a punishment.

Calming with other people present requires a different kind of strength from calming alone. It is not enough to feel your feet if you immediately use your next sentence as a weapon. It is not enough to keep your voice low if your words erase your boundary. It is not enough to say you are listening while privately building a prosecution. The skill is integrated: body anchored, attention open, speech restrained, position clear. That combination is rare, but it is trainable.

The route begins with listening under pressure, because many conflicts change direction at the point where listening collapses into counterattack. From there, the work moves to boundaries that are short enough to be heard and strong enough to hold without threat or apology overload. Then comes the most misunderstood skill of all: lowering intensity without conceding the issue, staying clear about your position while refusing to feed the heat around it.

The question is not whether you can remain perfectly composed while another person is difficult. That standard belongs in fantasy. The sharper question is this: when someone else's words begin to pull your body into defence, can you stay present long enough to hear one true thing, set one clean limit, or lower the temperature without giving away what matters?

Staying calm while listening

Listening is often the first skill to collapse under pressure.

Not because people are uncaring. Not because they have nothing to learn. Listening collapses because the body begins preparing for defence before the other person has finished speaking. A phrase lands badly, a tone feels accusatory, a facial expression seems dismissive, and attention shifts from receiving meaning to building a response. You are still looking at the person. You may even be nodding. But inside, you have stopped listening and started preparing.

This is the hidden turning point in many conflicts. The conversation does not break only when someone raises their voice. It often breaks earlier, when one person hears enough to feel threatened and then stops taking in the rest. From that moment, the exchange becomes less like dialogue and more like two private arguments happening aloud. One person is trying to be understood. The other is preparing to be vindicated, protected, excused, or released from discomfort.

Staying calm while listening is therefore not passive. It is active restraint.

It requires you to hold your body steady enough that the other person's words can arrive before your defence interrupts them. It asks you to notice the inner counterattack forming and not let it seize the wheel. It asks you to remain interested in meaning while your nervous system is searching for threat. This is difficult work, and it deserves to be treated as such. Listening under pressure is not the same as listening when everyone is polite, rested, and careful. It is listening while something in you wants to fight, flee, fix, please, explain, or disappear.

The first move is to anchor the body.

You cannot listen well if the body is entirely organised around defence. The jaw tightens, the breath shortens, the shoulders brace, the hands grip, the eyes fix, and suddenly the other person's sentence has become a battlefield. A physical anchor gives attention somewhere steadier to rest while the words continue. Both feet on the floor. One hand touching the table. Fingers lightly against a cup. Back against the chair. A slow exhale while the other person is speaking. These anchors do not make you agree. They make it possible to hear.

The distinction matters. Many people fear that if they soften their body, they are surrendering their position. They imagine that calm listening means absorbing blame, accepting unfairness, or making themselves smaller. That is not listening; that is appeasement. Real listening does not require agreement. It requires enough steadiness to know what you are agreeing or disagreeing with. Without that steadiness, you may reject something the other person never meant or defend against an accusation they never made.

A useful listening anchor is simple: feet, breath, meaning.

Feet: feel the ground.

Breath: let one exhale soften.

Meaning: ask, "What are they actually trying to say?"

That last question is crucial. In conflict, people often listen for danger rather than meaning. They listen for the unfair word, the exaggerated claim, the hidden accusation, the proof that they are being blamed. The mind becomes a prosecutor. It marks every weakness in the other person's case. It prepares rebuttals. It collects evidence. It may be accurate about some details and still miss the human message beneath them.

The other person may say, "You never listen to me." Taken literally, the word "never" may be untrue. A defensive listener will seize on that. "That is not fair. I listened yesterday. I always ask what you think." The correction may contain facts, but it misses the meaning: "I do not feel heard right now." If you respond only to the exaggeration, the conversation becomes a debate about wording. If you can hear the meaning beneath the imperfect wording, the conflict has a chance to slow.

This does not mean you must accept careless language without limit. If someone keeps using "always," "never," insults, or accusations, a boundary may be needed. But there is wisdom in not correcting the first imperfect phrase too quickly. People under emotion rarely speak in courtroom-quality language. If you demand perfect wording before you listen, most human conversations will fail the test. The skill is to hear the message without becoming trapped by the roughness of the delivery.

Another helpful question is: "What part of this could be true?"

Not all of it. Not the whole accusation. One part.

This question is powerful because it prevents all-or-nothing listening. When criticised, the nervous system often hears the statement as a total verdict. If one part is unfair, the whole thing must be rejected. If one word is exaggerated, the entire point can be dismissed. But many difficult conversations contain a mixture: something unfair, something clumsy, something emotional, and something useful. A calm listener does not swallow the whole thing. A calm listener looks for the one usable piece.

Perhaps the other person's tone is sharp, but they are right that you interrupted. Perhaps their timing is poor, but the issue has been avoided. Perhaps they are upset beyond what the moment deserves, but there is a pattern you need to acknowledge. Perhaps they are wrong about your motive, but accurate about the impact. Listening well means separating these strands without rushing into defence.

One micro-skill is to let the other person finish one full thought before you respond.

This sounds basic. It is not. Under pressure, the body often wants to interrupt at the first error. The interruption may feel necessary because the mind believes the wrong idea must be corrected immediately or it will become reality. But most conversations are not legal records. Letting someone finish does not mean you accept every word. It means you are gathering enough information to respond accurately.

A full thought is not the same as an endless monologue. If someone is escalating, repeating, attacking, or overwhelming you, you may need to interrupt with a boundary. But if they are simply expressing something difficult, practise staying with the sentence until it lands fully. Feel your feet. Let your hands remain still. Notice the first impulse to cut in. Do not obey it immediately. This is where listening becomes a 60-second skill: not grand empathy, but one withheld interruption.

Another micro-skill is reflecting one point before responding.

Reflection is not parroting. It is not a therapeutic performance. It is a brief signal that you have received at least part of the message. "You are saying the timing felt disrespectful." "You felt shut out when I went quiet." "You wanted me to check with you before deciding." "You are upset that I replied so late."

These sentences do not mean, "You are entirely right." They mean, "I understand the point you are making well enough to respond to it."

This one step can lower heat because many conflicts intensify when people feel unheard. If the other person believes you are preparing a defence instead of receiving the meaning, they may repeat themselves louder, sharper, or with more force. Reflection interrupts that spiral. It says, "I am not simply waiting to strike back." That can reduce pressure without requiring surrender.

A brief example shows the difference. Someone says, "You made that decision without even thinking about how it would affect me." The reactive response is immediate defence: "That is not true. I had to decide quickly, and you know I was under pressure." That may be accurate, but it starts with self-protection. A calmer response begins with one reflected point: "You felt left out of the decision." Then, after a breath: "I can understand why that would land badly. I also want to explain the pressure I was under." The second response does not concede everything. It simply places listening before defence.

That order changes the emotional weather.

It is important to avoid fake reflection. People can sense when "I hear you" is being used as a waiting room for disagreement. If your tone says, "I am performing listening so I can now prove you wrong," the phrase will not help. Real reflection requires a small pause in the inner courtroom. You are not just repeating words. You are allowing the other person's meaning to exist for a moment without immediately pushing it away.

This is uncomfortable when you feel misunderstood. The body wants to correct the record. It wants to protect your intention. It wants to say, "That is not what I meant," "You are twisting this," "You are ignoring what I did do," or "You are making me the villain." Some of these may be important later. But if they come too early, they often sound like refusal. The other person may then escalate, and the very misunderstanding you wanted to fix becomes deeper.

Listening under pressure requires tolerating temporary incompleteness.

For a few seconds, the other person's version is in the room and yours has not yet been fully stated. That can feel unsafe. But temporary incompleteness is not injustice. It is sequence. You do not have to say everything at once. You do not have to correct every detail before acknowledging one point. You do not have to defend your entire character before hearing the impact of one behaviour.

A helpful inner phrase is: "My turn is coming."

This phrase can calm the urgency to interrupt. It reassures the defensive part of you that listening is not permanent silence. You will have a chance to speak. You can clarify. You can disagree. You can set a boundary. You can correct a false assumption. But you do not need to do it before the other person has completed a thought. The phrase creates enough patience to stay present.

Another useful phrase is: "Listen for the need, not only the wording."

Behind anger, there may be a need for respect. Behind criticism, a need for reliability. Behind hurt, a need for repair. Behind panic, a need for reassurance handled wisely. Behind frustration, a need for change. The wording may be rough because the other person is activated too. Listening for the need does not excuse poor delivery, but it helps you respond to the living issue rather than only to the surface noise.

At the same time, staying calm while listening has limits. You are not required to remain available for insults, contempt, intimidation, humiliation, or relentless accusation. Calm listening is not endurance training for mistreatment. If the other person's speech becomes harmful, the listening skill shifts into boundary-setting: "I want to hear you, but I will not continue while I am being insulted." "I can discuss this if we slow down." "I am going to pause if this continues at this volume." Good listening includes knowing when the conditions for listening have broken down.

The body can help you recognise that line. There is ordinary discomfort, and there is overload. Ordinary discomfort feels unpleasant but workable: tight chest, heat, defensiveness, an urge to interrupt, but some ability to stay present. Overload feels like losing access to choice: blankness, panic, rage, shaking, dissociation, or a strong impulse to attack or escape. If you are overloaded, listening may no longer be the right task. A safe pause may be needed before any useful conversation can continue.

When listening is possible, pace matters. Slowing your response by even one breath can prevent the conversation from becoming a duel. Let the other person finish. Exhale. Reflect one point. Then respond. This rhythm is simple but powerful: receive, breathe, reflect, speak. The breath is the hinge. Without it, your reply may come from the pressure of being accused. With it, your reply has a better chance of coming from choice.

Eye contact also needs balance. Too much fixed eye contact can feel confrontational or intensify threat. Too little can feel dismissive or evasive. A softer gaze often works better. Look at the person while they speak, but allow your field to remain wide. Notice the room, the table, the floor, your hands. This prevents their face from becoming the whole world. You remain relationally present without becoming visually trapped.

Hands are another listening anchor. If you tend to interrupt, keep your hands still. If you tend to reach for your phone, place it face down or away. If you tend to clench, rest the hands open on your lap or a surface. The hands often act before the mind has decided. By settling them, you reduce the body's readiness to fight, flee, fix, or distract. Listening is not only in the ears. It is in the posture.

The mind will still prepare responses. That is normal. Do not expect perfect inner silence. The skill is to notice preparation without letting it replace listening. When you hear your inner defence begin, silently label it: "preparing." Then return to the other person's meaning. You may need to do this several times in one conversation. That is not failure. That is the practice.

A strong listener under pressure is not someone who has no reaction. It is someone who can keep returning.

Returning to the body.

Returning to the sentence being spoken.

Returning to the meaning beneath imperfect wording.

Returning to the present exchange rather than the old argument it resembles.

Returning to choice before replying.

This returning is especially important in long-standing relationships, where the present conversation is often crowded with history. A partner's complaint may sound like every previous complaint. A parent's comment may carry years of old tone. A colleague's challenge may touch earlier experiences of being underestimated. The body may begin reacting to the archive rather than the sentence. Listening calmly means asking, "What is being said now, in this moment, by this person?" The past may matter, but it should not always be allowed to write the response.

At work, calm listening can prevent status pressure from taking over. When someone questions your work, the body may hear threat to competence. You may feel the urge to justify immediately. A better move is to reflect or clarify before defending. "You are concerned about the timeline." "You want more detail on the decision." "Are you asking about the process or the outcome?" These responses buy time and show competence rather than panic. They also prevent you from answering a question that was not actually asked.

In family conflict, listening often fails because people assume they already know what the other person means. Familiarity becomes laziness. "Here we go again." "They always say this." "I know where this is heading." Sometimes the pattern is real. But assuming too quickly can lock both people into the old roles. Calm listening asks for one fresh data point. What is the exact concern this time? What is the one sentence I can reflect before I respond? Where is the current issue different from the old pattern?

In public-facing roles, listening under pressure can reduce heat without surrendering ground. A frustrated person may need to feel that their point has landed before they can hear limits. "You have been waiting longer than expected." "You are frustrated that the information was unclear." "You wanted this resolved today." These reflections do not promise what cannot be promised. They lower the intensity enough for the boundary or next step to be heard.

This is de-escalation through accuracy. Not appeasement. Not agreement. Accuracy.

When people feel accurately heard, they may not become happy, but they often become less driven to repeat themselves with increasing force. When they feel misheard, dismissed, or corrected too quickly, they often escalate. Listening calmly is therefore practical. It saves time, preserves dignity, and protects the next sentence.

Still, you must not use listening as a way to abandon yourself. Some people become excellent listeners because they are afraid to take up space. They reflect, validate, nod, and understand until their own position disappears. That is not the aim. The aim is to listen well enough to respond well. Your view still matters. Your boundary still matters. Your truth still matters. Listening is the doorway to a cleaner response, not a substitute for having one.

A useful structure is: reflect, then position.

"You felt left out of the decision. I understand that. I also need to explain why I had to act quickly."

"You are saying my tone was sharp. I can see that. The issue I raised still matters to me."

"You want an answer now. I hear that. I need time before I decide."

This structure reduces defensiveness because it proves reception before assertion. It also prevents self-erasure because your position is still named. Calm listening is strongest when paired with clear speech.

The next time you are listening and feel the counterattack forming, treat that as the cue. Not as failure. As the cue. Feel the feet. Soften the exhale. Keep the hands still. Ask, "What are they actually saying?" Let them finish one thought. Reflect one point before responding.

You do not have to agree.

You do have to hear enough to know what you are disagreeing with.

Setting boundaries quickly

A boundary loses power when it arrives as a lecture.

This is a difficult truth for people who care about being fair, understood, and not mistaken for rude. When pressure rises, they feel the limit inside themselves, but instead of stating it clearly, they wrap it in history, apology, explanation, justification, background, emotional proof, and sometimes a whole courtroom of evidence. By the time the boundary finally appears, it is exhausted. The other person may have stopped listening. The speaker may have talked themselves into shame or anger. What could have been one clean sentence becomes a long performance of distress.

A quick boundary is not a harsh boundary. It is not cold, aggressive, superior, or dismissive. It is a limit stated before the moment becomes too crowded to hear it. It tells the truth early enough to prevent escalation. It says what is acceptable, what is not acceptable, what you are available for, or what you will do next. Its strength comes from clarity, not force.

Many boundaries fail because they arrive too late. The person waits until they are overwhelmed, resentful, cornered, or furious. They endure the raised voice, the repeated demand, the intrusive question, the pressure for an instant reply, the sarcastic comment, the unfair assumption, the message after message after message. They tell themselves they are being patient. They try to calm down. They hope the other person will notice the limit without being told. Eventually the body can no longer hold the pressure, and the boundary erupts as a speech, an accusation, a withdrawal, or a threat.

This is not a failure of caring. It is often a failure of timing.

A boundary spoken early can be small. A boundary spoken late often has to carry the weight of everything that was not said sooner. That weight changes the tone. "I cannot talk while voices are raised" is clear. "You always do this, you never listen, and I am sick of having to be the only reasonable person here" may contain a real complaint, but it is no longer only a boundary. It is a boundary tangled with blame, history, and heat.

Quick boundaries work best when they are short because the nervous system under pressure cannot process a lecture well. Yours cannot. Theirs cannot. When tension is rising, the other person may be defensive, embarrassed, angry, panicked, or determined to get their point across. A long boundary gives them too many places to interrupt, debate, deny, or drag the conversation sideways. A short boundary is harder to misread.

"I will not continue while you are shouting."

"I need a minute before I answer."

"I am not discussing this by text."

"Please do not speak to me like that."

"I can talk about this, but not at this volume."

"I am going to pause and come back later."

These sentences do not explain everything. They are not meant to. A boundary is not a full moral argument. It is a line of participation. It tells the moment what conditions are needed for you to stay involved safely and respectfully.

The mistake many people make is trying to make the other person agree with the boundary before they hold it. They want the other person to understand why the boundary is reasonable, approve of the timing, validate the need, and reassure them that they are not being difficult. That desire is human, but it hands too much power to the very moment that needs containing. A boundary does not require the other person's immediate agreement in order to be real. It requires your willingness to act consistently with it.

This does not mean becoming rigid or punitive. It means knowing the difference between explaining a boundary and enforcing one. Explaining may be useful when everyone is calm. Enforcing is necessary when the line is being crossed. If someone is pressing for an answer and your body is escalating, the useful sentence is not a long defence of why you process slowly under emotional pressure. The useful sentence is, "I need time before I answer." If they continue pressing, the next useful sentence is not a bigger essay. It is repetition: "I am not answering this right now."

Repetition is one of the most underrated boundary skills.

People often repeat because they are losing control. Skilled repetition is different. It is calm structure. It refuses to add more fuel. The first boundary states the limit. The second repeats it. The third attaches action if needed. "I can talk if we lower our voices." "I am not continuing at this volume." "I am going to step away now and come back in twenty minutes." This sequence is firm without becoming theatrical.

A quick boundary should focus on your action more than the other person's character. "You are being disrespectful" may be true in your view, but it invites a debate about their intention. "I will continue when we can speak respectfully" is stronger because it names the condition for your participation. "You are harassing me with messages" may escalate into argument. "I am not replying again tonight" is clearer. "You are trying to control me" may or may not be accurate. "I am making this decision tomorrow, not under pressure now" gives you more ground.

This is the difference between accusation and limit. Accusation tries to define the other person. Limit defines your next move.

Tone matters. A boundary delivered with contempt becomes a provocation. A boundary delivered with apology overload becomes a negotiation against yourself. The ideal tone is not sweet. It is steady. Low enough in force that it does not inflame the room, clear enough in pace that it does not collapse into uncertainty. Say less. Slow slightly. Let the sentence end. Do not decorate it with nervous laughter, muttered resentment, or a final jab.

Apology overload weakens many boundaries. "I am so sorry, I know this is annoying, I feel terrible saying this, please do not be upset, but maybe could we not talk about it right now?" The limit is buried under fear. The other person may hear the apology more than the boundary, or they may sense that the boundary can be pushed. A cleaner version is, "I cannot talk about this well right now. I will come back to it later." No cruelty. No begging. No self-erasure.

A boundary can be kind and still inconvenient.

This is important because many people confuse kindness with keeping everyone comfortable. But a real boundary may disappoint someone. It may interrupt their preferred pace. It may prevent them from continuing a familiar pattern. It may say no when they wanted yes. It may end a conversation they wanted to keep pressing. If your standard is that a boundary must make everyone feel immediately pleased, you will rarely set one when it matters.

The point is not to control their feeling. The point is to keep your conduct clean.

Quick boundaries are especially useful when the other person is escalating. A long explanation gives escalation more material. A short boundary reduces the number of handles available for argument. "I will not be insulted" is stronger than a five-minute explanation of how insults affect your nervous system. "I am leaving this conversation if it continues like this" is stronger than a lecture about communication standards. The short sentence may feel too plain, but plainness is exactly what heated moments need.

There is also a difference between a boundary and a threat. A boundary names what you will do to protect the conditions of healthy participation. A threat tries to frighten or punish the other person into compliance. "If you raise your voice again, I will end this conversation and return later" can be a boundary if you mean it and follow through calmly. "Keep talking like that and you will regret it" is a threat. The emotional flavour matters. Boundaries create structure. Threats create fear.

A boundary should also be something you can actually carry out. "I will never speak to you again" may be a surge sentence, not a real limit. "I am not continuing this conversation tonight" is more credible. "I am done with all of this" may feel powerful and mean very little. "I am going to take space for the evening and speak tomorrow" gives the moment a shape. The more specific the boundary, the easier it is to trust.

In family arguments, quick boundaries prevent old roles from taking over. The explainer starts explaining. The fixer starts fixing. The pleaser starts softening the truth. The fighter starts prosecuting. The withdrawer disappears. A boundary can interrupt the family script. "I am not discussing this while we are both heated." "I will answer, but not if I am interrupted." "I am not taking sides in this conversation." "I need you to ask me directly, not hint." These sentences may not solve the family pattern, but they stop you from automatically playing your assigned part.

At work, boundaries often need to be even more concise. Too much emotional explanation can blur the professional line. "I can take this on next week, not today." "I need the request in writing." "I am available for this discussion until three." "I cannot respond properly without the missing information." "Let me pause before answering." These are not dramatic statements. They are clean limits around time, capacity, process, and quality of response.

In public-facing situations, boundaries need to be calm, repeatable, and behaviour-focused. "I want to help, but I cannot do that while I am being shouted at." "I can explain the next step." "I am going to pause this conversation if the language continues." The aim is not to win emotionally. The aim is to lower heat while keeping the line intact. A firm boundary can be de-escalating when it removes ambiguity.

The body must support the boundary. If your words say "I need a minute" while your body keeps leaning in, arguing, and continuing the exchange, the boundary will not hold. If your words say "I am not replying tonight" while your hands remain on the phone and you keep rereading the thread, the boundary is not yet embodied. Step back. Put the phone down. Unclench the hands. Lower the shoulders. Give the limit a physical form.

This is why quick boundaries pair well with breath and grounding. Feel both feet before speaking. Let one exhale lengthen. Say the sentence. Stop. The stopping is part of the boundary. Many people ruin a good boundary by continuing to talk after it. They state the limit, then justify it, apologise for it, soften it, repeat the whole story, and accidentally reopen the debate. A boundary needs an ending.

"I am not discussing this by text."

Then stop.

"I need time before I answer."

Then stop.

"I will continue when we can lower the volume."

Then stop.

The silence after a boundary may feel uncomfortable. Let it. Discomfort is not proof that the boundary is wrong. It may simply be the feeling of a new pattern entering an old moment. The other person may react. They may question it, dislike it, mock it, or push against it. That does not mean you need to produce a longer defence. It may mean you need to repeat the line and act on it.

A quick boundary should be connected to a next action. Without a next action, it can become a wish. "Please stop" is sometimes enough. But if the behaviour continues, you need the next step. "If this continues, I am going to leave the room." "I will reply tomorrow." "I am ending this call now." "I will discuss the issue, but not in this tone." The action is not punishment. It is follow-through.

Follow-through teaches your own nervous system that your words matter. This is often overlooked. Boundaries are not only messages to other people. They are messages to yourself. Every time you state a limit and abandon it immediately, the body learns that pressure wins. Every time you state a limit and follow it calmly, the body learns that you can protect yourself without exploding or disappearing.

There will be times when a boundary needs repair. You may set it too sharply. You may leave without giving a return point. You may sound colder than intended. Repair does not erase the boundary. It cleans the delivery. "I should not have snapped when I said that. The boundary still stands: I am not discussing this tonight." This is a mature sentence. It owns the tone without surrendering the limit.

There will also be times when the other person uses your boundary as evidence against you. "You are avoiding." "You are too sensitive." "You cannot handle a conversation." "You always shut things down." Some of this may be worth reflecting on later, especially if avoidance is your pattern. But during escalation, do not let accusation drag you into abandoning a needed pause. You can say, "I hear that you see it that way. I am still taking a pause." The sentence is brief because it does not enter the entire debate.

A quick boundary is strongest when it is aligned with your real purpose. Before speaking, ask yourself: what am I protecting? Time? Safety? Respect? Clarity? Capacity? A decision from being rushed? A conversation from becoming cruel? A relationship from further damage? When you know what the boundary protects, the sentence becomes cleaner.

If you are protecting time: "I cannot answer this today."

If you are protecting respectful speech: "I will continue when we can speak without insults."

If you are protecting a decision: "I am not deciding under pressure."

If you are protecting attention: "I can talk for ten minutes, then I need to return to work."

If you are protecting repair: "I want to discuss this, but not while we are both this heated."

The limit does not need to carry your entire emotional history. It needs to protect the next right action.

This is where boundaries become part of the 60-second calm. They are not grand declarations of identity. They are immediate tools for preventing escalation. A boundary gives the surge a container. It stops anger from becoming attack, panic from becoming over-compliance, stress from becoming over-commitment, and shame from becoming self-erasure. It allows you to stay in the room when staying is wise, and leave the room when leaving is necessary.

The best boundary is not always the strongest-sounding sentence. It is the sentence you can say early, clearly, and follow with action.

The next time you feel the limit rising in your body, do not wait until it becomes a speech. Notice the cue. Choose the cleanest sentence. Say it once. Repeat if needed. Act if necessary. Let the boundary be short enough to hold.

A line does not become stronger because you explain it for longer. It becomes stronger when you stand where you said it was.

De-escalating without conceding

De-escalation is often mistaken for giving in.

This misunderstanding causes enormous damage. People hear the word "de-escalate" and imagine becoming smaller, softer, more agreeable, less honest, less firm. They picture themselves absorbing unfairness in order to keep the peace, lowering their voice while abandoning their position, or offering soothing words that make the other person more comfortable while their own boundary quietly disappears. No wonder many people resist it. If calm means surrender, anger begins to look like self-respect.

But de-escalation is not surrender. It is the deliberate lowering of intensity so the issue can be handled without the conversation becoming the issue.

That distinction is vital. When heat rises, the original problem often vanishes behind the way people are speaking about it. A practical disagreement becomes a fight about tone. A request becomes a character trial. A boundary becomes a threat. A disappointment becomes a history lesson. Suddenly the issue is no longer the missed call, the late reply, the unfair comment, the unclear expectation, the household task, the decision at work, or the public complaint. The issue is now the escalation itself.

De-escalation protects the real issue from being buried under emotional wreckage.

It says, "This matters enough to handle carefully." Not "This does not matter." Not "You are right." Not "I withdraw my point." The aim is to reduce the force around the exchange while preserving the substance that needs attention. This is a more demanding skill than either attacking or appeasing. Attack lets the surge drive. Appeasement lets fear drive. De-escalation asks you to hold your position and lower the temperature at the same time.

Many people can do one of those things, but not both. They can stay firm by becoming hard, sharp, and increasingly absolute. Or they can lower the temperature by becoming vague, apologetic, and self-erasing. The real skill is steadier: firm without threat, calm without collapse, respectful without retreat.

The first principle is to separate intensity from content.

The intensity is the volume, pace, tone, urgency, repetition, facial expression, body posture, and emotional pressure in the exchange. The content is the actual matter being discussed. Under escalation, these two become fused. If the other person is loud, you may assume their whole point is unreasonable. If you are angry, you may assume your delivery is justified because your concern is valid. If someone is upset, you may rush to concede content just to reduce intensity. If you feel accused, you may attack the content because the intensity feels unbearable.

Separating the two gives you options. You can lower intensity without agreeing with the content. You can acknowledge a feeling without accepting an accusation. You can repair tone without withdrawing the boundary. You can say, "I want this to be calmer," while still saying, "I do not agree."

For example, someone says, "You never take this seriously." A reactive answer might be, "That is ridiculous. I take plenty seriously." The correction may be factually reasonable, but it increases heat. A self-erasing answer might be, "You are right, I am sorry, I will do whatever you want." That may reduce conflict briefly, but at the cost of accuracy. A de-escalating answer might be, "I can hear that you are frustrated. I do not agree that I never take it seriously, but I do want to understand what felt ignored." This lowers intensity without conceding the exaggerated claim.

Notice the structure. It receives the emotional signal, rejects the inaccurate absolute, and opens a path back to the specific issue. That is de-escalation with a spine.

A useful phrase is: "I can hear the feeling without accepting the whole conclusion."

This phrase is particularly important in family arguments, where language often arrives loaded with history. A parent says, "You do not care about this family." A partner says, "You always make it about you." A sibling says, "You think you are better than everyone." These sentences may be unfair, exaggerated, or painfully familiar. If you respond only to the unfairness, the fight intensifies. If you accept the whole statement, you disappear. The middle path is to hear the feeling beneath the accusation while refusing the inaccurate verdict.

"I can see you feel let down. I do care, and I am willing to talk about what happened."

"I hear that you felt overlooked. I do not accept that I always make it about me."

"You are angry, and I want to understand the specific issue. I am not going to continue with character attacks."

These responses are not magical. The other person may still push. But they protect your side of the conversation from becoming either attack or collapse.

The second principle is to slow the pace without becoming vague.

Escalation loves speed. People answer before listening, interrupt before understanding, repeat before reflecting, and decide before the body has settled. Slowing the pace can lower heat quickly, but only if it is done clearly. A vague pause can look like avoidance. A clear pause creates structure.

"I want to respond, but I am going to slow this down."

"Give me a moment. I am listening, and I do not want to answer sharply."

"We can discuss this, but not at this speed."

"I am going to take a minute so I can stay clear."

These sentences do not concede the point. They change the tempo. That tempo change matters because many conflicts escalate through rhythm as much as content. Fast speech invites faster speech. Interruptions invite interruptions. Sharp tones invite sharper tones. A slower pace is not weakness; it is leadership of the room.

The third principle is to use fewer words.

When people fear being misunderstood, they often explain too much. When they fear losing ground, they argue too much. When they fear conflict, they apologise too much. De-escalation usually improves when the sentence becomes shorter. Short sentences reduce the number of sparks in the air. They are easier for an activated person to hear. They are easier for you to deliver without becoming tangled in defence.

"I disagree."

"I need a minute."

"That is not okay with me."

"I want to keep this respectful."

"I can talk if we lower the volume."

"I hear you, and I am not deciding now."

These sentences may feel too plain. Good. Plain is often what heated moments need. A conflict does not always need a better speech. Sometimes it needs less verbal fuel.

The fourth principle is to stop trying to win the emotional courtroom.

Under pressure, the mind often imagines a judge somewhere in the room. Who is right? Who has the stronger evidence? Who was more hurt? Who started it? Who owes what? Who has behaved worse over time? The conversation becomes a legal drama, and every sentence is submitted as proof. This may feel powerful, but it rarely calms anything. In ordinary human conflict, the need to win often prevents the issue from being solved.

De-escalation asks a different question: what would help this moment become workable?

Workable does not mean comfortable. It means the conversation can continue without increasing harm. It may require a pause, a boundary, a shorter sentence, a lower voice, a change of setting, or a decision to return later. The goal is not to win the current emotional exchange. The goal is to preserve the conditions under which something useful can happen.

This is especially important at work. Workplace conflict often includes status, speed, reputation, and audience. A person who feels challenged may defend too quickly, while a person who feels dismissed may push harder to be recognised. De-escalation in that setting may sound like: "Let us separate the concern from the pace of this discussion." Or, "I hear the urgency. I need the specific decision you are asking for." Or, "I am happy to discuss the issue, but I want to keep the tone constructive." These statements lower heat without surrendering professional ground.

In public-facing roles, de-escalation is often about reducing intensity while maintaining a clear limit. An upset person may be angry, frightened, embarrassed, or frustrated by a process they cannot control. You may not be able to give them what they want. You may still be able to lower the temperature.

"I can see this is frustrating. I can explain the next step."

"I want to help, and I cannot do that while being shouted at."

"I hear that you want this resolved now. Here is what I can do."

"I cannot change that decision here, but I can tell you the options."

The words acknowledge pressure without promising what cannot be promised. This is crucial. False reassurance is not de-escalation. It is a loan taken from the future. The moment may soften briefly, but trust collapses when the promise fails. Real de-escalation is honest about limits.

The fifth principle is to distinguish relationship repair from issue resolution.

These are not the same. Relationship repair addresses the strain in the interaction: tone, impact, feeling unheard, a sharp word, a withdrawal, a misunderstanding. Issue resolution addresses the practical or moral matter: the decision, boundary, task, agreement, responsibility, or next step. Conflict often worsens because people try to solve both at once while escalated.

A person says, "You hurt me." You reply by explaining the logistics. They feel dismissed. You feel unfairly blamed. Heat rises. Or someone challenges your decision, and you respond by repairing the relationship too quickly: "Fine, forget it, I am sorry." The practical issue remains unresolved. Later, resentment returns.

De-escalation often begins by naming which layer you are addressing.

"I want to repair the way this conversation is going. Then we can return to the decision."

"I am sorry for my tone. I still want to discuss the agreement itself."

"I hear that you are upset with how I said it. That is separate from whether the boundary stands."

"I want us to slow down before we try to solve the actual issue."

This separation prevents a common error: using repair as concession. You can apologise for raising your voice without agreeing that your point was wrong. You can acknowledge someone's hurt without accepting their interpretation of your motive. You can soften the interaction without weakening the boundary. This is emotional precision.

The sixth principle is to avoid escalation language.

Certain phrases throw fuel even when the speaker feels justified. "You always." "You never." "Calm down." "You are overreacting." "That is ridiculous." "You are impossible." "Whatever." "Fine." "I am done." Some of these phrases may contain frustration that deserves attention, but their effect is often predictable. They turn the conversation towards defence, shame, or counterattack.

De-escalating language is more specific and less global. Instead of "You never listen," try, "I do not feel heard right now." Instead of "You are overreacting," try, "I want to understand what is making this feel so big." Instead of "Calm down," try, "I want us to slow this down." Instead of "That is ridiculous," try, "I do not see it that way." Specific language lowers the moral temperature. It leaves fewer insults for the other person to defend against.

Tone can still betray the words. "I do not see it that way" can be calm, or it can be contempt in formal clothing. The body must support the sentence: slower pace, lower volume, unclenched hands, breath not held, eyes not fixed like a challenge. De-escalation is not a script pasted over a hostile nervous system. It is speech supported by state management.

The seventh principle is to know when to stop.

Some moments cannot be de-escalated by staying longer. The other person may be too activated. You may be too activated. The setting may be wrong. The issue may require information you do not have. Continuing may only deepen the groove. In those moments, the de-escalating move is a pause with a return point.

"I want to continue this, but not while it is this heated. I am going to pause and come back later."

"We are repeating ourselves. I suggest we stop for now and return when we can think."

"I am not able to discuss this well at the moment. I will respond tomorrow."

"I am ending this call now. We can resume when the tone is respectful."

A pause is not concession. It is containment. The issue remains. The boundary remains. The values remain. What ends is the current escalation cycle.

This point is particularly important for people who believe they must prove sincerity by staying until everything is resolved. Some conflicts cannot be resolved from inside activation. Staying too long may look committed, but it can become destructive. A well-timed pause is often more respectful than an exhausted continuation.

The eighth principle is to keep your internal aim clear.

Before responding, ask: what am I trying to lower, and what am I trying to preserve?

You may be trying to lower volume, speed, accusation, panic, repetition, sarcasm, defensiveness, or urgency. You may be trying to preserve a boundary, a relationship, a decision, a value, a person's dignity, your own dignity, or the possibility of a later conversation. This question protects you from sliding into appeasement. It reminds you that lowering heat is only half the work. The other half is preserving what matters.

For instance, in a family argument, you may be trying to lower blame while preserving a boundary around how you are spoken to. In a workplace disagreement, you may be trying to lower defensiveness while preserving your professional concern. In a public complaint, you may be trying to lower frustration while preserving a policy or limit. In a partnership, you may be trying to lower tone while preserving the need for change.

This is why de-escalation without concession is not soft. It requires a clear spine and a calm surface. Many people can do one or the other. The craft is doing both.

A useful response pattern is acknowledge, anchor, assert.

Acknowledge the emotional or practical signal: "I can see this matters to you." "I hear that you are frustrated." "I understand you want an answer."

Anchor the pace or condition: "I want to slow this down." "I am going to answer carefully." "I will not continue while we are interrupting."

Assert your position: "I do not agree with that conclusion." "The boundary still stands." "I am not able to decide today." "Here is what I can offer."

The structure should not become robotic. It is a guide, not a script. Its strength is that it prevents the two common failures: reacting only to the emotion and losing the point, or asserting the point so sharply that the emotion escalates.

De-escalation also requires tolerance for being misunderstood briefly. This is hard. If someone says, "So you admit I am right?" or "You are just trying to avoid this," the body may rush to defend. You may need to clarify, but not with panic. "No. I am saying I want this calmer. I have not changed my position." Or, "I am not avoiding the issue. I am pausing the escalation." Short clarification is better than a long defence.

You do not need to over-correct every misreading. Some misreadings are attempts to pull you back into heat. Stay with the central line. Calmly repeated clarity is more powerful than frantic explanation.

There is also a moral reason to de-escalate without conceding. It protects truth from being distorted by fear. If you concede what you do not mean in order to end discomfort, resentment grows. If you attack in order to preserve truth, trust erodes. The mature path is to keep truth and reduce harm at the same time. It is not always satisfying in the moment. It is often the only path that leaves you with self-respect later.

The next time a conversation heats up, resist the false choice between winning and yielding. There is a third move. Lower the pace. Shorten the sentence. Acknowledge without swallowing the accusation. Set the limit without delivering a lecture. Repair the tone without abandoning the issue. Pause without disappearing.

De-escalation is not the art of giving ground.

It is the art of keeping the ground from catching fire.

Chapter 11
Tools for work and public pressure

Work pressure has a particular kind of sharpness. It does not always look emotional from the outside. It may look like competence, pace, professionalism, responsibility, or simply "getting on with it." Inside, however, the body may be doing something very different. A question in a meeting lands like a challenge. A call turns tense and the voice tightens. A message arrives with too little warmth and the mind fills the gap with threat. A notification appears during an already crowded day, and one small screen begins to dictate the state of the whole body.

The difficulty is that public and professional settings often allow less room for visible recovery. You may not be able to leave the meeting, close your eyes, explain your nervous system, or take a long pause without feeling exposed. You may need to answer while other people are watching. You may need to stay polite with someone who is being difficult. You may need to read a message without letting your face reveal the story your mind has started telling. In these moments, calm cannot depend on privacy. It has to become discreet.

This is where many people misunderstand workplace composure. They assume the goal is to feel untouched by pressure. That is unrealistic and, frankly, unnecessary. The real skill is to remain usable while pressure is present. Your body may still tighten. Your thoughts may still speed up. Your pride may still sting. Your panic may still offer a catastrophic interpretation. But the next visible move can still be slower, cleaner, and more deliberate than the surge wants it to be.

The stakes are high because work and public pressure often leave a record. A rushed reply can become an email trail. A defensive answer in a meeting can reshape how others hear your judgement. A sharp tone on a call can turn a practical issue into a relational one. A digital reaction can move faster than your steadier self can review it. In private life, repair may be possible through closeness and context; in professional life, the margin can feel thinner. This does not mean you must become stiff or artificial. It means your first minute matters.

There is also the quiet burden of status. At work, people are rarely reacting only to the stated issue. They may also be reacting to being interrupted, questioned, watched, evaluated, ignored, corrected, copied into an email, left out of a decision, or expected to respond immediately. Public pressure adds its own heat: the sense of being observed, judged, delayed, challenged, or unable to step away gracefully. The body reads these moments quickly. It may treat scrutiny as danger and speed as safety.

The most useful tools in these settings are small enough to hide in ordinary behaviour. A sip of water before answering. Both feet placed on the floor during a difficult call. A slower exhale while someone else is speaking. A glance at notes to buy a beat. A sentence that gives you time without sounding evasive: "Let me think about that for a moment." A decision not to answer a message from the first surge of interpretation. These are not tricks. They are professional self-protection.

The work begins with calm in meetings and calls, where status, timing, and visibility make pressure feel immediate. The body needs discreet ways to slow down without leaving the room. Then the focus shifts to digital triggers, because messages often create instant stories and instant replies, especially when tone is unclear and the body is already loaded. The aim is not to become detached from work or public responsibility, but to stop urgency from becoming your manager.

The question is not whether pressure will find you in public. It will. The sharper question is whether you can build a calm that does not require perfect conditions: a calm that can sit in a meeting, answer a call, read a difficult message, and still keep the next move under your own authority.

Calm in meetings and calls

Meetings and calls can make a calm person feel strangely exposed.

A question is asked, and the body hears challenge. A colleague interrupts, and the mind hears disrespect. A manager pauses before responding, and the silence begins to feel like judgement. Someone says, "Can you talk us through your thinking?" and although the words are ordinary, the nervous system treats them as a spotlight. The room may be polite. The agenda may be sensible. The pressure may still be real.

This is the particular difficulty of work surges: they often have to be managed while you are still expected to function. You cannot always step away. You cannot always explain that your chest has tightened, your jaw has locked, or your thoughts have begun moving too fast. You may be on camera. You may be in front of clients. You may be leading the call. You may be the youngest person in the room, the newest person on the team, the person expected to know the answer, or the person quietly afraid of looking unprepared. The body reacts, but the role continues.

That gap between inner state and outer expectation is where many workplace regrets begin.

Not always dramatic regrets. Sometimes the mistake is a defensive answer that makes you sound less confident than you are. Sometimes it is a rushed promise that creates extra work. Sometimes it is over-explaining because you fear being misunderstood. Sometimes it is silence that looks like disengagement when you are actually trying not to react. Sometimes it is a sharpness in your tone that makes the discussion harder than it needed to be. In meetings and calls, small changes in pace, voice, and timing can carry large meanings.

The aim is not to become untouched by professional pressure. That would be unrealistic. Work often involves scrutiny, uncertainty, competing priorities, status, deadlines, other people's opinions, and decisions made with imperfect information. The aim is to stay usable. Usable means you can hear the actual question, not only the threat inside it. You can buy a beat before answering. You can choose a shorter sentence instead of a defensive speech. You can notice the body accelerating without letting it write your next contribution.

The first tool is posture, because posture is available even when words are not.

Before answering, place both feet on the floor. Let the chair support you if you are sitting. If you are standing, feel the weight travel down through your legs. Rest your hands somewhere steady: on the table, in your lap, around a pen without gripping it, or lightly on your notebook. This does not need to look like a calming technique. It simply gives the body a structure that is not built entirely around defence.

Many people underestimate posture because it seems too small. But a meeting surge often appears first in the body: shoulders rise, breath shortens, jaw tightens, hands grip, eyes fix on the most threatening face or square on the screen. If the body takes a defensive shape, the mind often follows. A grounded posture sends a different signal. It says, "There is no need to answer from alarm." The question may still matter. The disagreement may still need handling. But the body is no longer being allowed to rush the room.

The second tool is the discreet exhale.

A long, obvious breathing exercise may feel awkward in a meeting. A discreet exhale does not. While someone is finishing their question, let your out-breath last slightly longer than your in-breath. Keep it comfortable. Do not perform calm. Do not inhale dramatically. Just allow the exhale to slow the pace before your voice enters. The purpose is not to make you peaceful. It is to stop the first word from carrying the full pressure of the body.

This is especially useful after interruption. Being interrupted can create instant heat because it touches status and respect. The first impulse may be to speak over the other person, correct them, or withdraw completely. A quiet exhale gives you one beat. That beat may allow you to say, "I would like to finish the point," rather than snapping, "Can I speak?" It may allow you to say, "Let me come back to that," rather than losing the thread. The breath protects the message from the surge.

The third tool is attention widening.

In a meeting, attention often narrows around the person who challenged you, the message in the chat, the unanswered question, the camera view of your own face, or the one phrase that sounded dismissive. When attention narrows, the mind may treat the moment as more dangerous than it is. Widening is subtle. Look at your notes. Notice the whole room, not just the person who spoke. On a video call, let your eyes move away from your own image. If possible, look at the edge of the screen, the table, the window, or the notebook in front of you. Bring more of the environment back into awareness.

This matters because a narrowed field produces narrowed answers. You may respond only to the sting, not the question. You may answer defensively rather than informatively. You may overstate certainty because uncertainty feels exposed. Widening gives the thinking mind more space. It reminds you that this is a meeting, not a trial; a question, not necessarily an attack; a pause, not necessarily condemnation.

The fourth tool is a beat-buying sentence.

Many work surges worsen because people believe they must answer instantly. They treat speed as proof of competence. But fast answers are not always better answers. In fact, under pressure, speed often produces the least accurate version of you. A beat-buying sentence gives you time without making you look lost.

"Let me think about that for a moment."

"I want to answer that clearly."

"Can I check I have understood the question?"

"Let me separate two points there."

"I will come back to the detail, but the short answer is this."

These sentences do something important: they place a small structure between the question and your reply. They also communicate thoughtfulness rather than panic. You are not stalling; you are improving the quality of the response. A person who can take a beat often appears more authoritative, not less.

The fifth tool is the clarifying question.

When pressure rises, the mind may answer the question it fears rather than the question that was asked. Someone says, "Why did the timeline change?" and you hear, "You failed." Someone says, "Can you justify that decision?" and you hear, "You are incompetent." Someone says, "I am not sure that works," and you hear, "Your idea is poor." A clarifying question slows the jump from words to threat.

"Are you asking about the timing or the decision itself?"

"Do you want the reasoning behind the change, or the next step from here?"

"Is your concern the cost, the risk, or the impact on the team?"

"Can you say which part feels unclear?"

These questions are useful because they move the conversation from vague pressure to specific content. Specific content is easier to handle. It also prevents you from wasting energy defending against an accusation that may not exist. In many meetings, clarity is calming.

The sixth tool is the short answer first.

Under scrutiny, many people over-explain. They try to prove competence by giving all the context immediately. This can backfire. The answer becomes crowded, and the speaker sounds less certain because the body is trying to outrun judgement with words. A calmer structure is to give the short answer first, then add detail only if needed.

"The main reason was capacity."

"The risk is manageable, but timing needs attention."

"My recommendation is to wait until we have the missing information."

"I do not have the final number yet, but I can confirm the direction."

Short answers create a frame. They help your own mind settle. They also help others follow you. Once the core answer is in place, you can add explanation without sounding as though you are building a defence in real time. A concise answer is not a shallow answer. It is an organised answer.

The seventh tool is the respectful hold.

This is useful when someone pushes for an answer you cannot responsibly give. Work pressure often creates false urgency. A person asks for a commitment, estimate, decision, or opinion before the conditions are right. The surge may push you to say yes, answer quickly, or make something up to avoid looking uncertain. A respectful hold protects judgement.

"I do not want to guess. I will confirm and come back to you."

"I need to check the detail before I commit to that."

"I can give a provisional view now, but not a final answer."

"I am not ready to decide that in this meeting."

This is calm in a professional form. It does not apologise excessively. It does not become defensive. It protects accuracy. The ability to say "not yet" clearly is a serious workplace skill.

Calls require a slightly different approach because the body has fewer visual cues. On the phone, silence can feel larger. Tone can be misread more easily. You may interrupt because you cannot see when someone is about to finish, or you may speak too quickly because pauses feel exposed. The same tools still apply, but they must become more verbal.

On a tense call, use audible structure. "I am going to pause for a second to think." "There are two points I want to answer." "Let me make sure I have this right." "I hear the concern." These phrases help both nervous systems. They reduce ambiguity. They make the pause less threatening. They give the conversation a shape when tone alone might escalate it.

Video calls have their own traps. Seeing your own face can increase self-monitoring. A delayed connection can make pauses feel awkward. Chat messages can split attention. The temptation is to perform composure while the body tightens behind the screen. Keep the tools physical. Feet on floor. Hands visible or settled. Screen at a comfortable distance. Eyes not locked on your own image. One exhale before unmuting. A beat before answering.

The mute button can be useful, but it should not become a hiding place. Muting gives you space to exhale, cough, sip water, or prevent a reactive noise. But if you use it to disengage completely, you may miss meaning and then respond poorly. Calm in a video call is not disappearing behind technology. It is using the technology to create just enough space for a cleaner response.

There is a particular surge that appears when you are challenged publicly. Someone questions your work in front of others. The body may interpret this as exposure. The urge may be to defend every detail, prove your competence, or show no weakness. In that moment, the strongest move is often to slow down and become specific.

"Good question. The reason for that choice was..."

"I can see why that needs clarification."

"There is a risk there, and this is how I suggest we manage it."

"I do not agree with that interpretation, but I understand the concern."

These responses do not collapse. They do not attack. They keep you in the role of someone who can think under scrutiny. That is more powerful than sounding invulnerable.

Sometimes the calmest move in a meeting is to postpone the answer. This can feel risky, especially if you worry about appearing unprepared. But there is a difference between not knowing and not pretending. A clean postponement protects trust.

"I do not have that information to hand. I will check and send it afterwards."

"I want to avoid giving an inaccurate answer."

"I need to look at the numbers before I respond properly."

"I can give a general view now, but I will confirm the detail later."

These sentences are stronger than bluffing. They also prevent the surge from making promises that your steadier self has to repair.

The next risk is emotional carry-over. A difficult meeting can end, but the body may still be activated. You may go straight into the next call carrying the tone of the last one. You may answer an email sharply because a colleague embarrassed you ten minutes earlier. You may bring work heat into family life at the end of the day. Meetings and calls need recovery margins, even tiny ones.

After a tense exchange, do a short reset before the next task. Stand up if possible. Exhale. Unclench the hands. Look away from the screen. Name one next action. If you handled the moment well, recover anyway. Restraint still costs energy. If you handled it badly, recover before repair. A repair sent from shame may become too much; a repair sent after downshifting can be clean and proportionate.

A brief work repair might sound like, "I was sharper than I intended in that discussion. I apologise. My concern about the timeline still stands, and I will set it out more clearly." This preserves both accountability and substance. You repair the delivery without abandoning the point.

Public pressure also includes customer-facing, service, teaching, care, leadership, and front-desk moments where another person's frustration lands on you. The calm skill there is to avoid absorbing the other person's pace. Their urgency does not have to become your urgency. Their volume does not have to become your volume. Their accusation does not have to become your defence. Use structure.

"I can help with the next step."

"I want to understand the issue."

"I cannot continue if I am being shouted at."

"Here is what I can do."

These sentences are deliberately plain. In public pressure, plain language is often safer than elaborate explanation. It lowers ambiguity and reduces the number of places where conflict can catch fire.

There will be moments when you cannot stay calm enough to continue well. That is not failure; it is information. The skill then is to pause professionally rather than push through poorly.

"I need a moment before I respond."

"Let us take a short pause and return to this."

"I am going to check the information and come back."

"I do not think this discussion is productive at the current pace."

A pause protects the work. It protects the relationship. It protects your judgement. It is better to create a clear interruption than to continue while your body is handing your voice to the surge.

Calm in meetings and calls is not a personality trait reserved for naturally composed people. It is a set of small behaviours practised until they become available under observation: feet down, exhale, widen, clarify, short answer, respectful hold, reset. None of these is dramatic. That is their strength. They fit inside ordinary professional behaviour. They do not require anyone else to know that you are regulating.

The next time pressure rises in a meeting or call, do not aim for flawless composure. Aim for one cleaner beat.

One breath before unmuting.

One clarifying question before defending.

One short answer before explaining.

One pause before committing.

One reset before carrying the moment into the next room.

That is enough to keep the surge from chairing the meeting.

Handling digital triggers

Digital pressure is dangerous because it feels private while it creates public consequences.

A message arrives, and the body reacts before the mind has finished reading. The screen is small, but the story it opens can be enormous. A short reply feels cold. A delayed response feels rejecting. A full stop feels hostile. A message with no greeting feels abrupt. Someone reads and does not answer. Someone answers too quickly. Someone copies in another person.

Someone asks, "Can we talk?" and the nervous system treats the words as an alarm.

Digital triggers are rarely about the device alone. They are about uncertainty, tone, timing, status, belonging, control, and the fear of what may be happening beyond the screen. The problem is that digital communication gives the body very little human information to work with. No full facial expression. No settled voice. No shared room. No reassuring context unless the sender has provided it. Into that empty space, the mind pours interpretation.

This is why a message can change your state in seconds.

The phone lights up. Your chest tightens. You open the message. The mind begins filling gaps. Why did they say it like that? Why so short? Why now? Why not earlier? Are they annoyed? Am I in trouble? Should I answer immediately? Should I explain? Should I defend? Should I apologise? Should I prove I am not bothered? The surge is no longer only emotional; it has become interactive. Your thumbs are available. The reply box is open. The send button is waiting.

Digital triggers collapse the gap between feeling and action. In face-to-face life, there may be natural friction. A person must finish speaking. You may need to breathe before answering. The room itself slows things down. With a phone, the body can convert a surge into a message almost instantly. Anger becomes a paragraph. Panic becomes repeated checking. Shame becomes over-apology. Defensiveness becomes a long explanation. Loneliness becomes a demand for reassurance. The feeling moves through the fingers before judgement has caught up.

The first rule of digital calm is therefore simple: do not let the first body reaction decide the first visible response.

A message is not an emergency simply because your body reacts as though it is one. It may require attention. It may even require firmness. But it does not automatically deserve an immediate reply from the most activated version of you. The body's urgency is information about your state, not proof about the message. That distinction protects you from turning digital discomfort into relational damage.

The one-minute protocol begins before you reply. In fact, it begins before you fully interpret.

When a message lands and you feel the surge, pause before opening it if possible. Feel both feet. Let one exhale lengthen. Notice the hand holding the device. This is not delay for the sake of delay. It is a small act of ownership. You are reminding the body that the phone has delivered information, not seized command.

If you have already opened the message, do not move straight from reading to replying. Read once for content, not tone. Then look away from the screen. This matters because staring at the message can intensify the story. The more you reread one phrase while activated, the more meaning the mind may attach to it. A neutral sentence can begin to sound hostile. A clumsy sentence can begin to sound cruel. A brief sentence can begin to feel like rejection. Looking away widens the field.

The next question is not, "What do I feel like saying?" That question belongs to the surge. A better question is, "What kind of response is actually needed?"

Some messages need no response at all. Some need a short acknowledgement. Some need time. Some need a factual answer. Some need a boundary. Some should not be handled by text. Some need to wait until you are calmer. Some need a conversation, not a thread. The body may want to answer everything with the full force of the state. Digital calm begins when you match the response to the need, not the intensity.

A useful distinction is between replying and reacting.

Replying serves the situation. Reacting serves the surge.

A reply may be brief, clear, and proportionate: "I have seen this and will come back to you later." A reaction may be a defensive essay written to reduce the discomfort of being misunderstood. A reply may say, "I do not agree with that, but I want to discuss it properly." A reaction may say, "I cannot believe you would say that after everything." A reply may set a boundary: "I am not discussing this by text tonight." A reaction may punish: "Fine. Do whatever you want."

The difference is not always the words alone. It is the state behind them.

Before sending, ask: "Am I trying to communicate, or am I trying to discharge?"

Discharge has a particular feel. The body wants the pressure out. The message feels necessary because holding it back is uncomfortable. You may imagine the other person reading it and finally understanding, finally feeling guilty, finally reassuring you, finally admitting they were wrong. This fantasy can be seductive. But digital messages are poor containers for emotional discharge. They travel without the full context of your body, your tone, your regret, or your complexity. They often land harder than intended.

A simple barrier can prevent damage: draft somewhere else.

Do not draft directly in the thread when you are activated. Use a notes app, a blank document, or paper. Remove the recipient if using email. Write the first version freely if you need to. Let it be sharp, needy, defensive, frightened, excessive, or messy. That first version is not communication. It is extraction. It gives the surge somewhere to put its language without giving that language to another person.

Then wait.

The waiting does not have to be dramatic. Put the phone down. Walk to another room. Drink water. Look outside. Feel your hands. Do one ordinary task. The aim is not to become perfectly calm. It is to let the first wave lose enough force that you can review the message as a person rather than as a state.

When you return, shorten. Most reactive messages are too long because the body is trying to secure safety through explanation, proof, or impact. Remove mind-reading. Remove insults. Remove sweeping claims. Remove repeated apologies. Remove old evidence that does not belong to the present message. Remove the sentence you added because you wanted them to feel the force of your feeling. Keep the actual point.

A strong digital response is often shorter than the surge wants and clearer than the surge can manage.

For example, the surge may write: "I do not understand why you would send that like this when you know how much pressure I am under. It feels like you are deliberately trying to make me feel bad, and I am honestly tired of always having to explain myself."

The steadier reply may be: "That message landed badly with me. I do not want to discuss it by text while I am upset. I will come back to it later."

The second message does not surrender. It also does not escalate. It names the impact, delays the medium, and protects the next conversation from the first surge.

Some digital triggers come not from messages received, but from messages not received. Silence can become a screen on which fear writes its favourite stories. They are angry. They are ignoring me. I have done something wrong. They do not care. Something bad has happened. I need to check. I need to send another message. I need to know now.

Silence is difficult because it offers no fresh information, only space. Panic, shame, and anger all dislike space. They try to fill it with certainty. But a delayed reply is not automatically rejection, disrespect, danger, or proof. It may be nothing more than delay. The body may hate that uncertainty, but hatred of uncertainty is still not evidence.

When silence triggers you, the tool is not another message sent from urgency. The tool is naming the state: "I am reacting to the gap." Then choose a boundary around checking. Put the phone down for a set period. Move it out of reach. Turn off the screen. Do not keep reopening the thread as though the next glance will give certainty. Each check asks the nervous system, "Are we safe yet?" and often keeps the alarm alive.

A practical rule is to check once, then act elsewhere.

Check the thread if you need to. Then leave it. Do something physical. Wash a cup. Walk. Open a different task. Speak to someone in the room. The body needs evidence that life is not suspended until the reply arrives. If the message truly requires follow-up, schedule it rather than chasing it: "I will follow up tomorrow," or "I will send one clear message later if needed." One planned follow-up is different from repeated anxious contact.

Group chats and copied emails bring their own pressure. They add audience. A message that might be manageable in private can feel exposing when others are included. The body may feel a sudden need to protect reputation. You may want to correct immediately, show competence, defend your position, or make sure nobody misunderstands. The danger is that public digital threads can turn a small surge into a visible performance.

In these moments, slow down even more. Ask, "Who actually needs this response?" and "What is the smallest professional or relationally clean reply?" Often the best answer is factual, brief, and free of emotional undertone. If the issue is charged, move it out of the group space: "I will respond to the detail separately," or "This may be better discussed directly." Do not use an audience as a court. Do not let the presence of witnesses turn your reply into a performance of self-defence.

Tone is difficult digitally because it must be built deliberately. In person, tone carries through voice, facial expression, and timing. In text, punctuation, length, speed, and word choice do much of the work. A short message may sound efficient to you and cold to someone else. A long message may sound thorough to you and overwhelming to them. A delayed response may be necessary for you and unsettling for them. This does not mean you must over-soften everything. It means you should choose tone consciously.

A useful practice is to read your message once as the recipient might read it while stressed. Not as a mind-reading exercise. As a humility exercise. Could this sound harsher than you intend? Is the main point clear? Have you added a sentence that belongs to irritation rather than information? Are you asking a question, or setting a trap? Are you apologising for the right thing, or apologising to make them soothe you? Are you being brief, or being cold? Are you being firm, or being punitive?

Digital calm often depends on medium choice. Not every issue belongs in text.

If the message is emotional, complex, easily misread, or likely to affect trust, consider whether text is the right container. A short holding message may be better than a full argument. "This feels important, and I do not want to handle it badly by text. Can we talk later?" Or, "I want to respond properly, but I need more space than a message thread." This is not avoidance. It is choosing a better medium for a difficult issue.

At work, the equivalent might be: "There is too much detail for a quick reply. I will send a clear response after reviewing it." Or, "This may be easier to resolve on a short call." The key is to avoid using the wrong medium simply because it is immediate.

Digital boundaries should be short. "I am not replying tonight." "I will answer tomorrow." "I do not discuss this by text." "Please send the request in writing." "I need time before responding." These sentences can feel abrupt if you are used to over-explaining, but they are often kinder than a long, activated message. A boundary that is clear early prevents resentment later.

Be careful with apology over text. A clean apology can repair. A panic apology can create more confusion. "I am sorry for the tone of my last message. I should have waited before sending it" is useful. "I am so sorry, I am awful, please do not hate me, I should never have said anything" turns the recipient into the manager of your shame. Repair digitally as you would in person: name the behaviour, acknowledge the impact if appropriate, state the next step, stop.

The same applies to anger. "That was not okay with me" is a boundary. "You clearly do not care and this is exactly what you always do" is a surge looking for a target. If you need to be firm, be specific. What happened? What do you need? What will you do next? The more global the statement, the more likely it is to escalate.

A practical digital reset can be used in under a minute.

Read.

Look away.

Feet on the floor.

One exhale.

Ask: reply, delay, boundary, or no response?

Draft elsewhere if charged.

Send only when the message serves the situation, not the surge.

This protocol is simple because digital triggers are fast. A complicated plan will not survive the moment when your thumb is already moving. You need a small interruption that can be inserted between reading and responding. The interruption is the point.

Handling digital triggers also requires managing the environment. Disable non-essential notifications if they repeatedly hijack your state. Keep the phone away during recovery after conflict. Do not read charged messages in bed if that is when rumination takes over. Avoid opening difficult threads while walking into a meeting, driving, trying to sleep, or already overloaded. Context matters. The same message read from a steadier body may produce a very different response.

This is not avoidance. It is timing.

A responsible person does not have to be instantly available to every emotional demand that arrives through a screen. Availability without boundaries becomes reactivity. You can be caring and not answer immediately. You can be professional and not reply from panic. You can be honest and not send the first draft. You can be firm and still wait until your voice on the page belongs to you.

There will be times when you send the reactive message anyway. Then the work becomes repair, not self-attack. Do not send five more messages trying to fix the first one from the same state. Downshift. Wait. Then repair cleanly: "I replied too quickly and the tone was sharper than I intended. I want to come back to the actual issue more carefully." This is enough. Do not bury the repair under a new flood of explanation.

The deeper skill is to stop treating your phone as an emotional emergency room. It is a communication tool, not a regulator. If you use it to discharge anger, chase certainty, seek repeated reassurance, or escape silence, it will train the very loops you are trying to break. Digital calm means returning the device to its proper size. It can deliver information. It should not be allowed to decide your state.

The next time a message lights up your body, pause before you let it light up your behaviour. The screen may be urgent. The story may be loud. The reply may feel ready.

Not yet.

Read with your feet on the floor. Let the first surge pass through your hands without becoming a sentence. Then choose the smallest response that your steadier self will still respect later.

Chapter 12
Your personal 60-second plan

Why does a person who knows ten calming tools often use none of them when the pressure rises?

The answer is rarely ignorance. By now, the problem is not that calm is mysterious, or that the body has offered no clues, or that the next safe action is impossible to imagine. The problem is excess. Too many options can become another form of pressure. In a surge, the mind does not want a library. It wants a handle. It wants the one breath you will actually take, the one grounding point you will actually feel, the one pause phrase you can say without sounding false, the one recovery move that brings you back into the day.

This is the final turn in the work: moving from understanding tools to owning a plan. A plan is not a performance of emotional sophistication. It is not a beautiful routine designed for an ideal morning. It is a small, sturdy arrangement built for the moment when your body is hot, your breath is tight, your attention has narrowed, your phone is in your hand, or your old pattern is already leaning towards the wheel. The aim is not variety. The aim is readiness.

Readiness requires honesty about your actual patterns. A person who attacks under pressure needs a different plan from a person who disappears. A person who panics around bodily sensations needs a different entry point from a person who over-explains in conflict. A person whose worst regrets happen by text needs more digital friction than someone whose difficulty is setting a boundary aloud. Copying someone else's routine can be oddly seductive, because it feels like certainty. But a plan that does not fit your surge pattern will fail precisely where it is meant to help.

The stakes are practical and deeply personal. Your plan is the bridge between the person you intend to be and the person who shows up under load. Without a plan, the familiar move often wins: the sharp reply, the rushed apology, the silence with no return point, the repeated checking, the argument rehearsed all evening, the decision made from heat. With a plan, the first wave may still rise, but it no longer meets an empty room. Something has been placed there in advance.

Many pressure moments are less random than they feel. They have favourite locations, favourite people, favourite times of day, favourite devices, favourite sentences. The car before entering the house. The phone after a long day. The meeting where you expect scrutiny. The family conversation that always tightens your chest. The bedtime replay. The particular silence that your mind fills with danger. Preparation reduces surprise by admitting that these moments are likely enough to deserve a pre-decided response.

The core plan begins with choosing a few tools small enough to survive escalation, then fitting them to the places where your surges actually happen. Predictable moments can be prepared with environmental changes, timed delays, and phrases rehearsed before the body needs them. Progress then has to remain humane, because a plan that becomes another way to attack yourself will eventually be abandoned. The practice is to return, adjust, and shorten the distance between surge and choice.

This is also where the definition of success must become more mature. Success is not never reacting. It is noticing sooner. It is sending fewer messages from heat. It is leaving the room with a return point rather than vanishing. It is repairing the sharp sentence without apologising for your whole existence. It is recognising panic as a pattern before the fear story takes command. It is having a hard day and still finding one small place where the old sequence did not complete itself.

A humane plan leaves room for imperfection without lowering the standard of responsibility. You will still have moments when you remember too late, speak too quickly, check too often, or replay too long. Those moments are not proof that the work has failed. They are information. The question is whether you can review them without turning review into punishment, and whether you can adjust the plan so the next cue is easier to catch. Calm becomes reliable not because you never lose it, but because you know how to return.

So the task now is precise: if the next surge arrived in its most familiar form, what would be waiting for it? Not a theory. Not a wish. Not a long menu of impressive techniques. One breath, one anchor, one pause, one recovery step, chosen well enough that your future self can reach them when the minute begins.

Choosing your core tools

A personal calm plan fails when it tries to be impressive.

This is one of the more useful disappointments in this work. After learning a range of techniques, the temptation is to build a large, elegant system: several breath patterns, multiple grounding methods, different scripts for every relationship, a digital protocol, a panic sequence, a recovery practice, a journalling method, and a set of rules for every possible trigger. It feels responsible. It feels thorough. It feels as though more tools must mean more control.

Under pressure, however, variety can become noise.

A surge does not give you the luxury of browsing a full menu. When the body is hot, breath is tight, attention is narrow, and an old impulse has already begun to move, too many options can paralyse the very part of you that needs simplicity. You may know several techniques and still use none, because the mind cannot sort them quickly enough. In a real pressure moment, the best tool is not the most sophisticated one. It is the one you can actually reach.

The aim is readiness, not variety.

Readiness means having a small set of familiar moves that match your patterns. Not someone else's perfect routine. Not a calming system that looks good on paper. Your plan must fit the way *you* surge: the earliest body cues, the default move, the places where you lose choice, and the kinds of consequences you most want to prevent. A person who sends reactive messages needs a different core plan from a person who disappears in conflict. A person who panics around breath sensations needs a different plan from a person whose anger arrives through sharp speech. A person who over-apologises needs different tools from a person who blames.

This is why the first task is selection. You are not collecting techniques. You are choosing your working tools.

A strong 60-second plan can begin with four essentials: one breath reset, one grounding method, one anger pause, and one recovery step. These cover the major transitions of escalation. The breath reset helps reduce intensity. The grounding method helps widen attention and return to the present. The anger pause protects speech and action. The recovery step prevents the surge from spreading into the next moment. Four tools are enough to begin because they give the pressured self a clear route: lower, locate, pause, return.

Your breath reset should be the simplest one your body accepts.

For many people, that means a comfortable longer exhale. Not a huge inhale. Not a complicated count. Not a breath that turns into performance. The reset might be: small inhale, longer soft exhale, shoulders lowering by a fraction. Or it might be a silent sigh before speaking. Or a pause-breath before answering. The right breath reset is the one that reduces speed without making you more self-conscious, dizzy, strained, or focused on whether you are doing it correctly.

Choose the breath reset according to your surge pattern. If anger makes you fast and forceful, choose a breath that creates a beat before speech. If panic makes you chase air, choose a small, steady breath that does not demand a dramatic inhale. If stress makes you rush, choose an exhale that slows your pace before the next task or message. Do not choose a tool because it sounds powerful. Choose the one your body will permit in public, in conflict, and in the first uncomfortable seconds.

A good test is this: could you use it without anyone noticing?

If the answer is yes, it belongs in real life. If the breath requires privacy, silence, perfect posture, and complete focus, it may still be useful at other times, but it is not your core 60-second tool. Core tools must survive ordinary human conditions: noise, interruption, embarrassment, fatigue, conversation, and a phone in your hand.

Your grounding method should be equally plain.

The purpose of grounding is not to escape the feeling. It is to reconnect with what is physically present so the surge does not become the whole world. Choose one anchor that works reliably: feet on the floor, hand on a surface, eyes naming neutral objects, texture under the fingers, temperature from a glass or tap. Do not choose five. Choose one main anchor and perhaps one backup.

Feet are often the best starting point because they are discreet and always available. Both feet on the floor. Weight down through the heels. Toes inside shoes. Ground meeting body. This is not poetic. It is practical. The feet interrupt the floating, rushing, bracing quality of escalation. They are especially useful when panic says "leave now," anger says "move forward," or stress says "hurry."

Hands are better for some people because their surges move through action. If you grip the phone, type too fast, clench fists, point, or reach for reassurance, a hand anchor may be your strongest tool. Place the hand on the table. Feel the cup. Touch fabric. Open the fingers. Let the hands stop carrying the surge forward. For digital triggers, hands may be the whole plan: phone down, palm on surface, exhale, wait.

Eyes are useful if your attention locks onto one threat target. Look away from the message. Notice the room. Name one neutral object. Let your field widen. This is particularly helpful when you reread a message until it becomes more threatening, stare at a person's face for signs of judgement, or monitor a bodily sensation until it feels larger. The eye anchor tells the mind: there is more here.

Your anger pause is the tool that protects the next sentence.

This matters even if you do not think of yourself as an angry person. Anger is not always shouting. It can appear as sarcasm, coldness, speed, correction, withdrawal, contempt, over-explaining, or the need to send one final message. Your anger pause should be a phrase short enough to say while heated and strong enough not to collapse into apology.

"I need a minute."

"I want to answer well."

"I am too heated to discuss this carefully."

"I am going to pause and come back."

"I can talk about this, but not at this volume."

Choose one that sounds like you. This is essential. A script that sounds unnatural will not survive pressure. If you are direct, use a direct sentence. If you tend to soften too much, make the sentence firmer. If you tend to sound sharp, choose wording that lowers the edge. If you tend to disappear, include a return point. The script is not there to make you sound like a therapist. It is there to keep your first surge from becoming the first wound.

For the person who attacks, the anger pause must slow the mouth.

For the person who withdraws, the anger pause must keep connection.

For the person who pleases, the anger pause must protect truth.

For the person who over-explains, the anger pause must stay brief.

For the person who performs competence, the anger pause must admit state without collapse.

This is why copying someone else's phrase rarely works. Your tool must meet your default move.

Your recovery step is the tool most people forget.

They focus on the moment of escalation but not the aftermath. Yet many regrets happen after the visible surge: the second message, the rumination loop, the displaced irritation, the panic checking, the shame attack, the apology that erases too much. A recovery step tells the body that the moment has ended and helps prevent the state from spreading.

A good recovery step is physical and ordinary. Wash your hands. Drink water. Walk to another room. Feel both feet and exhale. Put the phone away. Name the next small task. Look around the room and say, "That moment is over; this is the next one." The step does not need to be beautiful. It needs to mark the transition from impact to return.

Choose a recovery step that fits your common aftermath. If you ruminate, your recovery step might be: name the lesson, schedule any action, then do one ordinary task. If you carry work tension into home life, it might be a car reset before entering the house. If you panic and then check symptoms, it might be: no checking, cold water on hands, return to one simple activity. If you snap and then self-attack, it might be: downshift first, then repair only the behaviour.

The recovery step should answer one question: how do I stop this surge from becoming the rest of the day?

Once you have chosen the four tools, make them small enough to remember under pressure. Long plans fail because they require too much from an activated mind. Your plan might sound like this: exhale, feet, "I need a minute," wash hands. That is not simplistic. It is usable. The pressured self needs a handle, not an essay.

You can build the plan as a simple sequence.

When the surge begins, use the breath reset.

When attention narrows, use the grounding anchor.

When speech or action becomes risky, use the pause phrase.

When the moment ends, use the recovery step.

This sequence gives the body a path. It does not require you to decide from scratch each time. It does not require perfect calm. It simply gives the first minute a structure that has already been chosen by your steadier self.

The next task is to match the tools to your personal escalation map. Ask where your regrets usually happen. If your regrets happen before speaking, your breath and pause phrase are crucial. If your regrets happen through digital messages, your grounding method must include the phone: hand off device, draft elsewhere, wait. If your regrets happen through panic interpretation, your core tool must include present-fact language: "This is a panic spike; my feet are on the floor." If your regrets happen after conflict, your recovery step needs to be non-negotiable.

The best plan is not balanced in theory. It is weighted towards your actual risk.

A person who rarely sends reactive messages does not need the same digital rules as someone whose phone becomes the main route of escalation. A person who rarely raises their voice but often disappears needs scripts for return. A person who argues brilliantly but damages connection needs a listening anchor and a shorter boundary. A person who panics in public needs grounding that can be done discreetly with feet, hands, temperature, and eyes open. Your plan should be honest enough to be useful.

Do not choose tools to flatter yourself. Choose tools to protect your weak points.

This is not self-criticism. It is design. A good bridge is built for the load it must carry. Your 60-second plan should be built for the moments where you are least impressive, least patient, least flexible, least able to access your values. It should assume you will be tired sometimes. It should assume the other person may not speak perfectly. It should assume the message may arrive at a bad time. It should assume your body may move first. A plan that only works when you are already at your best is decoration.

Once chosen, the tools must be practised together. Not endlessly. Not as a ritual that becomes another burden. Practise the sequence in ordinary transitions: before opening messages, while waiting for the kettle, sitting in the car, entering a meeting, leaving a difficult conversation, standing in a queue. Exhale. Ground. Say the phrase quietly or in your mind. Do the recovery action. You are teaching the body that these moves belong together.

This matters because pressure reduces improvisation. The more familiar the sequence, the less you have to invent. Under stress, invention is expensive. Recognition is cheaper. A practised plan lets the body say, "I know this route." That familiarity may be enough to create the 60-second gap when it matters.

Keep the plan visible at first. Write it on a card, in a notebook, on a phone note, beside your desk, in the car, or on the inside of a journal. Use plain words. Not inspiring words. Working words.

Breath: soft exhale.

Ground: feet.

Pause: "I want to answer well."

Recover: water, walk, no replay.

This kind of note is not childish. It is a pre-decision. It removes work from the heated moment. The point is not to depend on the card forever. The point is to make the route familiar enough that eventually the body remembers.

Review the plan after real use. Not every tool will work equally well. You may discover that feet grounding is too subtle during panic and you need temperature. You may discover that your pause phrase is too polite and gets ignored. You may discover that your breath reset works in meetings but not in conflict with a partner. You may discover that your recovery step is too vague and needs a specific action. This is not failure. This is refinement.

A core plan should be stable enough to trust and flexible enough to adjust.

The danger is constantly changing tools because one difficult day made you doubt everything. If a tool does not produce instant calm, that does not mean it failed. Ask whether it protected the next move. Did it reduce the intensity slightly? Did it delay the message? Did it soften the first sentence? Did it stop the checking loop? Did it help you repair sooner? If yes, keep it. If it repeatedly adds pressure or remains unreachable, change it.

Another danger is turning the plan into a perfection contract. "If I have a plan, I should never react badly again." That thought will poison the work. Your plan is not a guarantee. It is a support. It increases the chance of returning to choice sooner. It does not remove emotion, history, fatigue, conflict, panic, or human imperfection. You will still miss cues. You will still sometimes remember late. You will still need repair. A humane plan expects this.

The true measure is not flawless execution. It is shorter distance.

Shorter distance between cue and recognition.

Shorter distance between anger and pause.

Shorter distance between panic and grounding.

Shorter distance between message and delay.

Shorter distance between conflict and recovery.

Shorter distance between mistake and repair.

That is what progress looks like in real life. Less drama. Fewer regrets. Faster return. More trust in your ability to interrupt the old pattern before it completes itself.

Your core tools should feel almost boring by the time they are working. That is a good sign. Under pressure, boring is reliable. You do not need novelty when the body is activated. You need the same exhale, the same feet, the same phrase, the same recovery step. Calm becomes available through repetition, not reinvention.

So choose small.

Choose honestly.

Choose for the body you have in real pressure, not the self-image you prefer in calm reflection.

One breath reset. One grounding anchor. One anger pause. One recovery step.

That is enough to meet the next surge with something ready.

Preparing for predictable moments

Many surges are not as random as they feel.

They may arrive suddenly, but they often arrive in familiar clothing. The same doorway after work. The same family topic. The same kind of message. The same meeting where you expect scrutiny. The same silence after a difficult text. The same late-evening tiredness that turns small comments into large threats. The body may still react as though the moment has come from nowhere, but if you look honestly, many of your pressure points have a pattern.

This is good news, though it may not feel flattering at first. Predictable moments can be prepared for. A pattern gives you a place to stand before the surge begins. Instead of waiting until you are heated, frightened, ashamed, or rushed, you can decide in advance what the first safe move will be. Preparation does not remove emotion. It reduces surprise. And surprise is one of escalation's favourite weapons.

A predictable moment is any situation where your nervous system has a history. Perhaps you know that certain conversations with a parent make you defensive. Perhaps you know that opening messages from a particular person makes your chest tighten. Perhaps you know that meetings after a poor night's sleep make you over-explain. Perhaps you know that driving home after a stressful day leaves you sharp with the first person who asks you a simple question. Perhaps you know that bedtime gives rumination too much space to perform its old theatre.

These moments deserve planning, not self-criticism.

Self-criticism says, "I should not react like this." Preparation says, "This is a known pressure point, so I will meet it with structure." That difference is enormous. Shame waits until after the surge and attacks you for being human. Preparation arrives before the surge and makes the next better move easier. It is not a guarantee. It is a kindness with discipline inside it.

The first step is to name the predictable moment plainly. Do not make it dramatic. Do not make it vague. "Family calls on Sunday." "Emails from my manager." "Entering the house after work." "Messages after ten at night." "Crowded shops." "Budget conversations." "Being corrected in public." "Waiting for replies." A good label is specific enough that you know when the moment has begun.

Once the moment is named, ask what usually happens in your sequence. What does your body do first? What story does your mind add? What is your default move? What is the usual regret? This is not an invitation to hold a private trial. It is practical mapping. If the predictable moment is a work meeting, perhaps your body tightens, your mind hears every question as criticism, and your default move is over-explaining. If the predictable moment is a partner's late reply, perhaps your stomach drops, your mind predicts distance, and your default move is checking or sending another message. The plan must fit the route.

Then decide what success looks like in that specific moment.

This is where many people aim too high and then abandon the plan. Success does not have to mean feeling calm, winning the conversation, being perfectly understood, or resolving the entire issue. In a pressure moment, success may be smaller and much more useful. Leaving the room kindly instead of storming out. Delaying a decision until morning. Asking one clarifying question before defending. Drafting without sending. Saying, "I need a minute," before your voice sharpens. Sitting in the car for one exhale before entering the house. Not checking the message thread for a short period. Repairing one behaviour without apologising for your whole self.

A realistic success definition gives the body a target it can reach. "Stay perfectly calm during the whole conversation" is too vague and too demanding. "If I feel heat rising, I will say, 'I need a minute before I answer,' and pause" is usable. "Do not panic in the shop" is not fully within your control. "If panic rises, I will feel my feet, hold the cold bottle, and name three objects before deciding whether to leave" is a plan. Good preparation turns a wish into a next action.

Environment tweaks can make the plan easier. Do not rely on willpower where design would do better. If you send reactive messages at night, keep the phone away from the bed or write replies in notes first. If you carry work stress through the front door, create a short transition before entering: hands off the wheel, one soft exhale, shoulders down, one sentence naming the state you want to bring in. If meetings make you defensive, keep a pen and notebook as anchors, with both feet on the floor before speaking. If family calls escalate, decide the pause phrase beforehand and choose where you will stand or sit.

The environment should help you remember before the surge becomes loud.

This is the value of cues. A cue is a predictable signal that starts the plan. The phone lighting up. The car engine stopping. The meeting link opening. The kettle boiling. The bedroom lamp switching off. The front door key in your hand. A cue removes some of the burden from memory. Instead of asking your pressured mind to invent a strategy, the cue says, "This is the moment. Use the plan."

Rehearsed phrases are part of the environment too, only they live in the mouth. Under pressure, language can vanish or become too sharp. A phrase practised beforehand is easier to reach. "I want to answer that carefully." "I am not deciding this while I am heated." "I can talk about this, but not at this volume." "I have read your message and will reply later." "I need a minute, then I will come back." These sentences are not elaborate because pressure does not need eloquence. It needs a line that holds.

The phrase must sound like you. If it feels artificial, change it until it fits. A sentence you would never naturally say will not appear when your body is activated. The best phrase is plain, short, and honest. It does not blame. It does not plead. It does not invite a long debate. It gives the next minute a safer shape.

Preparation is especially important for repeating relational dynamics. Some people can stay calm almost anywhere except with one particular person. This is not unusual. Familiar people carry familiar meanings. A small comment can arrive with years attached to it. A glance, pause, or phrase may touch old roles: the responsible one, the ignored one, the difficult one, the fixer, the failure, the child, the peacekeeper. The body reacts not only to what was said, but to what it has learnt that moment may become.

A prepared plan helps you stay in the present rather than falling automatically into the old role. If you know you become the defender, your plan may be to reflect one point before responding. If you become the pleaser, your plan may be to delay agreement: "I need to think before I answer." If you become the withdrawer, your plan may be to give a return point: "I need a break and will come back in twenty minutes." If you become the prosecutor, your plan may be one breath, one sentence, no history unless it is truly needed.

Digital moments need especially clear preparation because they move so quickly. Decide your rules before the message arrives. Perhaps charged messages are never answered from bed. Perhaps any reply longer than a short paragraph must wait. Perhaps you draft elsewhere if your face is hot or your thumbs are moving fast. Perhaps you read once, look away, exhale, and ask whether the response needed is reply, delay, boundary, or no response. The point is to make the safer route easier than the reactive one.

Public and work pressure also benefit from pre-planning. Before a meeting where you expect challenge, decide your beat-buying sentence. Before a difficult call, put both feet on the floor and have water nearby. Before a public-facing interaction, choose your boundary line: "I want to help, but I cannot continue while being shouted at." Before presenting, decide what you will do if criticism lands sharply: exhale, clarify the question, answer the content rather than the sting.

Preparation does not make you rigid. It makes you less available to panic improvisation.

There is a danger, however, in over-preparing. The mind can turn preparation into anxious rehearsal. It imagines every possible sentence, every possible response, every possible outcome. It tries to control the future by rehearsing it until the body is already activated before anything has happened. That is not preparation. That is rumination wearing a planner's coat.

Good preparation is brief and behavioural. It asks: what is the cue, what is the risk, what is the smallest safe move, and what does success look like? Then it stops. You do not need to script the entire conversation. You need one opening move and one recovery move. The future will not follow your script perfectly. It does not need to. Your plan is not there to control every variable. It is there to protect your first minute.

A useful pre-plan might sound like this: "When I get home from work, I will sit in the car for one exhale before going inside. Success is not being cheerful. Success is not bringing the first sharp tone through the door."

Another: "When I receive a message that feels cold, I will not reply from the first surge. I will draft elsewhere and wait. Success is sending nothing until I can read the message without adding a story to every word."

Another: "When my family brings up that topic, I will keep my feet on the floor and say, 'I am not discussing this if we start raising voices.' Success is setting the line early, not delivering a speech after I am already angry."

These plans are modest because modest plans work.

They also make repair easier. When you know what success looked like in advance, review becomes cleaner. You can ask, "Did I do the one thing I planned?" rather than "Was I perfectly calm?" If you did it, even clumsily, that is progress. If you did not, the next question is practical: was the cue too late, the phrase too unnatural, the environment too loaded, the success target too ambitious? Adjust the plan. Do not turn the miss into a character verdict.

Preparation also includes deciding what you will not do. This is often as important as deciding what you will do. You might decide: I will not send a final message while angry. I will not agree immediately to end discomfort. I will not discuss serious matters by text after bedtime. I will not keep checking symptoms once I have recognised the panic pattern. I will not continue a conversation where insults are being used. These "not" decisions remove dangerous routes before the surge starts arguing for them.

The strongest plans are written down and placed near the moment. A note in the car. A line at the top of a meeting page. A reminder beside the bed. A phone note titled "Read before replying." A small card in a bag. This is not weakness. It is external memory. Pressure narrows recall. A visible plan widens it again.

Over time, prepared moments become less surprising. The body still reacts, but not with the same helplessness. You recognise the doorway. You recognise the message. You recognise the tone. You recognise the evening pattern. Instead of thinking, "Here we go again," you can think, "This is the moment I planned for." That shift alone can reduce escalation. It turns the surge from an ambush into a known crossing.

You will not prepare for everything. Life will still produce fresh pressure, clumsy people, difficult timing, and unexpected bodily reactions. That is normal. The point of preparing predictable moments is not to eliminate uncertainty. It is to reduce unnecessary surprise where the pattern is already visible. Save your energy for what cannot be predicted. Do not keep being ambushed by the same room, the same thread, the same hour, the same cue.

The next time you notice a familiar surge beginning in a familiar place, do not waste the recognition. That pattern is information. Use it before the heat rises fully. Decide the cue. Choose the sentence. Place the barrier. Define the smallest success.

Predictable does not mean easy.

It means you can arrive prepared.

Keeping progress humane

Progress in calming skills is easily ruined by cruelty disguised as ambition.

A person learns the tools, practises the pauses, recognises the body cues, writes the plan, and begins to believe that this should mean they will never react badly again. Then a hard day arrives. Sleep is poor. A message lands at the wrong time. A familiar person says the familiar sentence. Panic rises in public. Anger moves faster than breath. The old reply is sent, the tone sharpens, the room goes quiet, or the rumination loop opens again. Immediately the mind turns on itself: "I should be past this." "I know better." "I have failed." "Nothing works."

That reaction may feel like accountability, but it is usually another surge.

Self-attack has the same narrowing quality as anger and panic. It reduces the whole picture to one piece of evidence. It treats a difficult moment as a verdict on your character. It forgets the times you paused, delayed, repaired, grounded, softened, or returned sooner than before. It demands perfection from a nervous system that is learning under real conditions. Then, because shame is itself a threat state, it makes the next pressure moment more loaded. You are no longer only dealing with the trigger. You are dealing with the fear of proving yourself hopeless.

A humane approach does not mean a soft standard. This is important. Humane progress is not indulgence, avoidance, or pretending that harmful words do not matter. It is the opposite of evasion because it keeps you capable of responsibility. A person drowning in shame often becomes less able to repair cleanly. They over-apologise, defend, disappear, or collapse into identity statements that make the other person soothe them. A steadier person can say, "I did not handle that well. I can repair the behaviour. I can adjust the plan."

That is the tone of real growth: clear, accountable, and not brutal.

Progress should be measured by shorter surges, fewer regrets, and faster repair. This is a more honest measure than emotional perfection. You may still feel anger, but perhaps it lasts less time before you recognise the heat. You may still panic, but perhaps you stop adding catastrophic meaning sooner. You may still send a message too quickly, but perhaps you repair the tone without sending five more from shame. You may still ruminate, but perhaps the loop closes before it owns the evening. These shifts may not look dramatic from outside. They are substantial.

The old standard says, "Did I stay calm?"

The better standard says, "Where did choice return?"

That question changes everything. Choice may return before the first sentence, which is excellent. It may return after one sharp sentence, which still matters. It may return after the message is drafted but before it is sent. It may return ten minutes into panic when you finally stop checking. It may return after conflict, when you downshift and repair only what is yours. Each return point is a place to strengthen. The goal is not to pretend the earlier part did not happen. The goal is to make the return more familiar.

A humane review begins with description, not judgement.

Description says, "My chest tightened when I read the message. I interpreted it as criticism. I replied too quickly." Judgement says, "I am ridiculous and defensive." Description says, "I went quiet because I felt overwhelmed and did not give a return point." Judgement says, "I always ruin conversations." Description says, "Panic rose in the shop, I checked my symptoms repeatedly, and that made the fear louder." Judgement says, "I cannot cope with anything." Description gives you something to work with. Judgement gives you a verdict and no path.

After description comes responsibility. Not blame. Responsibility.

Responsibility asks, "What was mine?" Perhaps your tone was sharp. Perhaps you interrupted. Perhaps you sent the message from heat. Perhaps you vanished without saying when you would come back. Perhaps you asked for reassurance again and again. Name it plainly. Do not minimise it. Also do not inflate it. You are not responsible for every emotion in the room, every misunderstanding, every reaction another person had, or every historical pattern that surfaced. You are responsible for your conduct and your next repair.

Then comes adjustment. Adjustment is the part that keeps progress alive.

A harsh mind asks, "What is wrong with me?" A skilful mind asks, "What needs changing in the plan?" Was the cue too late? Was the tool too complicated? Was the pause phrase unnatural? Did the message arrive at a predictable bad time? Did hunger, tiredness, or overload make the surge stronger? Did you need a firmer boundary rather than more breathing? Did you need grounding before breath because panic made breathing too charged? Did the recovery step fail because it was vague? These questions do not excuse the reaction. They improve the next design.

This is how calm becomes a practice you can return to, rather than a standard you either meet or fail.

Returning is the central word. You return to the breath after forgetting it. You return to the body after being swept into the story. You return to the conversation after taking space. You return to the plan after a hard day. You return to repair after defensiveness. You return to ordinary life after panic. A practice that cannot survive imperfection is too fragile for human use. The plan must be sturdy enough to be picked up again without ceremony.

There will be days when the best you can do is reduce the damage. That still counts.

A tired body will have less margin. A hungry body may be quicker to anger. A stressed mind may narrow faster. A person under repeated pressure may have fewer elegant responses available. This does not mean behaviour has no consequences. It means the review should include conditions. If you keep demanding peak performance from an exhausted system, you are not being disciplined; you are being unrealistic. Humane progress asks what support would make the next right action more reachable.

Sometimes the adjustment is not another technique. Sometimes it is sleep, food, space, a clearer boundary, a reduced commitment, a direct conversation, medical support where appropriate, therapy where needed, or less exposure to a dynamic that repeatedly overwhelms you. Self-regulation is powerful, but it is not meant to compensate forever for impossible conditions. A humane plan knows when the issue is not only your reaction, but the environment in which you are repeatedly trying to regulate.

This matters because some people use calming work against themselves. They assume that if they had better tools, nothing would affect them. They try to breathe through disrespect, ground through exhaustion, pause through overwork, and de-escalate every situation as though their only task is to become endlessly manageable. That is not calm. That is self-abandonment with good posture. The 60-second plan is meant to return you to agency, not make you more tolerant of what needs to change.

A humane plan includes repair without self-erasure. If you harm, repair. If you snap, acknowledge the tone. If you withdraw, clarify and return. If you over-apologise, correct the excess. If you panic and seek too much reassurance, name the pattern and adjust support. But do not use repair to erase your boundary, deny your need, or pretend the original issue was unimportant. Mature repair says, "I am responsible for how I handled that, and the underlying concern still matters."

A humane plan also includes celebration, though not in a sentimental way. Notice the quiet wins. The message not sent. The breath before the reply. The pause phrase that came out awkwardly but came out. The hand moved away from the phone. The panic spike recognised before the story became master. The argument ended without a second round. The apology kept short and accurate. These are not minor because they are invisible. They are the private architecture of change.

Many people dismiss progress because it does not feel triumphant. It often feels ordinary. Less heat. Less time lost. Less cleanup. Less dread of yourself afterwards. This is exactly the point. A calmer life may not announce itself as dramatic transformation. It may arrive as fewer unnecessary fires. More pauses. Cleaner words. Better endings. Faster returns. The absence of a familiar regret is a real outcome, even if no one else sees it.

The review after a difficult moment should therefore be brief and structured. Ask: what happened, what did I do, where did choice return, what needs repair, and what is one adjustment? Then stop. Do not turn review into rumination. Do not hold court against yourself for hours. The purpose of review is to build the next iteration of the plan. Once the lesson is extracted, return to the day.

A useful review might sound like this: "I was tired and read the message as criticism. My face got hot and I replied too fast. Choice returned after I saw the tone of my reply. I need to apologise for the sharpness, not for the concern. Adjustment: no charged replies after work until I have eaten and taken one exhale." That is humane progress. It is honest, specific, and usable.

Another might be: "Panic rose in the queue. I started checking my breath and that made it worse. Choice returned when I held the bottle and named objects. Adjustment: for panic, grounding first, breath second." Again, no drama. No verdict. A practical lesson.

Another: "In the argument, I needed space but went silent. Choice returned after I left the room. Repair: tell them I should have given a return point. Adjustment: use the phrase, 'I need ten minutes, then I will come back.'"

This kind of review builds trust because it proves that mistakes can become information. Without humane review, mistakes become evidence of failure. With humane review, they become instructions for the next version of the plan.

You will also need patience with uneven progress. Some patterns change quickly because they were waiting for one practical interruption. Others are older, deeper, or tied to relationships and environments that keep activating them. You may improve in work settings before family settings. You may manage digital triggers well and still struggle with panic sensations. You may pause during anger but still ruminate afterwards. Unevenness is not hypocrisy. It is the normal shape of learning under different pressures.

Do not compare one context with another too harshly. A tool that works in a meeting may not work with someone whose opinion touches a younger, more vulnerable part of you. A breath that helps with irritation may not be enough during panic. A boundary that is easy with a stranger may feel nearly impossible with family. This does not mean the plan is false. It means context matters. Adjust for the actual difficulty, not the difficulty you think you "should" have.

A humane plan is allowed to evolve.

Perhaps your first breath tool changes because you realise large breaths make panic worse. Perhaps your grounding anchor changes from feet to hands because hands are where your urge begins. Perhaps your anger phrase changes because the first version sounded too formal. Perhaps your recovery step changes because washing your hands works better than trying to sit still. This is refinement, not inconsistency. The plan serves the person. The person does not serve the plan.

There is a quiet confidence that comes from knowing you can begin again without making a ceremony of it. You miss the cue, then catch the next one. You react, then repair. You ruminate, then close the loop. You panic, then ground. You send the wrong message, then stop yourself from sending three more. You review, adjust, and continue. This is not glamorous, but it is resilient.

The worst thing a hard day can do is convince you to abandon the plan because you did not follow it perfectly. That is the old all-or-nothing pattern in a new costume. The plan is most needed on the day it is used clumsily. A tool remembered late is still a tool remembered. A pause taken after the first sharp sentence may still prevent the second. A repair made after shame settles may still restore trust. A recovery step used after rumination has already begun may still shorten the loop.

Progress is not purity. It is direction.

The humane standard is demanding because it asks for responsibility again and again. It does not let you hide behind "I was triggered" or "that is just how I am." It also refuses to let shame become the teacher. Shame is a loud teacher and a poor one. It narrows, exaggerates, and frightens. The better teacher is exact reflection: cue, state, move, outcome, adjustment.

Over time, the plan becomes less of a document and more of a relationship with yourself. You begin to trust that a surge is not the end of choice. You begin to know your early signs. You begin to expect hard moments without fearing that they will define you. You begin to recover faster from imperfection. Calm becomes less like a mood you must maintain and more like a route you know how to rejoin.

That is the final promise of the 60-second calm: not that you will never be angry, panicked, stressed, ashamed, defensive, rushed, or overwhelmed, but that these states will not always get the last word.

The next time you miss the pause, do not throw away the practice. Find the next opening. The next breath. The next grounded contact. The next honest repair. The next ordinary return to the day. Keep the standard. Drop the cruelty.

A humane plan does not ask you to become flawless.

It asks you to keep coming back sooner.

About the Author

Selma Ravik writes about the small, practical skills that help people stay human under pressure. Her work is grounded in a simple belief: intense feelings are not a character flaw, but the body doing its best to protect you with limited information and very little time. She is especially interested in the moments that do not look dramatic from the outside - the swallowed anger that turns into a sharp sentence, the spiralling thought that starts with a single notification, the sudden panic that arrives while you are meant to look composed.

Over years of collecting everyday coping strategies from ordinary lives, Selma has developed a clear, reader-friendly approach: explain what is happening, offer a tool you can use immediately, and make practice realistic enough to survive real schedules. She values language that reduces shame and increases choice, and she favours methods that can be done quietly at a desk, on a bus, or mid-conversation.

A subtle thread running through her writing is the old idea of "keeping your head" - a phrase that echoes through British public life, wartime diaries, and family sayings passed down at kitchen tables. For Selma, steadiness is not stiffness. It is the ability to pause, to notice, and to choose a next step that you can stand by later.

www.ingramcontent.com/pod-product-compliance
Lightning Source LLC
LaVergne TN
LVHW100725061126
851857LV00011B/393
* 9 7 8 8 1 6 9 8 8 8 3 5 6 *